£7.00   001331

KU-071-423

GENERA
ARD PROUDE
and DAVID SCOTT KASTAN

MUCH ADO ABOUT NOTHING

THE ARDEN SHAKESPEARE

* Third Series

THE ARDEN EDITION OF THE
WORKS OF WILLIAM SHAKESPEARE

MUCH ADO ABOUT
NOTHING

Edited by
A. R. HUMPHREYS

The general editors of the Arden Shakespeare have been
W. J. Craig and R. H. Case (first series 1899-1944)
Una Ellis-Fermor, Harold F. Brooks,
Harold Jenkins and Brian Morris (second series 1946-1982)

Present general editors (third series)
Richard Proudfoot, Ann Thompson and David Scott Kastan

This edition of *Much Ado About Nothing*, by A.R Humphreys,
first published in 1981 by
Methuen & Co. Ltd
Reprinted 4 times

Reprinted 1998 by Thomas Nelson & Sons Ltd

Thomas Nelson & Sons Ltd
Nelson House Mayfield Road
Walton-on-Thames Surrey
KT12 5PL UK

I(T)P® Thomas Nelson is an International
Thomson Publishing Company
I(T)P® is used under licence

British Library Cataloguing in Publication Data
A catalogue record for this book is available from
the British Library

Library of Congress Cataloguing in Publication Data
A catalogue record has been applied for

ISBN 0-416-17990-8 (cased)
ISBN 0-17-443482-0 (paperback)
NPN 9 8 7 6 5 4

CONTENTS

PREFACE

It is with a sense of honour and nostalgic affection that, though my introduction and text are not derived from hers, in much of this edition's illustrative material I follow Grace Trenery, the play's original Arden editor, in whom I, a very junior tutor in Liverpool University's Department of English Literature just before the war, found a warmhearted and encouraging friend. Working on the play I have been much reminded of her, as of other Liverpool colleagues and friends distinguished in Elizabethan and seventeenth-century fields—Leonard Martin, Archibald McIlwraith, and Arnold Davenport—now, alas, no more.

Grace Trenery's edition was richly annotated. To find room also for new material I have left out much that she included, yet the commentary still exceeds what normal annotation would require. A good many items I have kept, even if not strictly necessary, as good reading in themselves, and as reflecting Miss Trenery's enthusiasm for Elizabethan matters, to which her colleague Professor R. H. Case amply contributed.

I have often saved space by excising the commentator to whom a note was attributed; in any case, to ascertain the actual originator is often impossible. The lack of such attribution does not mean that I claim the credit myself; my debts to earlier editions, particularly—after the original Arden—to Furness's New Variorum, are very great. Wherever attribution would help further enquiry I have tried to give it.

Most of the work was done on a tenure of a Fellowship at the Huntington Library, San Marino, California, my wife valuably assisting. To Dr James Thorpe and his staff she and I are indebted beyond measure for unforgettable benefits at an institution which offered us resources, amenities, and the friendliness of scholarly society beyond all that might be hoped for.

The General Editors, Professors Harold Brooks, Harold Jenkins and Brian Morris, have been extraordinarily prompt, thorough and generous with bibliographical and many other kinds of guidance; to their very detailed advice I owe more than I can possibly say. My long absences from Britain while this edition was being prepared threw unusual burdens of checking on to them and the publisher's editorial staff. For help willingly rendered I should like, too, to thank the Shakespeare Centre and Shakespeare Institute, Stratford-upon-Avon, Professor Tony Fitton-Brown of the University of Leicester, and Dr Pamela Mason, whose MA thesis of the University of Birmingham, 'Much Ado' at Stratford, 1949–1976, furnished valuable information on which I have drawn in the section on stage history. My cordial thanks are due to two friends and colleagues at the University of Leicester, both enviably expert in the field of drama, Dr Lois Potter and Mr Roger Warren, for helpful and comprehensive criticism and illumination; from their much-appreciated promptings this edition has greatly benefited, and Mr Warren has been unstinting in his help with the proof-checking when I was far from my sources. The work, finally, has been harmoniously and felicitously furthered by my wife's investigatory diligence and the stimulus of discussion with her. For the faults that remain, the responsibility is mine.

University of the Bosphorus, 1981   A. R. HUMPHREYS

ABBREVIATIONS AND REFERENCES

The titles of Shakespeare's works are abbreviated as in C. T. Onions, *A Shakespeare Glossary*. Line-numberings and texts from other Shakespeare plays are normally from Peter Alexander's edition of the *Complete Works*. Q means the 1600 Quarto edition of the play, F the First Folio of 1623 (F1 when it needs distinguishing from F2, F3 or F4, the Folios of 1632, 1663, and 1685 respectively). S.D. means stage-direction. In the collations numerals are added after the names of editors only when an edition later than the first is intended; unnumbered references are to the first edition. Except where otherwise indicated the place of publication is London.

I. EDITIONS OF THE PLAY

Alexander	*William Shakespeare, The Complete Works*, ed. Peter Alexander, London and Glasgow, 1951.
Bennett	*Much Ado About Nothing*, ed. Josephine Waters Bennett, in *The Complete Works*, gen. ed. A. Harbage, revised Complete Pelican Shakespeare, Baltimore, Maryland, 1969.
Boas	*Much Ado About Nothing*, ed. F. S. Boas, Clarendon Select Plays of Shakespeare, Clarendon Press, Oxford, 1916.
Brooke	*Much Ado About Nothing*, ed. C. F. Tucker Brooke, in *The Works of William Shakespeare*, Yale edn, New Haven and London, 1917.
Camb.	*The Works of William Shakespeare*, ed. W. G. Clark and W. A. Wright, vol. II, Cambridge, England, 1863.
Capell	*Mr William Shakespeare His Comedies, Histories, and Tragedies*, ed. Edward Capell, vol. II, 1767.
Collier, 1, 2, 3	*The Works of Shakespeare*, ed. J. P. Collier, 1st edn, vol. II, 1842; 2nd edn, vol. II, 1858; 3rd edn, vol. I, 1876.
Deighton	*Much Ado About Nothing*, ed. K. Deighton, 1888.
Dyce	*The Works of William Shakespeare*, ed. A. Dyce, vol. II, 1857.
Evans	*The Riverside Shakespeare*, textual ed. G. Blakemore Evans, Boston, Mass., 1974.
Foakes	*Much Ado About Nothing*, ed. R. A. Foakes, New Penguin edn, Harmondsworth, Middlesex, 1968.
Furness	*Much Ado About Nothing*, ed. H. H. Furness, New Variorum edn, Philadelphia and London, 1899.
Globe	*The Works of William Shakespeare*, ed. W. G. Clark and W. A. Wright, Globe edn, 1864.
Halliwell	*The Works of William Shakespeare*, ed. J. O. Halliwell [-Phillipps], vol. IV, 1855.

xi

Hanmer	*The Works of Shakespear*, ed. Sir Thomas Hanmer, vol. I, 1743.
Hudson (Harvard)	*The Harvard Shakespeare*, ed. H. N. Hudson, Boston, Mass., vol. IV, 1881.
Johnson	*The Plays of William Shakespeare*, ed. Samuel Johnson, vol. III, 1765.
Kittredge	*The Complete Works of Shakespeare*, ed. G. L. Kittredge, Boston, Mass., 1936.
Knight	*The Works of William Shakspere*, ed. Charles Knight, Pictorial edn, vol. II [,1839].
Malone	*The Plays and Poems of William Shakespeare*, ed. Edmond Malone, vol. II, 1790.
NCS	*Much Ado About Nothing*, ed. Sir Arthur Quiller-Couch and J. Dover Wilson, New Cambridge Shakespeare, Cambridge, England, 1923.
Pope, 1, 2	*The Works of Shakespear*, ed. Alexander Pope, 1st edn, vol. I, 1725; 2nd edn, vol. II, 1728.
Riverside	*The Riverside Shakespeare*, textual ed. G. Blakemore Evans, Boston, Mass., 1974.
Rowe, 1, 3	*The Works of Mr William Shakespear*, ed. Nicholas Rowe, 1st edn, vol. I, 1709; 3rd edn, vol. I, 1714.
Staunton	*The Plays of Shakespeare*, ed. Howard Staunton, vol. I, 1858.
Steevens '93	*The Plays of William Shakspeare*, with notes by Samuel Johnson and George Steevens, ed. Isaac Reed, vol. IV, 1793.
Theobald, 1, 2	*The Works of Shakespeare*, ed. Lewis Theobald, 1st edn, vol. I, 1733; 2nd edn, vol. II, 1740.
Var. '78	*The Plays of William Shakespeare*, with notes by Samuel Johnson and George Steevens, vol. II, 1778.
Warburton	*The Works of Shakespear*, ed. William Warburton, vol. II, 1747.
Warwick	*Much Ado About Nothing*, ed. J. C. Smith, Warwick edn, 1902.
White, 2	*Mr William Shakespeare's Comedies, Histories, Tragedies, and Poems*, ed. R. G. White, 2nd edn, vol. I, Boston, Mass., 1883.
Wright	*Much Ado About Nothing*, ed. W. A. Wright, Clarendon Press, Oxford, 1905.
Yale	*The Works of William Shakespeare: Much Ado About Nothing*, ed. C. F. Tucker Brooke, Yale edn, New Haven and London, 1917.

2. OTHER WORKS

Abbott	E. A. Abbott, *A Shakespearian Grammar*, 3rd edn, 1870.
Bang's *Materialen*	W. Bang (gen. ed.), *Materialen zur Kunde des älteren Englischen Dramas*, 44 vols, Louvain, 1902–14.
Barton	Anne Barton, Introduction to *Much Ado About Nothing*, in *The Riverside Shakespeare*, textual ed. G. Blakemore Evans, Boston, Mass., 1974.
Brae	A. E. Brae, *Collier, Coleridge, and Shakespeare*, 1860.

Bullough	Geoffrey Bullough, *Narrative and Dramatic Sources of Shakespeare*, vol. II, 1958.
Capell (*Notes*)	Edward Capell, *Notes and Various Readings to Shakespeare*, vol. II, 1780.
Cotgrave	Randall Cotgrave, *A Dictionarie of the French and English Tongues*, 1611.
Craik	T. W. Craik, 'Much Ado About Nothing', in *Scrutiny*, ed. F. R. Leavis, vol. xix, Cambridge, England, 1952-3.
Davies (Grosart)	Sir John Davies, *Works*, ed. A. B. Grosart, 3 vols, Blackburn, 1869-76.
Douce (*Illustrations*)	F. Douce, *Illustrations of Shakespeare*, 1807.
Hazlitt	William Hazlitt, 'Much Ado About Nothing', in *Characters of Shakespear's Plays*, 1817.
Hazlitt's *Dodsley*	*A Select Collection of Old English Plays, originally published by Robert Dodsley*, revised by W. Carew Hazlitt, 15 vols, 1874-6.
Heath	Benjamin Heath, *A Revisal of Shakespear's Text*, 1765.
Holinshed	Raphael Holinshed, *Chronicles of England, Scotland, and Ireland*, 6 vols, ed. Henry Ellis, 1807-8.
Hudson (*Life*)	H. N. Hudson, *Shakespeare, his Life, Art, and Characters*, 2 vols, Boston, Mass., 1894.
Jonson (H. & S.)	Ben Jonson, *Works*, ed. C. H. Herford and Percy and Evelyn Simpson, 11 vols, Oxford, 1925-52.
Kinnear	Benjamin Gott Kinnear, *Cruces Shakespearianae*, 1883.
Linthicum	M. C. Linthicum, *Costume in the Drama of Shakespeare and his Contemporaries*, Oxford, 1936.
Lloyd	W. W. Lloyd, *Critical Essays*, 1856.
Mackenzie	A. M. Mackenzie, *The Women in Shakespeare's Plays*, 1929.
Madden	D. H. Madden, *The Diary of Master William Silence*, 1897.
Mason	Pamela Mason, '*Much Ado*' at Stratford-upon-Avon, 1949-76, M.A. thesis, University of Birmingham, England, 1976.
Nashe (McKerrow)	Thomas Nashe, *Works*, ed. R. B. McKerrow, 5 vols, 1904-10.
Noble	Richmond Noble, *Shakespeare's Biblical Knowledge*, 1935.
Onions	C. T. Onions, *A Shakespeare Glossary*, 2nd edn, revised, Oxford, 1919.
Rossiter	A. P. Rossiter, *Angel with Horns*, 1961.
Seymour	E. H. Seymour, *Remarks, Critical, Conjectural, and Explanatory*, 1805.
Spedding	James Spedding, 'On the Division of the Acts in . . . Much Ado About Nothing', in *The Gentleman's Magazine*, June 1850, and New Shakspere Society's Transactions, 1877-9.
Spurgeon	Caroline Spurgeon, *Shakespeare's Imagery, and What It Tells Us*, Cambridge, England, 1935.
Theobald 1726	Lewis Theobald, *Shakespeare Restored*, 1726.
Thirlby	Styan Thirlby, contributions in Theobald's edns.
Tilley	M. P. Tilley, *A Dictionary of the Proverbs in England in the Sixteenth and Seventeenth Centuries*, Ann Arbor, Michigan, 1950.
Vickers	Brian Vickers, *The Artistry of Shakespeare's Prose*, 1968.

Walker   W. S. Walker, *A Critical Examination of the Text of Shake-*
                            speare, 3 vols, 1860.

3. PERIODICALS, DICTIONARIES, SERIES

EETS   Early English Text Society.
ELH   *ELH, a Journal of English Literary History*, Johns Hopkins
                            University, Baltimore, Maryland.
NSS   New Shakspere Society.
OED   *Oxford English Dictionary*, Oxford, 1884–1928.
PMLA   *Publications of the Modern Language Association of America*,
                            Menasha, Wisconsin.
RES (N.S.)   *Review of English Studies* (New Series).
SAB   *The Shakespeare Association Bulletin*, New York.
ShQ   *The Shakespeare Quarterly*, New York.

INTRODUCTION

This edition follows the Quarto text of 1600 (on which see pp. 75–80), with minor modifications from the First Folio of 1623 and later editions.

I. PUBLICATION

Publication of the Quarto followed soon after two entries in the *Registers of the Stationers' Company*. The first runs as follows:

4. Augusti

As you like yt/a booke
HENRY the *FFIFT*/a booke } to be staied[1]
Euery man in his humour/a booke
The Commedie of much A doo about nothing /a booke

No year is given but the immediately preceding entries relate to plays registered in 1600 by the Lord Chamberlain's Men, the leading actors' company and Shakespeare's own. Why these four were 'to be staied' is not known: this may have been the company's attempt to forestall piratical publication of its property.[2] The same year, however, *Henry V* was piratically and faultily published by Thomas Millington and John Busby, and the players may have tried specifically to safeguard their rights. They kept *As You Like It* unpublished until the 1623 Folio, and the remaining pair they sold to authorized booksellers. *Every Man In His Humour*, registered for publication on 14 August 1600, was soon published in a good text by Walter Burre. Shortly after the quoted entry the *Register* carried the following notice:

23 Augusti

Andrewe Wyse   Entred for their copies vnder the handes of
William Aspley   the wardens Two bookes. the one called

---

1. *A Transcript of the Registers of the Company of Stationers*, ed. E. A. Arber (1876), Lib. C, occasional notes preceding the Register, vol. III, p. 37.
2. A. W. Pollard, *Shakespeare's Fight with the Pirates* (1920), p. 49.

> *Muche a Doo about nothinge*. Thother *the second parte of the history of kinge HENRY the iiii^{th} with the humours of Sir IOHN FFALLSTAFF*: Wrytten by master Shakespere. xij^{d1}

Since Puritan opponents of the drama had prompted the Privy Council on 22 June 1600 to limit the number of London's theatres to two, and the number of weekly performances to two at each,[2] the players might well need to supplement their income by selling play texts. Whatever the reason, that year Valentine Sims printed for Wise and Aspley the first and only Quarto of *Much Ado About Nothing*. The title-page read:

> Much adoe about / Nothing. / *As it hath been sundrie times publikely* / acted by the right honourable, the Lord / Chamberlaine his seruants. / *Written by William Shakespeare*. / [Ornament] / LONDON / Printed by V[alentine]. S[immes]. for Andrew Wise, and / William Aspley. / 1600.

It seems strange that until 1623 no reprintings were called for of these plays with such features as, on the one hand, 'the humours of Sir Iohn Ffallstaff' and, on the other, the wits of Beatrice and Benedick, but Elizabethan publication abounds in odd features. Eighteen of Shakespeare's plays remained unprinted until the 1623 Folio, including *Much Ado*'s companion comedies *As You Like It* and *Twelfth Night*, and some of the finest tragedies, among them *Macbeth*, *Julius Caesar*, *Coriolanus*, and *Antony and Cleopatra*. Of *Othello* there is one Quarto only, as late as 1622. So *Much Ado* is far from unique.

2. THE PLAY'S DATE

The play is not named in *Palladis Tamia*, the survey of notable works compiled by Francis Meres and entered in the *Stationers' Register* on 7 September 1598. Meres was in London in 1597 and 1598, seemingly mixing with literary men: his list is up to date enough to include Everard Guilpin's *Skialethia*, registered eight days after his own work. *Palladis Tamia* offers 'A comparatiue discourse of our English Poets with *the Greek, Latine, and Italian Poets*', and it rates Shakespeare 'the most excellent in both kinds for the stage' (i.e. comedy and tragedy). Of the comedies, it names

---

1. E. A. Arber, op. cit., vol. III, p. 170.
2. *Acts of the Privy Council, A.D. 1599–1600*, New Series, xxx, 1905, pp. 395–8.

'his *Gentlemen of Verona*, his *Errors*, his *Loue labors lost*, his *Loue labours wonne*, his *Midsummers night dreame*, & his *Merchant of Venice*'.

That '*Loue labours wonne*' was in fact the present play has been maintained[1] but is untenable: in August 1603 a London bookseller, Christopher Hunt, listed among his stock '*marchant of vennis, taming of a shrew, loves labor lost, loves labor won*',[2] and this rules out the idea that this last-named play was either *The Taming of the Shrew* or *Much Ado About Nothing*: any stock which Hunt had of the latter could only have been of the 1600 Quarto, the title-page of which bears its accepted name and no other. Meres, it must be concluded, did not mention *Much Ado*. The omission might be accidental, but it creates a strong supposition that the play was not known when he compiled his list, and so suggests the middle or latter part of 1598 as the earliest likely date of composition. A terminal date is fixed by the fact that Will Kemp the comic actor, whose name (variously rendered) appears in Dogberry's speech-headings in the 1600 Quarto (see the collation notes for iv. ii), left the Lord Chamberlain's Men early in 1599.

Stylistic evidence, though more subjective, supports such a date. The controlled energy of style, the integrity of thought and expression, and the masterly interrelating of diverse materials ally it with Shakespeare's full and confident maturity around 1598–9. As the original Arden edition noted, 'all the different

---

1. Originally by A. E. Brae, *Collier, Coleridge, and Shakespeare* (1860): he argued that the '*sundrie times publikely* acted' of Q's title-page might mean performances over some years, that Benedick and Beatrice look like 'COMPANION PICTURES' (Brae's capitals) to Berowne and Rosaline of *Love's Labour's Lost* (the '*finished portrait*' after the '*first sketch*'), that *Love's Labour's Lost* and *Much Ado* are contrasted in handling (the one 'obscure and euphuistic' in prevalent rhyme, the other 'plain and colloquial' in prevalent prose), and that 'Love's Labour' refers not to lovers' labour but labour of 'the deity Love . . . overcoming the apparently insuperable difficulties opposed to him' (pp. 138–9)—love's labour being *Lost* in the earlier play because Death finally frustrates Cupid, and *Won* in the later because Don Pedro succeeds in 'one of Hercules' labours', 'an achievement of great and supernatural difficulty, to be undertaken only by Gods and heroes'. These are mere surmises, not strengthened by alleged parallel phrases which prove equally insubstantial. Robert F. Fleissner, in '*Love's Labour's Won* and the occasion of *Much Ado*' (*Shakespeare Survey* 27, 1974), largely accepts the arguments of Brae and of A. H. Tolman (in *The Original Version of 'Love's Labour's Lost' with a Conjecture as to 'Love's Labour's Won*', 1918), for identifying the two plays and argues for a double title (*Love's Labour's Won*; *or, Much Ado About Nothing*) involving not only a pun on '*Nothing*' (see p. 4, below) but one also on '*Won*' (One) and '*Nothing*'. But the case is surely negatived by the fact that had Hunt had *Much Ado* in stock that is what he would have called it.

2. See T. W. Baldwin, *Shakspere's 'Love's Labor's Won*' (1957), p. 31.

elements of style and language, as of emotional interest, are reconciled . . . so harmonious[ly] as to render almost untenable the hypothesis of two different periods of craftsmanship' (as had been argued in the New Cambridge edition, 1923). *A Midsummer Night's Dream* seems likely to belong to 1595–6 (with, probably, a first performance on 19 February 1596; see the New Arden edition, p. lvi); *The Merchant of Venice* to 1596, the *Henry IV* pair and *The Merry Wives of Windsor* to 1596–7, *As You Like It* to early 1599, and *Julius Caesar* and *Henry V* to later that year. The latter part of 1598 offers a likely space for *Much Ado*, and to that period both factual and stylistic evidence rather decidedly points.

3. THE TITLE

Much Ado About Nothing sounds a title apt for some ephemeral diversion but hardly for a play whose comic and tragicomic power makes so momentous an impact. The reason for it may be Shakespeare's frequent nonchalance about his comedies' names.[1] But there may in fact be more to the matter. As Richard Grant White observed in his edition of 1858, in Elizabethan speech 'nothing' and 'noting' sounded much the same;[2] the play's plot, White argued, depends on 'noting'—watching, observing. Over-hearings are central to it, along with the consequent (and often erroneous) reportings or concludings, and certainly the main comic 'ado'—the gullings of Benedick and Beatrice—and the main serious one—the accusation of Hero—though resulting from 'noting' rest upon 'nothing'.

That 'nothing', colloquially spoken, was close to or identical with 'noting' is the basis of Shakespearean puns, especially in a context of musical 'noting'.[3] A similar pun, though non-musical, is conceivable here. Even this reinforcement of significance hardly produces a masterpiece of nomenclature; still, it fits the thematic awareness of dramatic crises prompted by rumours, mis-apprehensions, suspicions forming themselves into certitudes, molehills taken for mountains. Not that a sole 'noting/nothing' is the whole reason why Benedick and Beatrice are gulled so readily;

1. Titles with a take-it-or-leave-it air like *Much Ado About Nothing, As You Like It*, and *Twelfth Night; or, What You Will* suggest a dramatist 'very sure of his public' (J. Dover Wilson, *Shakespeare's Happy Comedies*, 1962, p. 121).

2. Presumably *noht*'n. 'Nothing' can still colloquially sound like *nut*'n.

3. Equivalence of sound is evident in this play at II. iii. 57—'*Note notes*, forsooth, and *nothing*'—and in *Wint.* IV. iv. 603—'my sir's song, and admiring the *nothing* of it'. Similarly 'moth' and 'mote' in *MND*; see New Arden edn, *Dramatis Personae* n. 8, p. [3].

the attraction they refuse to admit is already powerfully there, is very clearly 'something'. But the ploys which dislodge it from its hiding place are ingenious fictions ('nothings'); so, even there, the 'ado' of the result springs from 'noting', however contrived the fabrication. The play's title is, in fact, teasingly full of meaning.

4. SOURCES

(i) Claudio and Hero

General survey

Stories of the lover deceived by a rival or enemy into believing his beloved false are widespread and of great antiquity. An analogue of the Claudio–Hero plot has been traced back to a fifth-century Greek romance by Chariton, *Chaereas and Kallirrhoe*. Seventeen Renaissance versions, narrative or dramatic, are recorded before Shakespeare's, in Spanish, Italian, French, German, and English. They include the fifteenth-century Spanish *Tirant lo Blanch* (*Tirant the White*) by Juan Martorell, which probably lies behind Ariosto's version in the fifth canto of *Orlando Furioso* (1516).[1] Ariosto's lovers are named Ariodante and Genevra. His story, first translated into English and much elaborated in Peter Beverley's poem, *The Historie of Ariodanto and Ieneura* (*c.* 1566) (see Appendix I.i),[2] was further translated by Sir John Harington as *Orlando Furioso in English Heroical Verse* (1591). From Ariosto, Spenser derived his own very different version, which ends in disaster instead of the lovers' reunion; it tells how Squire Phedon, deceived by his supposed friend Philemon into thinking his adored Claribell disloyal, falls into the intemperance of killing her (*The Faerie Queene*, 1590, II.4.xvi–xxxviii; see Appendix I.iii.)

Meanwhile Matteo Bandello, the Italian ecclesiastic, diplomat, and man of letters, treated the subject in his own way in the twenty-second story of *La Prima Parte de le Novelle* (1554), naming his lovers Sir Timbreo and Fenicia. A French translation, morally and rhetorically elaborated, appeared as the eighteenth tale of the third volume of François de Belleforest's *Histoires Tragiques* (1569).

Versions in English other than those mentioned comprise, possibly, a 'matter of Panecia' (i.e. Fenicia?) play performed by

1. G. Bullough, *Narrative and Dramatic Sources of Shakespeare*, vol. II (1958), p. 62.
2. C. T. Prouty discusses and reprints this work, from the sole surviving copy in the Huntington Library, in *The Sources of 'Much Ado About Nothing'* (1950).

the Earl of Leicester's Men at Court on New Year's Day 1575 but no longer extant,[1] and, more evidently, an *Ariodante and Genevra* (also not extant), done likewise at Court, on 12 February 1583, by Merchant Taylors' schoolboys under their humanist headmaster Richard Mulcaster.[2] Other analogues or sources comprise George Whetstone's story of Rinaldo and Giletta, incorporating elements of Ariosto and Bandello in *The Rocke of Regard* (1576: see Appendix I.ii), and two plays, one—*Victoria*—in Latin (*c.* 1580–3) by Abraham Fraunce, the other—*Fedele and Fortunio, The Two Italian Gentlemen*—in English (1585) by one M. A. (Anthony Munday?).[3] Both are versions of a highly reputed comedy, *Il Fedele*, by Luigi Pasaquaglio (1579). In this, the would-be seducer Fedele, unable to win his desired Vittoria (who, though married, is enamoured of his rival, Fortunio), traduces her to her husband Cornelio and arranges that Cornelio shall see a servant (in love with her maid, like Borachio with Margaret in *Much Ado*) enter the house and court a supposed Vittoria. Cornelio, gulled, plans to poison his wife, but by a trick she mollifies Fedele and escapes her fate. With many variations as to its intrigues the story was widely popular, varying in tone from farce or Plautine comedy to tragedy.

Ariosto: 'Orlando Furioso', Canto V (*1516*)

Ariosto, translated by Harington in 1591, tells how the brave Renaldo, 'Of noble chivalrie the verie flowre' (v. 82), arrives in Scotland and learns that the Scottish princess Genevra must die accused of unchastity unless a champion comes forward to defend her. Resolving to do so he makes for the court at St Andrews and on the way saves a woman from murderous assailants. She is Genevra's maid Dalinda and she tells him that the princess is innocent.

Dalinda has been in love with Polynesso, Duke of Albany, and he has often met her secretly in Genevra's room, ascending by a rope ladder; Polynesso, nevertheless, has aspired to marry Genevra herself. But she loved the noble Ariodante, and was equally loved. Polynesso's desire for Genevra turning to hatred, he plotted to destroy the lovers' hopes. Though posing as

---

1. A. Feuillerat, *Documents Relating to the Office of the Revels in Time of Queen Elizabeth*, in Bang's *Materialen*, xxi. 238. 'Panecia' may be an error for 'Fenicia', the guiltless heroine of Bandello's version.

2. Ibid., xxi. 350.

3 Bullough, ii. 66, 68.

Ariodante's friend, he arranged that Dalinda (who had 'no reason, nor no wit, / His shamefull drift (tho' open) to perceaue'; v. 26) should dress herself as her mistress and admit him by night; he then placed Ariodante and the latter's brother Lurcanio where they could see him enter Genevra's window. The deception succeeded. Horrified, Ariodante disappeared, intending to drown himself, though in fact (unknown to anyone) having jumped from a cliff he thought better of it, swam ashore, and remained incognito. Lurcanio accused Genevra of unchastity, and she has been doomed to death.

To remove the unwitting accomplice Dalinda, Polynesso then planned the murder from which Renaldo has saved her. The two travellers reach St Andrews and Renaldo prepares to fight for justice. He finds a strange knight already engaging the deluded but honourable accuser Lurcanio, and he declares that neither contender should lose his life, Genevra's unknown champion because he fights for the right, Lurcanio because he is the victim of deceit. The combat ceases. Renaldo then accuses Polynesso and in the ensuing fight he mortally wounds him. Polynesso dies confessing his guilt; the strange knight reveals himself as Ariodante and is joyfully reunited with Genevra (to protect whom, though still thinking her guilty, he has even opposed his brother); and Dalinda betakes herself to a nunnery.

The similarities to Shakespeare's plot (though they show considerable variation) amount to Polynesso's mortal jealousy (for reasons different from Don John's in the play); his love affair with the maid and the ladder ascent to the disguised girl impersonating her mistress (though the play transfers these operations to the subordinate Borachio); the maid's ignorance of her action's bearing; the court's belief (in the play only temporary) in the heroine's guilt; the defending champion's challenge to the accuser; and the happy outcome after peril.

The most obvious of the differences from Shakespeare's plot are Ariosto's courtly-romance level; his Scottish location and quite different personal names; his sense of tragic danger and murderous violence (far outgoing anything in the play); his villain's motives (foiled jealousy in love) and initiatives in the deception (instead of through an agent's instigation); his deceived lover's reported suicide and secret reappearance; his accusation urged not by the lover (as a kind of vengeance) but by the lover's brother (as an act of justice); his wholly different handling of Genevra's plight (as compared with Hero's) and of the circumstances of the challenge (in the poem the deluded compassionate

Ariodante opposing his brother; in the play the deluded uncompassionate Claudio opposing the erstwhile friend Benedick) and the restoration of love; and the maid retiring to a nunnery (in the play, fully restored in social esteem). Shakespeare's particulars belong to a markedly different conception from Ariosto's.

Bandello: 'La Prima Parte de le Novelle', Novella 22 (1554)

Bandello's version is much racier, and far nearer to Shakespeare's. It tells how the knightly Sir Timbreo di Cardona, one of King Piero of Aragon's courtiers, and a valiant soldier while the King is capturing Sicily, falls in love during the victory celebrations in Messina with Fenicia, daughter of Messer Lionato de' Lionati, 'a poor gentleman and not his equal'.[1] Fenicia behaves so modestly that Sir Timbreo concludes that he can win her only by marriage (not at all his original plan). Her birth, he reflects, is lower than his but she is of good lineage, and through a friendly nobleman he gains her father's consent. The lovers rejoice and all Messina likewise, Lionato being highly regarded.

A rival, however, Sir Girondo Olerio Valenziano, has also fallen in love with Fenicia. Though basically honourable, and a friend of Sir Timbreo's, he resolves to break the betrothal, and he employs an agent, 'more pleased with evil than with good' (II.115), to tell Sir Timbreo that if he will hide in the garden he shall see Fenicia that very night playing him false. Suffering 'bitter (and as it seemed to him just) anger' (II.115), and 'blinded with the veil of jealousy' (II.116), Sir Timbreo does so, unaccompanied. The bedroom, in a remote part of the house, is entered by Sir Girondo's servant dressed as a gentleman. Sir Timbreo's love turns to 'cruel hate' (II.117), but bound by a vow of silence he leaves the scene without intervening.

Through the nobleman who arranged the betrothal he informs Lionato that Fenicia's misconduct has ended the engagement. Her whole family is shocked; Lionato, attributing the charge to Sir Timbreo's scorn at their reduced circumstances, vows his belief in her innocence and his trust that God will vindicate her. Fenicia herself, swooning, then recovering for a while, delivers a long and touching defence and prays that God will enlighten Sir Timbreo. She then lies apparently dead, but while awaiting burial she revives and her family take this as a sign that truth shall prevail. She is secretly sent to the country house of Lionato's brother and

1. Bullough, II. 118. Further references in this section are likewise to Bullough.

renamed Lucilla. The whole city grieves, obsequies are performed, and a sonnet is carved on her 'tomb'.

Sir Timbreo now begins to waver. He reflects that the bedroom in question is too remote to be hers, and that the intruder could hardly have been visiting her. More remarkably, Sir Girondo, struck with remorse at Fenicia's fate, offers Sir Timbreo his dagger before her tomb, confesses what his jealousy had driven him to, and begs for death.

Vengeance on him will not restore Fenicia, however, and Sir Timbreo nobly declines it. Valuing friendship before love he announces that had he known of Sir Girondo's passion he would have yielded Fenicia to him, or, he suggests, had they discussed the matter, Sir Girondo might have done likewise. They will, at any rate, publicly vindicate her, and this they do. Lionato exacts a promise that Sir Timbreo will take no other bride than one chosen for him.

Time passes. Fenicia completes her seventeenth year and blooms so beautifully as to be unrecognizable as her former self. She has, moreover, a younger sister Belfiore, almost as lovely. Lionato tells Sir Timbreo that he has a bride for him, and a gay company (including Sir Girondo) makes for the country house, attends Mass, and meets Fenicia-Lucilla and Belfiore. Though Sir Timbreo is reminded of Fenicia, in her enhanced beauty he does not recognize her. They are married, and at the wedding banquet he poignantly expresses his grief for the 'dead' bride, his joy in the living one, and his adoration of both; whereupon Lionato announces that the two are one. Joyful reunion ensues, Girondo begs for and receives forgiveness and the hand of Belfiore, and King Piero receives the party on its return to Messina with festivities, bestowing dowries on the brides and wealth and honour on Lionato.

This story is much nearer Shakespeare's than is Ariosto's. From it he derives the festive Messina setting, the names of Pedro and Leonato, Claudio's recent war service (different though the war's cause and course), the courtship conducted through a noble intermediary, the deceiver's disguised agent, the lover's seemingly justified public rejection of the supposedly false bride, the religious assurance buoying up the heroine's friends, her swoon, revival, self-defence, and presumed death, the obsequies and epitaph, Claudio's penitence and submission, Leonato's offering of the 'substitute' bride under his brother's auspices, the acceptance and marriage of the veiled and unknown lady, the revelation, and the concluding festivities under princely patronage.

The differences from Shakespeare's plot are, nevertheless, notable enough to testify to Shakespeare's selective and modifying intelligence. First, Bandello's King Piero has no part in the plot save as the victor during whose sojourn in Messina the wooing takes place, with no intervention from him, and as the patron of the eventual marriage. Shakespeare, instead, has Don Pedro presiding throughout and negotiating the betrothal. The story gains a more courtly air. Then, Bandello gives Fenicia a mother, whom Shakespeare discards, though including '*Innogen*' as Leonato's wife in the entry directions for i.i and ii.i. Since in Bandello the mother figures almost solely when the 'dead' girl is being prepared for burial, and Shakespeare makes no use of this scene, her part doubtless just naturally lapsed. Then again, Sir Timbreo is a sensual youth prepared to seduce Fenicia and turning to marriage only when seduction proves impossible: Claudio, quite on the contrary, rejects Leonato's surmise that he may have 'made defeat of [Hero's] virginity' and vows, convincingly, that he has shown nothing but 'Bashful sincerity and comely love' (iv.i.47, 54). Throughout he is a shy wooer, whose willingness to have Don Pedro negotiate for him seems due as much to social diffidence (so different from his military courage) as to the expected diplomacies of well-bred courtship.

Then again, jealous though Sir Timbreo is on thinking himself deceived, he shows no sign of the jumpiness that the callow Claudio evinces when Don John, almost as his first action, tricks him into thinking that Don Pedro has wooed for himself. True, Claudio is not too blameworthy in this, for Leonato's circle— Leonato, Antonio, even Beatrice and Benedick—all think the same; this Act II minor gulling portends the Act III major one, where Claudio's credulity is again endorsed by the similar error of the experienced Don Pedro. Wanting to give plausibility to the later crisis, Shakespeare differs from Bandello in making Claudio's temperamental instability a strand in the web of deceptions and misunderstandings integral to the play's fabric.

The motives for deception, next, are much changed from Bandello's. Rivalry over Hero, though credible were the events real, would in the world of the play be unfitting to so gentle and sheltered a heroine, so no element of rival love enters: Hero is to be virginal even to the extent of having no other wooer. From the rumbles of the concluded war Shakespeare picks up a different motive for Don John's envy—military jealousy and rancour—and saves Hero from any taint of competition; Don John's animus is against the 'young start-up' whose glory it is to have overthrown him (1.iii.62–3) and against the princely brother who has forgiven his rebellion.

The deceiver, moreover, is not Bandello's brave (though temporarily erring) knight who has loyally fought in King Piero's war but a rebel against his lord and brother; he has the wicked nature of Ariosto's Polynesso embodied in the saturnine, melancholic, minor Machiavel readily recognizable as the source of malice, and dramatically popular on the Elizabethan stage. He is, moreover, a bastard, in conventional corroboration of this evil humour, though on the stage the fact, set down in an entry direction (1.i.87), is not mentioned until Benedick reveals it after the church scandal (IV.i.188).[1] For Bandello's 'friend', treacherous only through love rivalry, Shakespeare substitutes a melodramatic rebel/foxy schemer, polarizes the two sides, sharpens the dramatic effect, and avoids the love-versus-friendship situation which had worked so dubiously in *The Two Gentlemen of Verona* and which in Bandello produces a Sir Timbreo and Sir Girondo each ready to hand over Fenicia regardless of her choice. Shakespeare rejects also the unlikely situation in Bandello when Sir Girondo, penitent after his appalling conduct, is again received into Lionato's family and shares in the wedding celebrations.

Among other main differences from Bandello are the equalizing of rank between Claudio and Hero, whose father is Governor of Messina, gracious and generous host of Don Pedro, not merely the head of a reduced though ancient family. This results in social cordiality all round among friends and eliminates any intrusive considerations of status. Of more importance are the different ways in which the accusation and its sequel are managed. In Bandello, Sir Timbreo alone sees the ladder trick. He then engages a friend to break off the betrothal before ever the wedding ceremony is reached. He wholly fails to convince Fenicia's family that she is guilty, and soon he begins to suspect his own judgement. Claudio on the other hand has fellow witnesses, in one of whom he has every confidence, and what they think they see is corroborated by Borachio. Then, though earlier he has had Don Pedro woo for him, Claudio himself takes up in church the role of accuser and performs it with highly dramatic effect; the impact is much stronger than with Bandello's breach negotiated by proxy, effected in Leonato's own household. So clear does the evidence

1. In *King John*, Philip Faulconbridge, bastard son of Richard Coeur de Lion, is a hero worthy of his father; bastardy, though conventionally thought synonymous with wickedness, was not necessarily so considered.

seem, and so authoritative are the witnesses, that Leonato is convinced, and even Benedick is 'attir'd in wonder' (IV.i.144) until Beatrice makes his mind up for him. And Claudio, far from coming to suspect his own judgement, has to behave with egregious tactlessness, to be challenged by Benedick (analogously to the situation in Ariosto, though this one is differently handled), and have his error dispelled by Dogberry.

Neither Bandello nor Shakespeare intends the tragic shock to be unbearable; both provide assurance of relief. But this happens in quite different ways. Bandello has Lionato's family confident that God will reveal the truth; Shakespeare has Dogberry's Watch discover it beforehand, and the Friar give spiritual comfort in church. The passions of Claudio and Leonato stretch the nerves in one direction: knowledge that enlightenment will soon dawn relieves them in the other (though Benedick's challenge to Claudio, instigated by the marvellously welcome indignation of Beatrice, maintains the potential of tension). Finally, Dogberry's bumblings produce an enormously enjoyable sense of relaxation.

As for Claudio's conduct, from accusation to clarification, it is far more disturbing than Sir Timbreo's. Whatever psychological reasons may be offered (callowness, shattered idealism, hyperemotional self-justification, the choking intemperateness to which adolescents are liable, and so on), it is difficult to forgive such behaviour. Yet, as *The Merchant of Venice* had recently shown, Shakespeare was fascinated even in comedy by dramatic intensification whenever tragic potential is present. This kind of comedy is a sunny day over the afternoon of which looms the blackness of storm, to yield to the glow of evening. (Not long before, the end of *Love's Labour's Lost* had shadowed the sunshine with death delaying the fulfilment of love.)

So—and here Shakespeare differs dramatically from Bandello —the church scene explodes with power. Making the bridegroom central in the denunciation of the bride, springing this theatrical coup amidst the happy expectancies and solemnities of the church scene, Shakespeare achieves a scene so startling that the inmost natures of the participants disclose themselves in a way alien to mere comedy.

As for the dénouement, in the sources either the maid, if there is one, or the repentant deceiver discloses the truth. In Shakespeare, things are quite different. Margaret (one feels if one finds time to reflect, but none is allowed) ought to do so but does not, and Don John certainly will not. So Dogberry steps in, an incomparable *deus ex machina*, and turns grief and anger into irresistible mirth.

The interlinking

The main ingredients Shakespeare finds in Ariosto, then, are the following: the intriguer of unredeemed wickedness; the lady's maid involved in an affair with the villain (or his agent), in the ladder trick, and in the impersonation of her mistress, while ignorant of the guile which prompts this; the joint witness, by the lover and his supporter, of the furtive entry; the shared belief in the heroine's guilt; the challenge by a defender; and the villain's punishment.

In Bandello he finds the setting in Messina and its elegant society; names for the visiting prince and his host; the young lover's prowess in his prince's war; the courtship conducted through a noble intermediary; stress on social honour blotted by supposed feminine frailty; the intriguer's scheming subordinate who effects the night entry; the heroine's swoon, revival, self-defence, apparent death, concealment, unrecognized re-appearance, and finally revealed identity; the religious context promising the proper outcome; and the final festivities re-establishing the initial gaiety.

Interweaving Bandello's materials with Ariosto's, Shakespeare shows a mind ranging over elements loosely similar but so markedly variant in tone and incidents that only the shrewdest of judgements could co-ordinate them into a theme of such tragi-comic force. Of course, his treatment shows one fundamental difference from both Ariosto's and Bandello's: those, though ending with love satisfied, are not comedies. In *Much Ado*, Beatrice, Benedick, and Dogberry affect the tenor of the serious plot throughout, enriching and brightening it in its happy phases, qualifying its severity in its grave ones, and doing this not merely by concurrent presence but by the most integral of plot-relationships. *Much Ado* is indeed superbly devised.

Belleforest: 'Le Troisiesme Tome des Histoires Tragiques Extraictes des oeuvres Italiennes de Bandel', Histoire XVIII (1569)

Belleforest's narrative closely follows Bandello's, particularly in its later stages, from the crisis of the broken engagement to the end. The main difference lies in much sentimental and moralizing embellishment; Belleforest is about half as long again as Bandello, a difference for which the embellishment largely accounts. To relate his plot would be virtually to recite Bandello again.

On which version Shakespeare drew can hardly be determined with complete certainty, since the differences between them, in so far as they belong to the story and not to the sentimentalizings of Belleforest, are insignificant; none, anyway, has any bearing on Shakespeare's treatment. The likelihood, though, is in favour of Bandello. Momentarily, Belleforest's 'le Roy Pierre d'Aragon' may look closer than Bandello's 'il re Piero di Ragona', but this detail is too slight to support any deduction.

What seems more significant is that, while in neither version does King Piero/Pierre figure as more than detachedly present at start and finish (at the start as the victor whose entourage is enjoying life in Messina, at the finish as benefactor of Lionato's family), Belleforest's prince enters the story much less favourably than Bandello's, as 'ce roy inhumain Pierre d'Aragon'. This is because Belleforest's French patriotism is outraged by the slaughter suffered by the French at the Sicilian vespers of 1283, which occasioned the King's arrival with his army to take the island over. If this had been how Pierre was brought to Shakespeare's attention, the transformation into the gaily participating, courteous, and kind Don Pedro of the play would be most unexpected. It is true that in Bandello also King Piero occupies Sicily (being induced to do so by the Pope), and then defeats an invasion by the King of Naples with great difficulty and much slaughter on both sides. But nothing is said to his disadvantage, and much is made of the joyful victory celebrations, so he forms a far likelier original for Shakespeare to transform into the noble friend who furthers the young hero's suit.

The odds, then, seem decidedly to favour Bandello as the actual source. For all practical purposes, in any case, he must be so considered, since Belleforest—if against likelihood his was the version Shakespeare had before him—merely transmits, as far as all material points go, what his precursor furnished him with.

(ii) Beatrice and Benedick

Beatrice and Benedick themselves, though not referable to precise sources, owe much to two traditions. These are those of the scorner of love, rejecting suitors, and of the witty courtiers in many Renaissance stories exchanging debate or badinage.

The scorner of love

This tradition is familiar in romance and popular narrative. The scorner, the love-heretic, often finds his or her hauteur a prelude to conversion and surrender. In *Troilus and Criseyde*, having derided Cupid as 'lord of thise fooles alle', Troilus is foreseeably subjected to the anguish and ardour of desire. Shakespeare's own Valentine opens *The Two Gentlemen of Verona* by teasing the amorous Proteus on being 'yoked' in a state 'where scorn is bought with groans, / Coy looks with heart-sore sighs' (I.i.29–30), only himself soon to be mocked by Speed as being 'metamorphis'd with a mistress', Silvia (II.i.16–28). The King and lords of *Love's Labour's Lost* suffer similarly for their hubris, and admit defeat. An instance very recent at the time when Shakespeare was working on *Much Ado* is that in Spenser's story of the haughty Mirabella, the widely adored but scornful beauty who vows that, born free, she will ever remain so.[1] 'With the onely twinckle of her eye' (stanza 31) she torments her admirers until Cupid enquires why his servants suffer so, and then condemns her to wander the world until she has saved as many loves as she destroyed. Since in two years she manages to redeem two only as against the scores she has slain, the sentence looks interminable. Her steed is led by the tyrannous Disdain cruelly abusing her, and followed by Scorn with a whip (Beatrice, we may recall, is 'Lady Disdain', in whose eyes 'Disdain and scorn ride sparkling').

A nearer suggestion of Beatrice, however, occurs in Castiglione's *Il Cortegiano* (1528) (see pp. 16–18): Shakespeare may well have known it:

> I have also seene a most fervent love spring in the heart of a woman, towarde one that seemed at the first not to beare him the least affection in the world [This appears to mean 'towards one for whom she seemed not to bear the least affection'; Ed.], onely for that she heard say, that the opinion of many was, that they loved together.[2]

Nothing could better foreshadow Beatrice's self-discovery.

Shakespeare had himself treated the related though different figures of Katherina the beautiful termagant of *The Taming of the*

1. *The Faerie Queene*, VI.vii. The parallel was pointed out by A. F. Potts in 'Spenserian "Courtesy" and "Temperance" in Shakespeare's *Much Ado About Nothing*', *SAB* XVII (1942), and developed by C. T. Prouty in *The Sources of 'Much Ado About Nothing'*, pp. 53–5.
2. Op. cit., ed. W. Raleigh (1900), Tudor Translations series, p. 279.

Shrew, the witty ladies of *Love's Labour's Lost* routing the lords who think themselves superior to love, and Portia in *The Merchant of Venice* deriding her flock of suitors as gaily as Beatrice could do. Shortly, in *As You Like It*, Rosalind would mock affected lovers. All these in due course yield, like Beatrice herself, but before they do they all (save for Katherina) deploy the shrewd wisdom and witty malice which are their invincible weapons against male pretension.

Patterns of courtesy and wit

What was needed for wit comedy was a literary genre of intellectual equality between the sexes in a sophisticated spirit of challenge and debate; this is the basic theme of George Meredith's classic essay *The Idea of Comedy*.

The traditions of courtesy literature which came to provide this did not begin with the Italian Renaissance,[1] but for the present purpose the seminal inspiration was that of Baldassare Castiglione's *Il Cortegiano*, the outstanding example of Renaissance social doctrine.[2] Castiglione (1478–1529) entered the service of the Duke of Urbino in 1504 and proved accomplished in war and the humanities. He recorded the tone of his circle in a work which Dr Johnson was to recommend to Boswell on 2 October 1773, while they were in Skye, as 'the best book that ever was written on good breeding'.[3] It celebrates the ducal circle in 'the lytle

1. For medieval precedents see John Lawlor (ed.), *Patterns of Love and Courtesy* (1966).

2. See Mary Augusta Scott, '*The Book of the Courtyer*: a possible source of Benedick and Beatrice', *PMLA* xvi (1901), p. 476. The article argues: (*i*) that Shakespeare could well have known the work, since it had had three editions by 1588; (*ii*) that prior to *Much Ado* he had done nothing in dialogue comparable to the freedom and ease of the *conversazioni* in *Il Cortegiano* (a dubious point); (*iii*) that, wishing to brighten the semi-tragedy of Claudio and Hero, he found in *The Courtyer* 'a charming witty pair [Lord Gaspare Pallavicino and the Lady Emilia Pia] in a dramatic dialogue'; (*iv*) that though in their witty sparrings (like *Much Ado*'s 'merry war'), Lord Gaspare (like Benedick 'a professed tyrant to their sex') takes a lively anti-feminist stance and Lady Emilia counter-attacks, all this happens in a mutually appreciative spirit. 'It is impossible to speak too highly of the artistic setting of the four evenings' conversation, sparkling with every variety of graceful interlude, from grave to gay; now a pleasing metaphor, now a jest, a drollery—a skirmish of wit, a dramatic episode' (op. cit., p. 487). The resemblances noted are, however, merely general parallels, sometimes quite loose, and not specific enough to prove a direct debt owed by Shakespeare to Castiglione.

3. Its influence rapidly spread. In England Thomas Hoby translated it (1552–4) and published the result in 1561 as *The Courtyer of Count Baldassar*

Citye of Urbin', a principal feature of which is the distinction of the women. Among them Lady Emilia Pia, 'endowed with so lovely a wytt and judgment as you shall knowe, seemed the maistresse and ringe leader of all the companye'. The spirit of the place is one of intelligent happiness—'pleasaunte communication and merye conceytes, and in every man's countenaunce . . . a lovynge jocoundness'.[1] The men are brave, honourable, and athletic, the women charming, lively, and intelligent:

> For right as it is seemlye for [the man] to showe a certain
> manlinesse full and steadye, so doeth it well in a woman to
> have a tendernesse, soft and milde, with a kinde of womanlie
> sweetnes in every gesture of herres.[2]

They dance, cultivate music, and enjoy 'wytty sportes and pastimes'. Accomplishments are achieved 'rather as nature and trueth leade them, then study and arte'.[3] Their speech is cultured, neither archaic nor affected, their utterances well turned. Debating on love and kindred matters the women distinguish themselves as much as the men, for 'who woteth not that without women no contentation or delite can be felt in all this lief of ourse?'[4] In particular the sprightly contentions between Lady Emilia and Lord Gaspare Pallavicino reflect their ideal of mental and temperamental equality. The Tudor Translations edition admirably sums up what the book could offer to Elizabethan playwrights. First, in general terms:

In one notable regard *The Courtyer* may well have served as a

---

Castilio; further editions followed in 1577 and 1588, before the date of *Much Ado*. Roger Ascham, in *The Scholemaster* (1570), remarked that it should be more noted in the English court (he died in 1568, before it had had its full effect), since 'advisedlie read and diligentlie folowed but one yeare at home in England [it] would do a yong jentleman more good then three yeares travell abrode spent in Italie' (ed. J. E. B. Mayor, 1863, p. 61). John Florio's *Second Frutes* (1591: dedication) reports that the most commonly studied books for those learning Italian were this, together with Guazzo's dialogues (see below, p. 18). In John Marston's first *Satire* (ll. 27–50) the punctilious courtier is 'the absolute Castilio,— / He that can all the points of courtship show'. Everard Guilpin's *Skialethia* (1598) invites the reader to Court, where '*Balthazer* [*i.e.* Baldassare Castiglione] affords / Fountaines of holy and rose-water words' (Sig. C4). Gabriel Harvey paid repeated Latin tributes (*e.g. Rhetor*, 1577, prefatory letter, and fol. 1.ii; also *Gratulatio Valdinensium*, 1578, IV.3, 17, 18). Ben Jonson's *Timber: or Discoveries* (1641) recommends Castiglione's book, along with Cicero's *De Oratore*, as a model for the '*Life*, and *Quicknesse*, which is the strength and sinnewes of your penning, by pretty Sayings, Similitudes, and Conceits' (ed. G. B. Harrison, 1923, pp. 86–7).

1. Op. cit., ed. W. Raleigh (1900), p. 32.
2. Ibid., p. 219.   3. Ibid., p. 59.   4. Ibid., p. 264.

model for the nascent Elizabethan drama. The dramatic form
of colloquy in which the book was cast was the most popular of
literary forms at the time of the Renaissance. . . . To escape
from the appointed order, the categories, partitions, and theses
of scholasticism into a freer air; to redeem the truths of morals
and philosophy from their servitude to system, and to set them
in motion as they are seen in the live world, . . . was in itself a
kind of humanism, a reaching after the more perfect expressiveness of the drama.

Then, in more specific terms:

The civil retorts, delicate interruptions, and fencing matches of
wit that are scattered throughout the book had an even higher
value as models for English writing. Where could English
courtly comedy learn the trick of its trade better than from
this gallant realism? . . . The best models of courtly dialogue
available for Lyly and Shakespeare were to be sought in Italy;
not in the Italian drama, which was given over to the classic
tradition, but in just such natural sparkling conversations as
were reported in the dialogue form of Italian prose.[1]

The inspiration of *The Courtyer* was extended by other works.
George Pettie translated Stefano Guazzo's *La Civile Conversazione*
(1574) out of Italian as *The Civile Conversation of M. Steeven Guazzo*
(1581, Books 1 to 3; 1586, Book 4, translated by Bartholomew
Young). This consists of discussions between Guazzo's brother and
the brother's friend, discussions 'rather familiar and pleasant,
than affected and grave, . . . with carefull diligence and skilful
art; mary yet so that . . . the whole seemeth to be done by
chaunce'.[2] Particularly notable in Guazzo's cultivation of social
courtesies is the comment on the animating spirit of women in
society:

If you marke the order of feastes, playes, and merie meetings
of friends, you will saye, that all these assemblies are colde
and nothing delightfull, if there bee no women at them. For . . .
men in their presence plucke up their spirites, and indevour by
woordes, jestures, and all other wayes to give them to under-
stande howe desirous they are of their favour and good will. . . .
To be shorte, women are they whiche keepe men waking and in
continuall exercise. . . . [And] women do the verie same, who I

1. Ibid., pp. lxxi–lxxii, lxxxiv.
2. Op. cit., ed. E. Sullivan (1925), Tudor Translations, 2nd series, 1.24, 27.

warrant you woulde not be so fine, so trimmed and tricked up, so amiable every way, but of a desire to please men.[1]

No very original discovery, perhaps; yet to establish such a code was to set the tone for Shakespeare's world of courtly comedy.

Lyly

In comic drama the strongest influence on Shakespeare was that of John Lyly's euphuistic fiction and plays.[2] Their effects on Shakespeare's prose will be suggested later (see pp. 25-6 and Appendix II); here what is in question is the technique of comic management. Lyly's is a gay, trim world of (if one took them seriously) affected clevernesses, in an elegantly mannered society which would be speechless were epigrams disallowed. Each phrase must have its point, each utterance its poise and pattern like the figures in a dance; each speaker must, whatever his alleged emotion, be self-possessed.

Lyly's plays develop epigrams and antitheses as their specific mode. The brisk logic-chopping of his pert pages and banterers foreshadows that of Shakespeare's cheerful impertinents like Moth, Costard, Launce, Speed, and Launcelot. His suavely witty exchanges among young elegants are heard again in Shakespeare's courtly comedies (see Appendix II). The aim is to achieve, as Silvia remarks in *The Two Gentlemen of Verona*, 'a fine volley of words, gentlemen, and quickly shot off', except that the ladies are as adept as the gentlemen and often more so, and the volleys, with Shakespeare's development, consist not of words alone but of perceptive analyses and the sparkling rallies of active minds.[3]

Shakespearean precedents

Shakespeare had already brought to a high point of stage effectiveness the sexual rivalry for mastery in *The Taming of the Shrew* (for instance at II.i.179-270) and the wit contest over love and other matters among the lords and ladies of *Love's Labour's*

---

1. Op. cit., 1.235-6.
2. There is an excellent chapter, 'Lyly and Shakespeare', in G. K. Hunter's *John Lyly: the Humanist as Courtier* (1962).
3. Of *Love's Labour's Lost* G. K. Hunter remarks, 'Shakespeare has written a courtly play, a play which exposes to our admiration the brilliant life of a highly civilised community bent on enjoying itself. . . . Shakespeare, like Lyly, centres his picture of Cortegiano-like brilliance on what is also known as courtship—the verbal technique of wooing' (op. cit., p. 334).

Lost, Berowne and Rosaline in particular (as at II.i.113–27 and
179–92). In Berowne, moreover, he had already drawn a precursor
of Benedick, rallying on all but equal terms with the wittiest of the
women; 'a merrier man / Within the limit of becoming mirth / I
never spent an hour's talk withal,' Rosaline testifies, one whose
'eye begets occasion for his wit' so that his tongue turns to jest
whatever it touches. Shakespeare had also shown the self-
confident Berowne, suddenly subject to love, breaking out into
comically exasperated soliloquies in verse and prose which are
hardly distinguishable from the idiom of Benedick:

> And I, forsooth, in love; I, that have been love's whip;
> A very beadle to a humorous sigh;
> A critic, nay, a night-watch constable;
> A domineering pedant o'er the boy,
> Than whom no mortal so magnificent!
>   . . . Go to; it is a plague
> That Cupid will impose for my neglect
> Of his almighty dreadful little might.[1]

The King he is hunting the deer: I am coursing myself. They
have pitched a toil: I am toiling in a pitch—pitch that defiles.
Defile! a foul word. . . . I will not love; if I do, hang me.
I'faith, I will not. O, but her eye! By this light, but for her eye,
I would not love her—yes, for her two eyes. Well, I do nothing
in the world but lie, and lie in my throat. By heaven, I do love;
and it hath taught me to rhyme, and to be mallicholy; and
here is part of my rhyme, and here my mallicholy. Well, she
hath one o' my sonnets already; the clown bore it, the fool sent
it, and the lady hath it: sweet clown, sweeter fool, sweetest
lady![2]

Prefiguring Benedick, Berowne boasts himself superior to his
fellows:

> I am betray'd by keeping company
> With men like you, men of inconstancy.
> When shall you see me write a thing in rhyme?
> Or groan for Joan? or spend a minute's time
> In pruning me? When shall you hear that I
> Will praise a hand, a foot, a face, an eye,
> A gait, a state, a brow, a breast, a waist,
> A leg, a limb?—[3]

this, of course, immediately before proving as vulnerable as they.

1. *LLL*, III.i.164–8, 191–3.   2. Ibid., IV.iii.1–15.   3. Ibid., IV.iii.175–82.

If Benedick has his forerunner in Berowne, Beatrice has hers among the witty ladies first of Lylyan and then of Shakespearean comedy. Of them all, only Katherina of *The Taming of the Shrew* compares with her in combativeness (and she is acrimoniously rather than attractively 'witty', greatly outdoing Beatrice in belligerence, though Beatrice shares the impulse to dominate which makes Katherina shrewish, as Beatrice, except in fun, is not): but others like Rosaline, Portia, and Rosalind delight in their intelligent high spirits. When they are satirical they are appreciatively so, enjoying the extravagances they mock but desiring no more in the way of reform than the prevalence of affectionate esteem and good humour. Each is, as Beatrice is for Don Pedro, 'By my troth, a pleasant-spirited lady', and each might say, as Beatrice does, 'There was a star danced, and under that was I born'.

(iii) Dogberry

John Aubrey (1626–97) collected materials for his *Brief Lives* from sources more or less connected with Shakespeare, and among them the report that

> The Humour of . . . the Constable in a *Midsomernight's Dreame*, he happened to take at Grendon [i.e. Grendon Underwood] in Bucks . . . whiche is in the roade from London to Stratford, and there was living that Constable about 1642 when I first came to Oxon. Mr. Jos. Howe is of that parish and knew him.[1]

A Midsummer Night's Dream boasting no constable, this may be meant for Bottom the weaver, but since the Grendon notable is specifically constabulary Aubrey probably erred over the play's name rather than the character's function. One cherishes the thought of some actual Dogberry, in his own world anything but mute and inglorious. More 'sources' than this cannot be expected, save in the general sense that exuberant mismanagers of the English language, of the logic of evidence, and of the processes of discourse have always been found comic; Shakespeare had shown Dull, the constable of *Love's Labour's Lost*, 'reprehending' the Duke and wishing to 'see his own person in flesh and blood' (Dull's part is brief, however), Bottom lording it over his fellows, Launcelot Gobbo and his father bemusing Bassanio by interrupting each

---

1. Aubrey's *Brief Lives*, ed. O. L. Dick (1949), p. 334.

other,[1] and Mistress Quickly unleashing her dazingly voluble malapropisms.

John Payne Collier, who included a biography of Will Kemp, the original Dogberry, in his *Memorials of the Principal Actors in the Plays of Shakespeare* (in the Shakespeare Society's publications for 1846), printed in that society's papers for 1844 a letter from Lord Burghley to Secretary Walsingham dated 10 August 1586, at a time when it was pressingly important to arrest conspirators in the Babington plot against the Queen. In his urgency Burghley marked his missive 'hast hast hast hast Post', and what he was so agitated about were ludicrous shortcomings he had discovered in the measures to (as Dogberry would have it) comprehend all aspicious persons. No actual connection is suggested between the Watch at Enfield (whence the complaint arose) and that at Messina, but real life may have furnished Shakespeare with inspirations over and above any he found at Grendon. The letter runs as follows:

> Sir—As I cam from London homward, in my coche, I sawe at every townes end the number of x or xii, standyng, with long staves, and untill I cam to Enfeld I thought no other of them, but that they had stayd for avoyding of the rayne, or to drynk at some alehowse, for so they did stand under pentyces [i.e. penthouses—like Borachio!] at ale howses. But at Enfeld fyndyng a dosen in a plump, when ther was no rayne, I bethought my self that they war appointed as watchmen, for the apprehendyng of such as are missyng; and there uppon I called some of them to me apart, and asked them wherfor they stood there? and one of them answered, 'To take 3 yong men.' And demandyng how they should know the persons, one answered with these wordes: 'Marry, my Lord, by intelligence of ther favor.' 'What meane you by that?' quoth I. 'Marry', sayd they, 'one of the partyes hath a hooked nose.' 'And have you,' quoth I, 'no other mark?'—'No', sayth they. And then I asked who apoynted them; and they answered one Bankes, a Head Constable, whom I willed to be sent to me. Surely, sir, who ever had the chardge from yow hath used the matter negligently for these watchmen stand so openly in plumps, as

1. *Mer. V.*, ii.ii; cf. *Ado* iii.v. Muriel Bradbrook sees Dogberry and Verges as 'clearly incarnations of Gobbo and his father' (in Leonard F. Dean, ed., *Shakespeare: Modern Essays in Criticism*, 1957, p. 105), but the resemblance is limited to this particular scene. Gobbo and Old Gobbo, Bottom and Quince, Dogberry and Verges, are all comedy duos, the leading comic man and his 'feed'.

no suspected person will come neare them; and if they be no
better instructed but to fynd 3 persons by one of them havyng a
hooked nose, they may miss thereof. And thus I thought good
to advertise yow, that the Iustyces that had the chardge, as I
thynk, may use the matter more circumspectly.[1]

The fact that in the play Borachio brings Conrade under the
penthouse out of the rain is doubtless sheer coincidence. But one
treasures the light thrown on constabulary practice by Bankes's
men, to whom Dogberry's charge might well have been directed,
who seem likelier than not to let 'vagrom men' steal out of their
company, and who have merely a hooked nose on which to hang
their case. Messina's Watch, conjuring up the mysterious
Deformed, a vile thief this seven year, who wears a key in his ear
and hath a lock hanging by it and borrows money in God's name
without repaying it, could hardly surpass the earnest confusions
of Enfield's.[2]

Dogberry's 'source', if seminally in some worthy of Grendon,
lies rather among these anticipations, combined with certain stage
precedents,[3] together (it is a major consideration) with the
cherished abilities of Will Kemp, the role's original performer.
Kemp, leading comedian of the 1590s, figures in the anonymous
Cambridge satire *The Returne from Parnassus*, Part 2 (*c.* 1601) as
instructing a student, Philomusus, in stage delivery, and declaring
that his face 'would be good for a foolish Mayre or a foolish
iustice of peace';[4] he could presumably have trained him, too,
for a foolish constable. Whatever Kemp's skills as a comic actor,
Shakespeare would certainly envisage them in his conception of
Dogberry.[5]

1. *Shakespeare Society Papers* 1 (1844), pp. 3–4.
2. Babington and other conspirators were in fact arrested on the day Burghley
wrote his letter, though in different circumstances, so some parts of England's
law-and-order system worked quite as well as Messina's.
3. For a precedent in Lyly's *Endimion* see below, III.iii.i, n.
4. *The Three Parnassus Plays*, ed. J. B. Leishman (1949), pp. 341–2.
5. For Kemp's qualities see W. A. Armstrong, 'Actors and theatres', in
Shakespeare in his Own Age, Shakespeare Survey 17 (1964), p. 195. This suggests
that as Kemp was notorious for upstaging his fellow actors with extem-
poral witticisms Shakespeare provided him with a part devised to absorb
such sallies: 'As for Dogberry, . . . the bumbling discursiveness of the charac-
terisation seems designed to accommodate . . . such digressions, by-play, and
improvisations as Kempe may have brought to the role. That Shakespeare's
clowns were shaped to fit the actors who played them seems beyond question.'

(iv) Old play?

That an earlier play lurks behind some of Shakespeare's texts is
certain, and some commentators, particularly John Dover Wilson
in the New Cambridge Shakespeare, have extended the assump-
tion widely. In respect of *Much Ado* Dover Wilson held that

(*a*) the Quarto's stage-directions introduce characters with no
function, either at all or at the point of entry;[1]
(*b*) some stage-directions are eccentric or idiosyncratic;[2]
(*c*) in the speech-prefixes for iv.ii Dogberry and Verges are
named in a variety of forms;[3]
(*d*) verse lines have allegedly been cut or revised;[4]
(*e*) loose ends and unexplained allusions occur (e.g. to earlier
encounters between Beatrice and Benedick); in particular,
explanations are needed for the Borachio–Margaret intrigue.

The 'old play', it is supposed, would have been largely, perhaps wholly, in verse. The fact that Beatrice is gulled in verse
(iii.i) 'shows that Beatrice and Benedick provided a comic
underplot in the old play';[5] the 'surviving' verse is judged to
resemble the early styles of *The Two Gentlemen of Verona* and *Romeo
and Juliet*; and in revision, it is argued, some of the 'original' verse
was cut.

 Such shaky 'evidence' does not warrant such confident
deductions. Certainly there were earlier Ariosto- or Bandello-
derived plays, but that any was Shakespeare's, or that any not
his offered him anything worth taking over, is quite un-
demonstrated. Irregular directions and speech-headings are as
likely when an author is drafting a new play as when he is
reworking an old one: he will not get everything right first time.
The alleged verse-cuttings are merely typographical uncertainties
over line-settings or other practical problems. The verse is by no
means immature; much in *As You Like It* (also largely a prose
play) is similar, and so are parts of *The Merchant of Venice* a little
earlier, and of *Julius Caesar* a little later. As for Margaret, in the
sources Shakespeare found a lady's companion unaware that her

---

1. See below, p. 77. 2. See below, pp. 77–8. 3. See iv.ii, nn.
 4. In iv.i, Benedick's lines at ll. 143–5 and the Friar's at 155–8; these are
prose in QF, rearranged as verse from Pope onwards. The latter speech Dover
Wilson considered 'certainly' obscure—which it is not. At v.i. 106–9 he thought
that further lines on the quarrel had been cut, since in the existing text Leonato
and Antonio leave so abruptly.
 5. NCS, p. 104.

folly affected her mistress, and no 'old play' explaining her state of mind need be conjured up.

5. STYLE

(i) Precedents

'Elizabethan thought was more linguistically alive than ours.'[1] The comment is George Wilson Knight's, writing on the expressiveness of Lyly's style. Manipulating a dramatic prose intently alive, Shakespeare owed much to Lyly, as he did in comic tone and technique, though transforming Lylyan artifice into inimitable vitality. Lyly's main gift to Shakespeare might be said to be that of dramatic form through auditory form: as Wilson Knight puts it, in Lyly at his best 'You are jerked into a stage awareness. . . . Instead of listening, you see; instead of knowing, experience'.[2] Many a passage springs to mind in *Much Ado* where sound and sense are integrally one, and combine with thought, attitude, and impulse.[3]

This view amends the conventional one, that Lyly offers merely a kaleidoscope of superficialities. His showier traits, admittedly, soon provoked parody, and in his plays he toned them down as compared with *Euphues*.[4] But the discipline they exacted in poise and control was healthy for dramatic prose, as the courtly decorum of the plays was healthy for romance comedy.

Before Lyly it is hard to find dramatic prose aspiring to art except for that of George Gascoigne's *Supposes*, acted in 1566. This is a translation of Ariosto's *Gli Suppositi* and benefits from its sophisticated original. Its prose is clear and civilized, neatly turned, spiced with alliteration, antithesis, simile, and phrasal pattern, and its characters are not more mannered than its status as a work of neat artifice requires. During the next twenty years little of promise evolved from this lone example, but by 1590 a young dramatist could find in Lyly an intoxicating range of stimuli. For dramatic style there was an endless quarry of pointed elegances, gnomic tags, and heady phrasal flourishes;

1. G. Wilson Knight, 'Lyly', *RES* xv (1939), p. 146.
2. Ibid., p. 148.
3. On the evolution of witty style see Appendix II.
4. Michael Drayton in *Of Poets and Poesie* defines them as 'Talking of Stones, Stars, Plants, of Fishes, Flyes, / Playing with words, and idle Similes'. For other critical views by Sidney, Nashe, Harvey, and others see Lyly, *Works*, ed. R. W. Bond (1902), I. 134, and G. K. Hunter, *John Lyly*, pp. 280 ff.

for temperamental analysis, there were the resourcefulness of repartee, virtuoso self-quizzings in dilemmas, and, not least, delicate emotional graces. If Lyly offered display, he offered also tenderness and sympathy when emotions were to be touched, 'an essential humility and purity before direct human experience that bring [him] closest to Shakespeare'.[1]

(ii) Shakespeare's evolution in comedy

While in Shakespeare's early comedies the character groupings and interplay of social levels follow Lylyan precedents in their witty pages, quipping clowns, and young sophisticates, often paired with or against each other, his assimilation of phrasal refinement is often thought to have waited until *The Merchant of Venice*, where certainly Portia's quick, often antithetical phrasing, sometimes of proverbial quips (as in I.ii), shows a shimmer as elegant as Lyly's own, and far richer. Yet earlier plays such as *The Two Gentlemen of Verona*, *The Comedy of Errors*, and *Love's Labour's Lost* had caught the pleasures of witty artifice, of epigram, the play of metaphor and pert riposte. Thence there pass into later work techniques of inventive spiritedness, into Ford's jealous ruminations in *The Merry Wives of Windsor* (III.ii.26 ff.), Rosalind's mockery of love in *As You Like It* (III.ii.346 ff.), and Falstaff's royal parody in *1 Henry IV* (II.iv.387 ff.), to choose among many examples. This is 'word-play [which] sees similarities in opposites',[2] and is ideal for intellectual duelling and the canvassing of witty alternatives.

(iii) The play's style

Nothing about the play's style is casual or characterless.[3] Falling on the ear with spirited assurance, it is always so fresh as to seem spontaneous, the minting of minds commanding their resources. Nevertheless, it is very artful. Of Beatrice it has rightly been said that she 'exploits the effect of repartee by which replies are made to seem like improvisation'.[4] Even Dogberry is as self-approving a virtuoso as his betters with his gnomic tags and felicitous malapropisms; to affect a more high-falutin' vocabulary than he

1. G. Wilson Knight, 'Lyly', in *RES* xv (1939), p. 163.
2. Ibid., p. 146.
3. Shakespeare's dedications to *Venus and Adonis* and *The Rape of Lucrece*, brief though they are, reveal a delightfully elegant sense of phrase.
4. Vickers, p. 174.

can master is part of his sense of status.[1] For courtliness, the prose manages such discreet and charming Lylyan artifices as Leonato and the Messenger exchange at the outset. These forecast many kinds of surefooted phrasing. There is a lovely trimness (an actor's delight, surely) in such things (they are too many for counting) as 'How much better is it to weep at joy than to joy at weeping!', or 'Rich she shall be, that's certain; wise, or I'll none; virtuous, or I'll never cheapen her', or 'What your wisdoms could not discover, these shallow fools have brought to light'. But in its precision it is equally apt for such differing effects as Claudio's touchingly lucid 'In mine eye, she is the sweetest lady that ever I looked on' (I.i.174–5), Don John's acidulous slanders (III.ii.84–111), and Beatrice's diatribes (IV.i.314–23). Speech so alert with pattern and play, with aphorism and antithetical sparkle, is alive for stage delivery of the most calculated naturalness, everything falling rightly for the voice.

The main mood is hospitable and appreciative, animatedly expressing a sense of vivid appearances. A sampling of a single scene (II.i) yields a characteristic harvest of sprightlinesses—'like my lady's eldest son, evermore tattling'; 'overmastered with a piece of valiant dust'; 'a clod of wayward marl'; 'wooing, wedding, and repenting is as a Scotch jig, a measure, and a cinque-pace'; 'I can see a church by daylight'; 'What fashion will you wear the garland of? About your neck, like an usurer's chain? Or under your arm, like a lieutenant's scarf?'; 'as melancholy as a lodge in a warren'; 'duller than a great thaw'; 'She speaks poniards, and every word stabs'; 'there was a star danced, and under that was I born'. Writers like Voltaire and Shaw practise the wit of intellectual point; Shakespeare's wit is that of aptly surprising natural and human notation, allied with brilliant leaps of unexpected analogy, wit pleasantly likened by Coleridge to

> the flourishing of a man's stick while he is walking, in the full flow of animal spirits, a sort of exuberance of hilarity which . . . resembles a conductor, to distribute a portion of gladness to the surrounding air.[2]

The examples quoted above all come from Beatrice and Benedick,

---

1. Anne Barton pleasantly remarks, 'There is . . . something almost touching in Dogberry's unrequited passion for words in a play in which the others possess a mastery of language' (Riverside, p. 331). But who is to call the passion unrequited? If, like Keats, Dogberry looks on fine phrases like a lover, he certainly feels his wooing rewarded.

2. Coleridge, *Shakespearean Criticism*, ed. T. M. Raysor, vol. II (1960), p. 91.

some measure of what these two contribute. F. P. Wilson's praise
of them is happy:

> If they speak in prose, no one thinks of them as prose characters.
> ... More than any characters in high comedy, they rise above
> verbal wit and pit mind against mind in dialogue that surprises
> in sense, image, and cadence, giving to character both body and
> beauty.[1]

But such qualities are not theirs alone. Mental vitality pervades
the play, whether wittily good or tetchily evil, so that it dances
with dexterities of antithesis, in meaning, tone, colour. The
euphuistic patterns, the epigrammatic points, the complimentary
courtesies, depend on these. Beatrice's exchanges with Benedick
or Benedick's with the love-struck Claudio are virtuoso pointings
of contrasting tenets. Claudio's own pleasantest speech is
devotedly alert with them: '*Silence* is the perfectest *herald* of joy;
I were but *little* happy, if I could say how *much*. Lady, as *you* are
mine, *I* am *yours*; I give away *myself* for *you* and dote upon the
exchange' (II.i.288–91).

Words of charm, tenderness, and grace set up their appreciative
tone, to be challenged by those of witty or malevolent aggression.
The heartening spirit is evoked by many 'generous' words,
praising the sweet, modest, merry, valiant, or honourable nature
of most of the participants. Any number of brief speeches offer
themselves with sprightly pointing and dancing rhythm. But the
technique may be interestingly seen in two longer discourses,
both apparently improvisations yet both beautifully designed,
from speakers as different as Benedick and Borachio. When set
out in phrasal shape they suggest how aptly for stage delivery
(and actor's memory) Shakespeare has evolved the prose forms
of which Lyly had given more artificial yet still salutary examples.
Benedick reflects on Claudio (II.iii.7–21):

> I do much wonder that one man,
> seeing how much another man is a fool
> when he dedicates his behaviours to love,
> will,
> after he hath laughed at such shallow follies in others,
> become the argument of his own scorn
> by falling in love:
> and such a man is Claudio.

---

1. *Shakespearian and Other Studies*, ed. Helen Gardner (1969), p. 86

I have known
when there was no music with him
but the drum and the fife,
and now had he rather hear
the tabor and the pipe.

I have known
when he would have walked ten mile afoot
to see a good armour,
and now will he lie ten nights awake
carving the fashion of a new doublet.

He was wont to speak plain and to the purpose,
like an honest man and a soldier,
and now is he turned orthography—
his words are a very fantastical banquet,
just so many strange dishes.

Borachio is never credited with Benedick's rhetorical resources, yet his narration to Conrade is equally athletic and sinewy (III.iii.149–58):

Two of them did, the Prince and Claudio,
but the devil my master knew she was Margaret;
and partly by his oaths,
which first possessed them,
partly by the dark night,
which did deceive them,
but chiefly by my villainy,
which did confirm any slander that Don John had made,
away went Claudio enraged;
swore he would meet her as he was appointed
next morning at the temple,
and there, before the whole congregation,
shame her with what he saw o'er-night,
and send her home again without a husband.

These are the rhythms of dramatically activated meaning. The voice carries with it, here and elsewhere, meaning and action, whether gracious, combative, sharp,[1] or (like Dogberry's)

---

1. 'Throughout the play, Don John's prose suggests, by means of its controlled Euphuistic pattern, that his blind hatred of all the others is accompanied by a systematic pursuit of villainy' (Craik, p. 303). Don John—'a brutal user of language'—formulates symmetries which 'not only convey the necessary information about his character, but by their very rigidity show up his uncompromising egotism' (Vickers, pp. 177, 171).

unctuous. The stresses seem inevitable; the rhythms arise from thinking and feeling. Yet they imply a masterly control: what looks spontaneous falls into clarifying form.

The style may be delicately ornate, as it is at the beginning. But it may also be dynamically spirited, and, after Leonato's diplomacies with the Messenger, Beatrice's voice rings with inspiriting energy, eager as she is to surprise by dashing forays: 'the rather slow start establishes a norm against which Beatrice's wit stands out'.[1] While the courtly decorum reflects courtesy-book tradition, where everything must please and nothing offend, the different tradition of wit rivalry demands a gay asperity. To Beatrice and Benedick repartee is 'a way of life, a mutual witty antagonism', in which as well as the provocations of repartee 'there is the more difficult task of catching up metaphors and developing them as if by free association'.[2] To this end, the contestants prove their resourcefulness by cadenzas of unpredictable invention. The tonal counterpoint between decorum and vivacity is evident in Benedick's exchanges with Claudio and Don Pedro (I. i. 150–269), or in Don Pedro's courteous straightforwardness and Benedick's hyperbolic extravagances (II. i. 196–258), 'spoken at high speed and in a burlesque fury.'[3] The sequence of connections and leaps, as of electric sparks across gaps, in Benedick's protestations from 'O, she misused me past the endurance of a block!' (II. i. 223) to his exit with 'I cannot endure my Lady Tongue' (II. i. 257–8) is fascinating. The dazzling invention whirls through its manoeuvres, springing from 'block' to 'oak' to 'green leaf', taking in the paradox of the speaking oak and transforming this metaphor into that of the loquacious visor (reactivating the 'mask' scene of a hundred lines earlier), flinging in the unexpected 'duller than a great thaw', then pouring out a flurry of aggressive images (jests like arrow flights at targets, sentences as poniards, words as daggers, breath as pestilence), switching the metaphor from lacerating weapons to decimating 'terminations' and stretching these latter to the North Star, turning then from geographical to chronological comprehensiveness and from biblical to classical heroics, tossing off the hyperbole-paradox of the willing sinners making for hell as a refuge, and finally rising to the virtuoso flourish of 'Antipodes / furthest inch of Asia / Prester John's foot / great Cham's beard / Pygmies'. All this is carried on phrasing which, far from labouring, becomes lighter footed the further it goes,

1. Vickers, p. 174.   2. Ibid., pp. 175, 176.
3. Milton Crane, *Shakespeare's Prose* (1951), p. 195.

up to the 'dish-Tongue' metaphor on which the actor bounds
off into the wings.

Most of the play is in prose; chances for lyrical enrichment are
few, since the major part is comic manoeuvring about love, and
the mocking of attitudinizing. But to ask how its appeal would
change were it entirely in prose is to awaken to the sensitive
qualities of the verse. Prose may show the main strengths but it
has no monopoly of effectiveness. The verse, too, offers courteous
decorum on the one hand and impulsive energies on the other.

The lucidities of Claudio's exchanges with Don Pedro prove
that unruffled sincerities need no loading with effect, no
embellishment more than delicate figurative heightening.
Compared with characteristic verse of, say, *The Two Gentlemen of
Verona* they show the maturity of assured gracefulness. Their
gentle colourings mellow a play of which the bright wit or dark
venom could otherwise seem over-assertive—colourings such as
characterize Claudio's

> How still the evening is,
> As hush'd on purpose to grace harmony! (II.iii.38–9)

or Hero's

> For look where Beatrice like a lapwing runs
> Close by the ground, to hear our conference (III.i.24–5)

or Ursula's

> The pleasant'st angling is to see the fish
> Cut with her golden oars the silver stream (III.i.26–7)

or Don Pedro's

> Good morrow, masters; put your torches out.
> The wolves have prey'd, and look, the gentle day,
> Before the wheels of Phoebus, round about
> Dapples the drowsy east with spots of grey (v.iii.24–7)

(a delicate aubade, dispelling the gloom and grief of Act IV).
Beatrice's dizaine (III.i.107–16) is a charming lapse into lyric
convention from one so professedly unlyrical and unconventional.
And the epitaph and song at the tomb (v.iii), though no striking
specimens of Claudio's 'sad invention', are formally grave in a
way which music would well sustain.

Then, too, there are moving simplicities, touchingly limpid
within the run of delicately-voiced metre, like Hero's 'He is the
only man of Italy, / Always excepted my dear Claudio,' or

Leonato's 'Being that I flow in grief, / The smallest twine may
lead me'. Stylistic assurance is evident in unadorned single-line
speeches going straight to the point, like Leonato's 'As freely, son,
as God did give her me', or 'Are these things spoken, or do I but
dream?'; or Hero's 'And seem'd I ever otherwise to you?', or
'Is my lord well that he doth speak so wide?'; or the Friar's 'Lady,
what man is he you are accus'd of?', or 'There is some strange
misprision in the princes'. Unremarkable though these may seem,
they fly straight to their targets, and it is typical of Beatrice's
directness and power that she releases a similar shaft into the
very bull's-eye: 'O, on my soul my cousin is belied!' The eight
words compress a theatreful of tension.

It is against the unmannered centrality of such verse, equally
far from artlessness and artfulness, that certain enrichments stand
out—Hero's portrayal of Beatrice, for instance, unexpectedly
vivacious in her lines about the 'pleached bower' and the presumptuous honeysuckles, and her brilliant rendering of her
cousin's nature (III.i. 1–80). A different but still stronger effect is
that of Claudio's and Leonato's histrionics in church, the whole
nature of which is to burst through the norms of courtesy and
decorum. Antonio's astonishing vehemence is another example
(v.i. 80–99). The serviceable politeness of most of the verse and
the sparkle of most of the prose saunter along with practised
self-possession; against these the upsurges of rich comic style or of
strong tragic style form impressive contrasts, bold prominences
thrusting through a cultivated landscape.

Like the prose the verse actively responds to the voice. As Hero
and Ursula gull Beatrice, as Hero crowds trait on trait in
describing Beatrice, every demurely mischievous inflection is
rendered, of mock concern, mock indignation, mock regret. As
Beatrice and Benedick go for the last time through their duelling
routines (v.iv. 72–97), the verse in its trim economies sounds its
delicious mimesis of their witty wariness. The church scene and its
successors ring with vigorous utterance, in Claudio's
melodramatic poignancy, Don Pedro's corroborative regret,
Hero's forthright honesty, Leonato's shocked despair, the Friar's
measured considerateness, and so on. One cannot mishear the
rhythm of Leonato's distress in

> But mine, and mine I lov'd, and mine I prais'd,
> And mine that I was proud on—mine so much
> That I myself was to myself not mine,
> Valuing of her—(IV.i. 136–9)

or that of Antonio's voluble fury in v.i. The actor must surely
relish the infallible stressing of

> He shall kill two of us, and men indeed:
> But that's no matter, let him kill one first.
> Win me and wear me, let him answer me.
> Come follow me, boy, come, sir boy, come follow me,
> Sir boy, I'll whip you from your foining fence,
> Nay, as I am a gentleman, I will. (v.i.80–5)

Verse and prose both sound with Shakespearean music, not (in
general) by romantic lyricism but by vitality playing expressively
on the ear. Bernard Shaw, deriding the alleged intelligence of
Beatrice and Benedick, allowed nevertheless that their vocal
felicities amply compensate for any mental shortcomings. 'No
matter how poor, coarse, cheap, and obvious the thought may
be,' he observed, 'the mood is charming, and the music of the
words expresses the mood. . . . Not until the Shakespearean music
is added by replacing paraphrase with the original lines does the
enchantment begin. Then you are in another world.'[1] The
analysis is (mock?) naive; the tribute is true.

6. STAGE HISTORY

Though not reprinted between 1600 and 1623 the play was
evidently popular. The Quarto's title-page proclaims it as
'*sundrie times publikely* / acted by the right honourable, the Lord /
Chamberlaine his seruants', and it figures prominently in the tribute Leonard Digges prefixed to the 1640 edition of Shakespeare's
poems. Comparing Jonson's plays with Shakespeare's, Digges
wrote:

> Though these [Jonson's] have sham'd all the Ancients,
> > and might raise
> Their Authours merit with a crowne of Bayes,
> Yet these sometimes, even at a friends desire
> Acted, haue scarce defrai'd the Seacoale fire
> And doore-keepers: when let but *Falstaffe* come,
> *Hall, Poines,* the rest, you scarce shall have a roome
> All is so pester'd: let but *Beatrice*
> And *Benedicke* be seene, loe in a trice
> The Cockpit, Galleries, Boxes, all are full.

1. *Shaw on Shakespeare,* ed. Edwin Wilson (1969), pp. 156–7.

Seeming allusions or echoes in near-contemporary works confirm this popularity. The *Shakspere Allusion Book* points to Thomas Heywood's *The Fayre Mayde of the Exchange* (1607) as apparently reflecting Benedick in its 'I could not indure the carrier of her wit' (cf. *Much Ado*, II.i.257–8) and 'I am horribly in love with her' (cf. II.iii.226–7), and Dogberry in "'tis most tolerable and not to be endured' (cf. III.iii.36); and to a further apparent Dogberry echo in Robert Armin's dedication to *The Italian Tayler* (1609): 'a Beggar, who hath been writ downe for an Asse in his time' (cf. IV.ii.83–4). Such phrases, it would seem, had become popular currency.

The Lord Chamberlain's accounts record £93. 6s. 8d. as paid to John Heminge on 20 May 1613, for 'presentinge [at Whitehall] before the Princes Highnes the Lady Elizabeth and the Prince Pallatyne Elector fowerteene severall playes': these included 'Much Adoe abowte Nothinge'. £40 more, together with 'his Maiesties rewarde' of £20, was paid the same day for six other performances, including 'Benedicte and Betteris',[1] and, odd though the difference in titles is, this must surely be the same play; the alternative name attests the predominance the comic plot has almost always had over the serious. Robert Burton refers to lovers 'like *Benedict* and *Betteris* in the Comedy',[2] and Charles I wrote 'Benedik and Betrice' against the title in his copy of the Second Folio.[3]

Seventeenth-century records of it are scanty. A regulation from the Lord Chamberlain's office on 12 December 1660 assigned it to the playwright Sir William Davenant and the Duke's Company, with eight other plays, which Davenant proposed to 'reform and make fitt'.[4] The results included the amalgamation of *Much Ado* with *Measure for Measure* in a work Davenant entitled *The Law Against Lovers*, first performed on 15 February 1662 (see Appendix III). When *Much Ado* itself re-emerged, among John Rich's Shakespearean revivals at Lincoln's Inn Fields in February 1721, it was billed as 'Not acted these Thirty Years': it may, therefore, have been played up to about 1690, but specific evidence is lacking.[5] The 1721 revival bore no fruit, and the next production was apparently that by Rich at

1. E. K. Chambers, *William Shakespeare* (1930), vol. II, p. 343.
2. *The Anatomy of Melancholy*, Pt 3, 2, 2, 4. The reference first appeared in the 3rd edn, 1628.
3. J. O. Halliwell-Phillipps, *Memoranda*, 59, quoted in Furness, p. 6.
4. Cited in NCS, p. 159.
5. NCS, p. 160.

Covent Garden in 1737—'Never acted there before'[1]—with further performances in 1739 and 1746.[2] But while itself off the stage *Much Ado* contributed to two adaptations, Charles Johnson's *Love in a Forest* (at Drury Lane in 1723), incorporating bits of Benedick into a version of *As You Like It*, and James Miller's *The Universal Passion* (also at Drury Lane, in 1737), which combined a much altered *Much Ado* with Molière's *La Princesse d'Elide*, with insertions also from *The Two Gentlemen of Verona* and *Twelfth Night*.[3]

Thereafter it fared much better, under Garrick's sponsorship. He rehearsed as Benedick for two months before satisfying himself, and then put the play on at Drury Lane on 14 November 1748 with Hannah Pritchard as Beatrice. Francis Gentleman, in his *Dramatic Censor* (1770), though unconvinced that, as often reputed, Benedick was Garrick's finest part, admitted not only that popular feeling 'authorized the warmest encomiums' on him in the role but also that though Garrick was then past his best 'the pre-eminence of his significant features, the distinct volubility of his expression, and his stage manoeuvres' were outstanding. Mrs Pritchard, for her part, was 'so excellent . . . that her uncharacteristic corpulence was always overlooked'.[4] A fair run followed up to 16 May 1749, with a revival on 28 October at which, Garrick having that summer married, 'the Jests in Benedick were receiv'd with uncommon applause'.[5]

Garrick and Drury Lane monopolized the play until on 9 May 1776 he retired, having played it there also in October 1769 as part of a Shakespeare season following the historic Stratford-upon-Avon festivities which he inaugurated that summer. About a hundred performances took place during his time as Benedick (1748–76), and about ninety more by the end of the century. The Kemble brothers, John Philip and Charles, continued it with distinction from a Haymarket revival in 1788 until well into the nineteenth century: in *Characters of Shakespeare's Plays* (1817)

1. A. H. Scouten (ed.), *The London Stage 1660–1800*, Pt 3, *1729–1747* (1961), p. 690.

2. C. B. Hogan, *Shakespeare in the Theatre, 1701–1800*, vol. 1 (1952), pp. 342–4.

3. J. Genest, *The English Stage* (1832), vol. III, p. 493.

4. Op. cit., II. 318, 319, 321. Of the Beatrice–Benedick forays it is recorded that 'every scene between them was a continual struggle for superiority, nor could the spectators determine to which of them the preference was due' (Thomas Davies, *Dramatic Miscellanies*, 1783–4, quoted in NCS, p. 161).

5. Quoted in G. W. Stone (ed.), *The London Stage 1660–1800*, Pt 4, *1747–1776* (1962), p. 140, from the Drury Lane prompter (also actor and playwright), Richard Cross.

Hazlitt commented that 'This admirable comedy used to be frequently acted till of late years'. It formed part of John Philip Kemble's first managerial season at Covent Garden in 1803–4, and at Charles Kemble's final appearance as Benedick in 1836 he chose as his Beatrice a fledgeling actress, Helen Faucit, who for forty years was to prove an outstanding interpreter of the part. Charles Kean, too, mounted it, with great splendour, in his last season at the Princess Theatre in 1858.

Two developments in particular stand out during the nineteenth century. One was the distinction brought to the performance of Beatrice by Helen Faucit, followed by Ellen Terry, and to that of Benedick by Henry Irving. The other was the increasingly sumptuous style of production. These features call for a word.

By the early nineteenth century Beatrice's part had settled, it seems, into a generally shrewish tone, that of either 'a hoyden, or a vixen, or that still more repulsive personage, a compound of the two'.[1] This may explain why Anna Jameson found in her 'a slight infusion of the termagant' and Thomas Campbell thought her 'disagreeable, . . . a tartar, . . . and, if a natural woman, . . . not a pleasing representative of the sex'.[2] She was rescued primarily by Helen Faucit and then by Ellen Terry,[3] and with occasional variants[4] the practice of playing Beatrice as warmly feminine has continued into the twentieth century.

---

1. George Fletcher, *Studies of Shakespeare* (1847), p. 282, quoted in Furness, p. 386.

2. Anna Jameson, *Characteristics of Women* (1832), vol. I, p. 62; Thomas Campbell (ed.), *Dramatic Works of Shakespeare* (1838), p. xlvi, quoted in Furness, p. 351. The tradition of 'talkative misogynist' and 'terrible termagant' engaged in a 'cat-and-dog fight ending in a union that will only result in "a predestinate scratched face"' evidently persisted until late in the nineteenth century; see Clement Scott, *From 'The Bells' to 'King Arthur'* (1897), quoted in G. Rowell, *Victorian Dramatic Criticism* (1971), pp. 118–19.

3. That other aspects of the part also needed redeeming is indicated by Ellen Terry's story that during rehearsal at the Lyceum an old actor, Thomas Lacy, told her that, when Benedick rushes forward to aid the swooning Hero, Beatrice must indignantly shoo him away. She replied, 'Oh, nonsense, Mr Lacy', and refused, whereon he remarked that it was always done, and always raised a laugh: *Four Lectures on Shakespeare*, pp. 95–6.

4. Geraldine McEwan's Beatrice at Stratford-upon-Avon in 1961 was described as 'dispens[ing] almost entirely with the airs and graces of the traditional Beatrice, . . . a modern young woman who thoroughly enjoys the Elizabethan notion of repartee, . . . a little hoydenish . . . but . . . in her prosaic way extremely effective' (*The Times*, 5 April 1961), and as 'pretty, pert, un-poetic, and hard', 'attractive rather than endearing' yet 'completely successful' (*Leamington Spa Courier*, 7 April 1961).

Helen Faucit, writing (under her married name of Lady Martin) *On Some of Shakespeare's Female Characters* (1885), tells how, young and inexperienced, she was chosen by the retiring Charles Kemble to play opposite him in 1836: she was 19, he 61—a very odd conjunction, one would think, but one which proved wholly successful. She shone in the part throughout her career until her last appearance in it, when in 1879 she performed it at the opening of the Shakespeare Memorial Theatre at Stratford-upon-Avon. The tenor of many reviews is that of the *Manchester Courier* of 9 May 1846:

> a performance of rare beauty, . . . less buoyant, less boisterous [than her precursors', with neither] the hearty laugh of Mrs Jordan, that made the listener doubt if such a woman could ever be unhappy;[1] nor the biting sarcasm and fire-eating of others we could name.

She herself later mentioned with particular pleasure a *Liverpool Journal* critique (2 May 1846) which found her Beatrice 'a creature overflowing with joyousness, raillery itself being in her nothing more than an excess of animal spirits, tempered by passing through a soul of goodness'.[2] Twenty years later the *Manchester Courier* (11 April 1866) was still praising 'the beautifully modulated voice, [harmonizing with] each studied gesture, and . . . the felicitous manner in which both combine to express each varying thought'.[3] A *Liverpool Daily Post* review by Sir Edward Russell (16 December 1870) commented vividly on the climax of her part:

> '*Kill Claudio*' cries Beatrice in a wonderful voice, earnest and thrilling, startling to the depths every one within hearing, and yet not a whit more fierce than the voice of Beatrice so moved might be, nor in any way, in spite of its tremendous bitterness and force, inconsistent with her character. This was the finest triumph of the night.[4]

Ellen Terry's Beatrice was in the same spirit of witty warmth and generous beauty, 'the incarnation of light-hearted mirth

---

1. Dorothea Jordan (1761–1816), noted for impetuous playing. Hazlitt, however, reports that 'Mrs Jordan, we have understood, played Beatrice very delightfully'.

2. Furness, p. 358, records her delight at this appraisal.

3. Ibid., p. 388.

4. Ibid., p. 390.

which is never heartless, and of gay coquetry which never loses the charm of spontaneity'.[1] To quote a contemporary tribute,

Surely never such a buoyant, winsome, merry, enchanting personality was ever seen on the stage—or off it. She was literally compact of merriment till her anger with Claudio blazed forth in a brief tragic moment half passion and whole pathos that carried everything before it. And as for tragic strength, none who have ever seen or may ever see it can forget her futile helpless anger, the surging, choking passion in her voice, as striding to and fro with long paces, her whirling words won Benedick to her as in answer to his query: 'Is Claudio thine enemy?' she broke out, 'Is he not approved in the height a villain . . .?'[2]

Reflecting on her part, she herself commented:

I have played Beatrice hundreds of times, but not once as I know she ought to be played. I was never swift enough, not nearly swift enough at the Lyceum where I had a too deliberate, though polished and thoughtful, Benedick in Henry Irving. But at least I did not make the mistake of being arch and skittish.[3]

This Lyceum revival opened on 11 October 1882; it ran for 212 successive performances there, went on Irving's first American tour, and returned for thirty-one more London performances in 1884. Its sumptuous presentation is described below (pp. 39–40). That Ellen Terry's estimate of Irving's Benedick (and who better able to judge?) as 'too deliberate, though polished and thoughtful', was well founded seems confirmed by reviewers' comments, wholly laudatory in intention, that 'the chivalry of the part suits him, and so does the graciousness of the character, and so does its quiet and self-analytical wit' and that he appeared 'a soldier first, a lover next, and always a gentleman'.[4] With this

1. *Saturday Review*, 21 October 1882, quoted in Furness, p. 392.

2. Bram Stoker, *Personal Reminiscences of Henry Irving* (1906), vol. i, p. 101. Stoker relates that John Penberthy, a cousin of Henry Irving's just back from a South American mining career, was so struck by the scene that, 'his face blazing with generous anger, [he] said in his native Cornwall accent which he had never lost: "It was a damned good job for that cur Claudio that I hadn't my shootin' irons on me. If I had I'd soon have blasted hell out of him!"' (ibid., p. 103).

3. *Four Lectures on Shakespeare*, p. 97.

4. Frederick Wedmore in the *Academy*, 21 October 1882, quoted in Furness, p. 390; Clement Scott, *From 'The Bells' to 'King Arthur'* (1897), quoted in G. Rowell, *Victorian Dramatic Criticism* (1971), p. 122. Bernard Shaw commented on Irving's deliberation.

one may contrast a recent reviewer's account of Donald Sinden's splendidly exuberant Benedick in the Stratford-upon-Avon Anglo-Indian production of 1976, as 'at every opportunity . . . down front, his terminal consonants popping like champagne corks, [handling] text and character like a heavyweight requiring furious bursts of energy'.[1] The result was wonderfully funny, but certainly quite different from Irving's manly and impressive distinction.

As for the other nineteenth-century phenomenon, sumptuous production, *Much Ado* had no monopoly. Victorian (and Edwardian) designers vied with each other in enrichment and later ones have followed suit, though less lavishly. But the lure of an Italian location heightened the prevailing taste for embellishment. When, along with *The Merchant of Venice* and *King Lear*, Charles Kean offered it in his farewell season in 1858, the effects were very fine:

> The opening view, the harbour of Messina, was quite a pictorial gem. The gradual illumination of the lighthouse and various mansions, in almost every window, the moon slowly rising and throwing silver light upon the deep blue waters of the Mediterranean, were managed with imposing reality. Then followed the masquerade, with its variegated lamps, bridge, gardens, and lake, seen through the arches of the palace.[2]

The 1882 Lyceum production already mentioned was superbly mounted. It opened on Leonato's house, 'a classic structure, supported by columns and steps of yellow marble', with blue sea and sky beyond, and the foliage of the orchard. The ballroom was 'crimson and gold, relieved by soft tapestry hangings', its light 'softened by the appearance of rose-trees'.[3] The church scene, 'one of the grandest stage-pictures that has ever been presented', inspired some ecstatic prose:

> The altar stands at the left-hand side of the stage, and the beautifully ornamented roof is supported by massive pillars. These accessories, the massive pillars, the figured iron gates, the decorated roof, the pictures, the stained glass, the elaborate and costly altar, the carved oak benches, the burning lights, and the perfume of incense, all combine to render this a scene

1. Irving Wardle in *The Times*, 9 April 1976.
2. J. W. Cole, *The Theatrical Life and Times of Charles Kean, F.S.A.* (1959), vol. II, pp. 333-4.
3. Austin Brereton, *Dramatic Notes*, October 1882 (1883), p. 50.

of such richness and grandeur as at first to arrest all thought of the play and to delight only the eye with the beautiful sight.[1]

Laurence Irving, in his account of his father, gives further details of the church scene, with

> its real built-out round pillars thirty feet high, its canopied roof of crimson plush from which hung the golden lamps universally used in Italian cathedrals, its painted canopy overhanging the altar, its great ironwork gates, its altar with vases of flowers and flaming candles rising to a height of eighteen feet, its stained glass windows and statues of saints.[2]

Such scenes might well tend 'to arrest all thought of the play and to delight only the eye', and a swing to simplicity could be expected.[3] Ellen Terry revived the play on 23 May 1903, her son Gordon Craig designing a newfangled sober setting which *The Times* on 25 May commended for eschewing 'overgorgeous trappings', though many spectators probably shared the *Athenaeum*'s view (30 May) that much of it, 'especially the scene of Leonato's garden, with an enormous structure of apparent wickerwork, fail[ed] to convey . . . any intelligible idea'. Bernard Shaw, in a letter of 3 June to Ellen Terry about this production, commented that *Much Ado* is 'a shocking bad play [which] can only be saved by Dogberry picking it up at the end, when Benedick and Beatrice are worn out after the church scene'. This sounds like coat-trailing but probably also reflects the production's weaknesses. In any case, older preferences persisted, and when Beerbohm Tree staged a revival at His Majesty's in January 1905 Shaw joked about its 'fair ladies, Sicilian landscapes, Italian gardens, summer nights and dawns (compressed into five minutes), Renascential splendours, dancing, singing,

1. Ibid., p. 51.
2. Laurence Irving, *Henry Irving*, quoted in J. C. Trewin, *Shakespeare on the English Stage, 1900–1964* (1964), p. 27. In the particulars of the church ceremonial Irving was concerned to suggest religious solemnity without so much authenticity as might be deemed blasphemous (a theatre, after all, is not a church) or be disturbing to Protestant sensibilities (Bram Stoker, *Personal Reminiscences of Henry Irving* (1906), vol. 1, p. 105). A painting of the church scene by Johnston Forbes-Robertson (reproduced in G. Rowell, *The Victorian Theatre*, 1956) shows a positively cathedral-like magnificence and amply confirms the quoted descriptions of its splendour. Bernard Shaw called the whole production 'expensively mounted and superlatively dull' (*Saturday Review*, 25 May 1885).
3. Helena Faucit herself protested about the performer's task of competing with 'gorgeous scenery', 'dresses extravagant in cost', and over-active extras; cf. Furness, p. 361.

masquerading, architecture, orchestration tastefully culled from Wagner, Bizet and German, and endless larks in the way of stage business'.[1]

The twentieth century has seen productions too many to particularize; comment has to be confined to a few with representative significance, staged since the second world war and mostly at Stratford-upon-Avon. The starting-point must be the almost legendary version directed by John Gielgud at Stratford in 1949, with Diana Wynyard ('gay, charming, and fiery'; *Daily Telegraph*, 20 April) and Anthony Quayle ('engaging and manly'; ibid.) as Beatrice and Benedick, Harry Andrews as Don Pedro ('pleasing and genial, . . . blessed with an innate dignity'; *Stratford-upon-Avon Herald*, 22 April), and Philip Guard as Claudio ('very spirited and earnest'; *Stage*, 21 April). The sets by the Spanish designer Mariano Andreu were widely praised as gay, fantastic, and ingenious; to quote the *Birmingham Post* of 20 April: 'The scenery opens, shuts, wheels, and turns inside out. Gardens become banqueting halls, and by a turn of the hand gaily attired ushers transport us from the pillared exterior of a church porch to the Byzantine reaches of a far-flung nave'. Very rich and delightful, the production was revived at Stratford in 1950, with Gielgud and Peggy Ashcroft as Benedick and Beatrice, and in London in 1952 and again in 1955 after an extensive continental tour. Settings and costumes were early Renaissance,[2] deliciously decorative, and the spirit of the whole so captivating as virtually to annul qualms about questionable elements in the plot; the sense of romantic, indulgent comedy chimed with the postwar mood of hedonism.[3] One reviewer, however, while praising its beauty, hinted that something might be missing: 'Designers, producers, and actors combined to catch and hold every lightest romantic breath that blows . . . from the springtime of the world when belief was innocent and love credulous', but was it not all 'lulling us with style', 'really too smooth'?[4]

1. *Saturday Review*, 11 February 1905.

2. Gielgud prescribed 'scenery and dresses of the Boccaccio period', since he felt that Elizabethan costume was difficult for modern actors to wear and overweighted the action, as well as making the play too specifically Elizabethan (*Stage Directions*, 1963, p. 39.) His book contains a lively account of the effects he and his designer achieved.

3. The *Stratford-upon-Avon Herald* (22 April 1949) represents the general tenor, elated that 'all the beauty of this happy play' was captured 'as joyously as the holiday sunshine, and with something of the serene gaiety of the first appleblossom'.

4. *New Statesman*, 30 April 1949. The *Birmingham Post*'s man found himself 'slightly distracted' by the scenic ingenuity (20 April).

The desire for beautiful sophistication after years of war gave a special elegance and warmth which made this production the standard of judgement for two decades but, by its very seductiveness, perhaps glossed over the play's provocations. Ivor Brown's review of the 1955 continental tour production suggests a more combative Benedick and Beatrice from Gielgud and Peggy Ashcroft than the warmly agreeable ones of Anthony Quayle and Diana Wynyard in 1949, though still within a manner of evident suavity:

> That the 'merry war' of Beatrice and Benedick would be fought with the utmost neatness of verbal fence was assured. Benedick is a part in which Sir John had displayed his perfect marksmanship with the arrow of a well-barbed line, and Peggy Ashcroft had been no less adroit in returning the bolt with the most dexterous contrivance of stage archery. Here was the riposte of 'conceits' that so delighted the Elizabethans with their keen appetite for word-play, and here were the best players of this pit-a-pat comedy and best speakers of a mannered prose and verse that our theatre contains.[1]

The first postwar phase, then, with its continental undertaking to show British theatre at its most distinguished, attained what *The Times* (22 July 1955) called 'a sort of classic status'. But this it did at the expense of somewhat obscuring the major 'nothing' about which there is the gravest 'ado'.

Certain trends have emerged in more recent productions. The most notable have been, first, experiments with period and locale; second, interpretations of moral bearings; and third (sometimes combined with this last) rebalancings of the play to bring into reasonable equipoise its graver and gayer elements.

The 1949 to 1955 productions were set in an Italian Renaissance appropriate to the Sicilian scene, to the play's assumed era, and to the myth of a romantically elegant society. To claim some originality of approach later productions have often sought a different time and place. This trend became notable enough for the *Guardian*'s reviewer, Michael Billington, to open his account of John Barton's Anglo-Indian production at Stratford-upon-Avon in 1976 with the words, 'I have seen *Much Ado About Nothing* set in Risorgimento Italy, Pancho Villa's Mexico, and even, in one experimental version, Elizabethan England' (9 April 1976). Reviewing this same production, Irving Wardle in *The Times* (9 April) recalled a 1971 Stratford (Ontario)

1. Ivor Brown, *Shakespeare Memorial Theatre 1954–56* (1956), p. 11.

setting in Edwardian *art nouveau*, which apparently 'worked
wonders for Beatrice as a bicycling New Woman' but which rather
suggests the spirit of *Man and Superman*. The 1958 Douglas Seale
production at Stratford-upon-Avon, in elegant early nineteenth-
century styles, conveyed

> the spirited pleasure everyone takes in a Messina of crinoline
> and parasol and flowered waistcoat, of epaulette and sash and
> whisker, of smoking cap and frogged velvet jacket, of cheroots
> and tight lacing, of cheerful period embellishment.[1]

This production, Regency or early Victorian in mode (*The Times*
thought it 'Risorgimento' or 'neo-Napoleonic'), was very
beautiful, less sumptuous than those of the nineteenth century
discussed above but similar in decorative appeal. The designer,
Tanya Moiseiwitsch, provided stage pictures (the word is
appropriate) of great charm by the simple device of dropping in
behind a solid-built front 'frame' of trellis a series of exquisitely
detailed backcloths of house, garden, bedroom, street, church, in
a kind of distillation of nineteenth-century scenic enrichment.

> The settings with their radiant sunlight and sparkling nights are
> Italian to the core, and nostalgic at that. We have fairy lights,
> the masked waltz, the lancers danced with pennants, flowered
> waistcoats, tasselled smoking-caps, flowing black cloaks lined
> with scarlet, eavesdropping not from a garden arbour but from
> behind parasols red and white, and challenges to duels where
> visiting cards are handed over.[2]

Michael Langham in 1961 went back a little earlier, to pure
Regency, with Wellingtonian uniforms for the men and Jane
Austen dresses for the women. Zeffirelli's sensational National
Theatre production in 1965 had a dashingly bravura montage, as
if for a comic opera, of 'Sicily about the turn of the nineteenth–
twentieth centuries, with its hot sun, its lively temperament, its
gaiety, its easy tears, its constant play of gesture':[3] its aim,
Zeffirelli announced, was to banish 'terribly bored' feelings
resulting from a 'very dull play'.[4] The result delighted many,
infuriated some, and bored none. As if by drastic reaction Trevor
Nunn's Stratford production in 1968 was homebred Elizabethan
English, but again as if by another drastic reaction John Barton's

1. *Birmingham Post*, 27 August 1958.
2. *Liverpool Daily Post*, 27 August 1958.
3. *Daily Telegraph*, 18 February 1965.
4. Retrospectively reported in the *Guardian*, 29 October 1977.

in 1976 was as emphatically unhomebred as Zeffirelli's, which it rivalled in controversial impact. Set in British India amid the officer-class conventions of the British Raj, it offered an extra-ordinary extension of imaginative relevance, yet one challengingly plausible.

To what end, all this? The quest has been for a setting both fittingly decorative for a love comedy and fittingly authentic for the melodrama of the plot. The high-romantic Gielgud pro-ductions may have left the Claudio–Hero crisis implausible, the postwar celebratory spirit being alien to its heartlessness. But why should Regency, Victorian, Edwardian or Anglo-Indian settings validate the melodrama any more than others? They have no monopoly of aptness; a Restoration or eighteenth-century setting might serve as well if its glamour were not allowed to obscure the play's penetrating humanity—or indeed one in imperial Moscow or Vienna (where even Dogberry could be as much at home as in Sicily, or as little). What is sought is a setting where the pastime flirtations of affluent leisure can be congenially accommodated. Renaissance Messina is seemingly thought too escapist a milieu. What producers seek is some Chekhovian equivalent which may familiarize and authenticate the wilfulness of feeling and the conventionalities of conduct on which the plot depends.

In some ways settings in the Regency–Victorian–Edwardian eras have suited the tragic comedy as well as the comic.[1] Of the 1958 Regency–Risorgimento version *The Times* observed that 'the period chosen was a source of profit to the more serious scenes', that Claudio with his 'fierce young egotism' might have figured in a Stendhal novel or Don John in a Delacroix portrait (27 August 1958). The Italianate military-romantic convention helped to carry the church scene. Another critic stressed the aptness of such a period for melodramatic sensations (Don John's gleeful malice, for instance): 'The producer's problem is to find a convention which will persuade his modern audience to say, We do believe in villains! Mr Seale's answer is, Villains are Victorian: this will produce in a modern audience the same kind of theatrical acceptance given originally to the plot.'[2] Zeffirelli's Sicilian

---

1. On the other hand, Sir John Gielgud expresses amazement at nineteenth-century settings, since 'Surely the period between 1800 and 1900, when women barely showed their ankles, and conversation between the sexes was intensely prudish and reserved, is in direct contradiction of Shakespeare's whole intention in the text' (*Stage Directions* (1963), p. 43).

2. Muriel St Clare Byrne, 'The Shakespeare Season at Stratford-upon-Avon, 1958' in *ShQ* IX (1958), p. 528. Gareth Lloyd Evans attributes to Don John and

extravaganza could accommodate in the context of Mediterranean exuberance (as parodic Italian melodrama) Don John's postures, Claudio's histrionic jealousy, Don Pedro's and Leonato's affronted honours, and Beatrice's avenging 'Kill Claudio!'

> Instead of [her] being the proponent of a distant ethic of love that now lies pickled in troubadour poetry, Hero becomes a wretchedly believable girl trapped in a perfectly recognisable Sicily where the same ferocious code of chastity endures to this day. . . . Beatrice for once seems credible as her cousin, . . . a product of the same culture who simply happens to have more spirit and a pelting tongue. . . . This at once makes sense of the Hero–Claudio drama; in logic it is absurd that the accusation against Hero is unanswered, . . . but in Sicily a slur is enough.[1]

The Regency–Victorian–Edwardian versions also have found settings in which carefree affluence made intrigues, malevolent or benevolent, credible enough. Rethinking the time and place has paid dividends beyond the merely decorative.

To pass, now, to the next theme—moral bearings. Often in the past taken as escapist entertainment, *Much Ado* has recently been reassessed as turning a critical eye on the manners and motives it reveals. Viewed thus, it has been thought to present

> largely superficial people in a superficial society; [so that] what is important is that the society should be real and recognizable. These young men, lounging in smoking jackets, puffing cheroots, dancing to the undisguised music of the waltz — we know precisely the world to which they belong, [that of] regulated frivolity.[2]

There is a onesidedness here that ignores the play's depth and warmth, but it is a sign that *Much Ado*, like *The Merchant of Venice*, is in its central phases morally disturbing. The anguish of the church scene and the shock of its brutality forbid romance-escapism (however relieved for the audience by prospects of comic reversal). The relief with which we hear Beatrice denouncing 'Princes and counties' is a measure of the depth to which we feel morally engaged. At any rate, the critic just quoted, reviewing a later production (in 1961), again thought he perceived 'frivolous

---

his cronies 'the half-absurd qualities of bare-faced melodramatic villainy' (*Shakespeare III, 1599–1604* (1971), p. 17).

1. *Observer*, 21 February 1965, quoted in Mason, pp. 82–3.

2. *Leamington Spa Courier*, 29 August 1958. Is undisguised waltz music, one wonders, more reprehensible, or less, than the disguised kind?

people in a frivolous society, . . . a world of social artifice more familiar and so more concrete in its meaning than the remote, unimaginable world of Renaissance Messina'.[1] Trevor Nunn's 1968 production was even held to reveal 'a world of sombre and often sinister grandeur, a world of spies and peepers, [with] a disturbing ambivalence, that undercurrent of malignity or impotence which marks the grown world in this play'.[2] Later views again, on the 1976 British Raj version, saw Messina, or Messina's updated equivalent, in a dubious light:

> At a safe distance from the mother country Don Pedro and his cronies are released from social restraint. Their manners remain perfect, but they give not a damn how much damage they do. Everything is a game; cricket, shooting the wild life, framing an innocent girl.[3]

> In this world of privileged impishness, Don John's pointless destructiveness is simply an extension of the prevailing officers' mess ethical code.[4]

Productions prompting such judgements are far from the lush indulgences of the Kean–Irving–Alexander–Tree tradition. They are meant not to relax with entertainment but to cut through to the core of moral judgement. May we hope before long to find *The Importance of Being Earnest* responsibly interpreted for the castigation of dandyism?

Is this, in fact, at all what the play is about? Or does it tendentiously impose an extraneous prejudice? There is the ground here, but not the time, for a major debate: if to validate a play it is translated into a 'real and recognizable' society, what distortion does it suffer when that society's defects are reflected back upon it? Plays differ much in the degree to which they show the age and body of the time his form and pressure, and a critique of such judgements as have just been recorded appears below (see pp. 51–3, 72–3). To put the quoted views into perspective, however, it should be added that the critics applauded the productions in question by no means solely for sociological and moral scrutiny.

1. Ibid., 7 April 1961.
2. *Spectator*, 25 October 1968. For the masked dance 'the stage was dimly lit, and the soldiers wore menacing half-face visors with long, viciously pointed noses. . . . They brandished drawn swords which were struck menacingly at the end of the masque. This emphasized that while the military brought colour, splendour, and activity to Messina, bound up with this was the potential for evil' (Mason, p. 96).
3. *The Times*, 9 April 1976.   4. *Guardian*, 9 April 1976.

As well as trying for apt location and moral focus, recent productions have sought to harmonize the play's gayer and graver elements. Traditionally, Benedick and Beatrice have had most of the limelight, no one else (save Dogberry) very much.[1] What can or should be done to balance the play? Three things, mainly: Hero and Claudio can gain in prominence; Benedick and Beatrice can be less salient; and within both pairs there can be shown true feeling, masked in Benedick and Beatrice at first by the passages at arms but progressively revealed as real and strong, so that their alliance in church is felt to have behind it a long perspective, the comic plot thereby gaining a poignancy which gravitates towards the serious one.[2]

Producers have tried to enhance Claudio and Hero, partly by stressing how much they reflect the conventions which have conditioned their conformities (as against the nonconformist Benedick and Beatrice); they gain thereby a kind of representative dimension. Hero, moreover, almost imperceptible in most traditional representations, has been encouraged to make a more noticeable impact, though hardly living up to Hazlitt's billing of her as 'the principal figure in the piece, [who] leaves an indelible impression on the mind'.[3] Barbara Jefford in 1950 is reported as playing her with 'grace, beauty, and feeling' (which counts for much);[4] and in 1968, as 'the adored daughter round whom her father's house revolves' so that even Beatrice 'takes second place', Helen Mirren ensured that Hero's suffering in church made this the play's 'dark centre'.[5] In 1976 Cherie Lunghi gave her 'an emphatically animated performance'.[6] Relatively subdued though her share of the text is, it holds sufficient content to allow her considerable prominence. (For the sincerity of her love see below, pp. 61–2; for the degree of Shakespeare's interest in her and Claudio, pp. 50, 60.)

Claudio offers something of a problem. Interpretations lean to

1. It may be assumed that Victorian/Edwardian scenic elaboration in the church scene gave the serious plot, at least at the crisis, much more prominence than it might have had. In a thoughtful comment on the tomb scene J. R. Mulryne points out how deep and serious could be its effect when seen and heard (*Shakespeare: 'Much Ado About Nothing'* (1965), pp. 9–10).

2. Henry Irving and Ellen Terry played Benedick and Beatrice as 'echoes of one another as much at the outset as when they are discovered at the close writing verses to one another' (Clement Scott, *From 'The Bells' to 'King Arthur'*, quoted in G. Rowell, *Victorian Dramatic Criticism* (1971), p. 121).

3. *Characters of Shakespear's Plays* ('*Much Ado About Nothing*').

4. *Birmingham Gazette*, 7 June 1950.

5. *Spectator*, 25 October 1968.

6. *The Times*, 9 April 1976.

one of two procedures. One is to stress his youth, inexperience, and essential decency, understandably vulnerable to seemingly authenticated deception. In Gielgud's production he was 'very spirited and earnest' (*Stage*, 21 April 1949), in Douglas Seale's in 1958, a tense young egoist, 'both likeable and convincing', so hurt in grief that his violent reaction was understandable, even forgivable (*Stratford-upon-Avon Herald*, 29 August). In 1971, 'distraught with anger and insecurity' (*Stage*, 22 December), he earned a measure of sympathy. The other course is to colour him with the faults of his milieu. Of the 1958 Claudio, so sympathetically viewed above, Robert Speaight observed that the only thing that prevented us from judging him a cad was the fact that he was 'a stupid military blockhead', hardly blameable since 'military service [had] blunted the accepted decencies'.[1] In 1976 he was a self-centred prig governed by the conventions of the officers' mess.[2] But at least, treated in any of these ways, Claudio makes more of an impact than when seen merely as the callow hanger-on of a leisured prince; he gains a nature and a context. And the serious plot gains in conviction, though it suffers misrepresentation. (For further analysis of Claudio see pp. 54-9.)

As Hero's and Claudio's parts have gathered strength, those of Benedick and Beatrice have sometimes been presented in quieter fashion than those of scintillating virtuosi. Older than Claudio and Hero, they have been seen (for instance, by Derek Godfrey and Elizabeth Spriggs in 1971) as poised on the verge of lifelong singleness instead of the union they half-consciously yearn for, with a touch of experienced sadness under the assured surface, and—Beatrice particularly—with a depth of nature as movingly responsive to the crises in her own plot as to those in Hero's. This has produced a notable concentration and gravity at the notorious point where the plots most dramatically knit together, her cry of 'Kill Claudio'. It is a moment dangerously liable to explode the audience into laughter, perhaps because so unexpectedly sensational, so unlikely to turn out as she wishes, and so intense that Benedick's instinctive rejection chimes incongruously against it. Gielgud and Peggy Ashcroft steered skilfully past it:

> We observed how the passage was lifted gradually to that
> 'Bid me do anything for thee'; how Beatrice paused for

1. *Tablet*, 13 September 1958.
2. 'They are a heartless lot, these officers; they will no doubt be moving to another station shortly; they continue as coldly frivolous after the interrupted wedding as before it, no doubt thinking themselves lucky to have got out of an embarrassing entanglement' (*Financial Times*, 9 April 1976).

a moment in a charged silence until the words 'Kill Claudio' were forced from her; and how Benedick's 'Ha! not for the wide world' was quick, low-toned, the almost incredulous exclamation of a man who had not realised how friendship must struggle with love and honour.[1]

The precedent has been generally followed: it is significant less as a means of outflanking a danger than as evincing care for consonance of tone (or rather, avoidance of dissonance) in so far as the play's disparate elements permit. Tragic potential within prevalent comedy is of the play's essence.

The solution is to keep in due proportion the principal figures— Benedick and Beatrice, of course, but also Claudio, Don Pedro, Hero, Don John, Leonato, and not least the Friar; Dogberry and Verges pose no problems, infallibly conveying as they do the former's irresistible absurdity and the latter's eager second-fiddling. The play is one of close-knit relationships. Without lessening Benedick's and Beatrice's comic force one must give the others real substance—Don Pedro sufficient authoritative presence to count for more than the mere leader of 'frivolous people in a frivolous society', Don John sufficient dangerousness to figure notably, Claudio sufficient youthful virtue to excuse his inexperience, Hero sufficient charm and spirit to be noticeably appealing, Leonato sufficient stature to carry the graces of hospitality and the humiliations of anger, and Friar Francis sufficient spiritual power to provide the play's 'steadying, sane mind, its *punctum indifferens*'.[2]

In short, one welcomes attempts to balance the grave and the gay, and to make all parts seem credible outcomes of a credible society, provided nothing is lost of its heady vitality. It offers a large, rich, appreciated world, not a small, censorious one. To present it, as more than one reviewer found more than one production doing, as a world of glossy triviality or of 'the prankish

1. J. C. Trewin, *Shakespeare on the English Stage 1900–1964* (1964), p. 220. *The Times* observed that John Gielgud and Peggy Ashcroft had kept their love-declarations in a low key of new-found seriousness so that this cry was felt as deepening an existing tone (22 July 1955). Later it called this 'Gielgud's inspired treatment of the episode' (5 April 1961).

2. NCS, p. xv. V. S. Pritchett, reviewing the 1958 production in which, it seems, the Friar was too amiably pious, was provoked into drawing a wholly different and indeed unrecognizable portrait of him—'there is plenty in the part to show the wily man of action, the worldly plotter of the confessional' (*New Statesman*, 5 September 1958). This is as far adrift as any amiable-sentimentalist presentation. But, however wrong, it does invite the actor to find elements of commanding thoughtfulness which indeed the part offers.

practical jokes of a bored officer class' (no one is in the least bored,
not even the restively disgruntled Don John; for good or ill they
all act with irrepressible zest)—to present or interpret the play's
tone thus is to distort its warm and compelling humanity.

7. THE WORLD OF MESSINA

(i) *The prevalent spirit*

As such stage interpretations make clear, Messina's world has not
struck everyone as essentially good-natured. Yet essentially
good-natured is surely what it is. Predominantly it is a lively,
sociable world presented through its etiquettes and enjoyments,
and framed in a context of companionable localities, convincing
times and places, shared witticisms, familiar exchanges of popular
allusions and phrases, and a network of plans, clues, and
reminiscences creating a close-knit scene for the cheerful
manoeuvres of affluent leisure. This is not the fancy-free world of
pastoral comedy; until unsettled by alien influence it is a scene of
social engagement, courtly diplomacies, and festive pleasure, a
cheerful world of carnival.

Generous affection is natural to it, and this fact is crucial.
Without it, Leonato's query about how many 'gentlemen' had
been killed, and the Messenger's reply, 'But few of any sort, and
none of name', would be heartless, and the exchanges between
Don Pedro and Claudio as to whether Hero was Leonato's heir
(a topic revived when Leonato commends Antonio's 'daughter'
as sole heir to both) would be worldly-wise.[1] But such things are
quickly absorbed into contexts of praise and affection, the former
into the uncle's tearful joy and the appreciation of 'pleasant'
Benedick and the 'merry war', the latter into Claudio's tribute to
his 'modest young lady', the sweetest he ever looked on; and
Messina's good nature remains unimpaired. The play abounds in
kindly feeling—Benedick's sympathy for Claudio as the 'poor
hurt fowl' creeping into sedges, Beatrice's infallible touch whenever she thinks of true affection, Hero's 'I will do any modest
office, my lord, to help my cousin to a good husband' (ii.i.352–3),
or 'He [Benedick] is the only man of Italy, / Always excepted my
dear Claudio' (iii.i.92–3). Such pleasantness of nature casts a

1. Critics have on both these points taken an unfavourable view of Messina's
outlook: yet no similar fault has been found with Benedick for saying, of a
hypothetical wife, 'Rich she shall be, that's certain' (ii.iii.30); his jocular
tone doubtless carries off the mercenary sentiment.

charm which makes 'regulated frivolity' a misleading definition of Messina's world.

(ii) The impact of Don John

Yet is not this picture too indulgent? After all, Don John's slanders are readily accepted, and Claudio, Don Pedro, and even Leonato spurn the suffering Hero. Is the contrast between the gaiety—at the beginning and end—and the intervening violence merely theatrical sensation, or does it point to a hard self-centred-ness beneath the attractive social surface?

The Elizabethans in general worried little about dramatic consistency: like Polonius, they would swallow almost any tragical-comical-historical-pastoral mixture. But later commentators have sometimes been either uneasy about *Much Ado's* variety of tone (like E. K. Chambers diagnosing 'inconsistency of purpose and . . . clashing of dramatic planes')[1] or concerned to lessen the disparity. This might be done by demoting Don John to Coleridge's minor villain 'merely shown and withdrawn',[2] so eclipsing the serious theme behind the comic, or by seeking to assimilate the two sides. But however this is done, the church scene must always raise sharp questions as to character and motive, and its unhappy sequel is distasteful when early in Act V Don Pedro and Claudio, showing no concern over Hero's fate and little over Leonato's distress, continue jesting over Benedick.[3]

That comic and serious plots are in fact structurally inter-related is suggested below (see 'Form and structure', pp. 59 ff.). Here the question is in what spirit the world of Messina is to be interpreted. Some misreadings of the play take Don John to be less extraneous to its spirit than integral to it; they hold that Don Pedro partly shares his brother's nature, that Leonato's anger arises less from his shock over Hero than from that to his self-centred pride (*'mine*, and *mine* I lov'd, and *mine* I prais'd, / And *mine* that I was proud on'; IV.i.136–7), and that Claudio shows a prickly sense of prestige and a willingness to wound not unlike Don John's own. If Messina's world is really one of 'privileged impishness', and Don John's malice an integral part of 'the

1. E. K. Chambers, *Shakespeare: A Survey* (1925), p. 128.
2. *Shakespearean Criticism*, ed. T. M. Raysor (1960), vol. I, p. 200.
3. The scene can be effectively played, and the sense of heartlessness some-what mitigated, if Don Pedro and Claudio show so much embarrassment before Leonato and Antonio that they seize the chance to jest at Benedick as a relief from a painful strain.

military garrison's careless arrogance',[1] Messina is a radically
divided world, heartlessly sophisticated on the one hand (the
princes and Claudio), honestly generous on the other (Beatrice
and Benedick).

But that view cannot stand. Don John's malevolence and
unsociability, marked by images of sickness, festering poison, and
incompatibility (the canker-rose, the thief of love, the muzzled
dog, the caged bird) and by themes of resentment and moroseness,
are defined by his being a rebel and bastard. A villain within a
comedy, he is bound for defeat, yet real in his humiliated
fractiousness and hatred of social love.[2] His acridity stands out.
He casts himself as the outsider, barely acknowledging any
invitation into the social world.[3] He and his allies stress death as
against life, vexation as against pleasure, sickness as against
health. It is true that if he 'cannot hide' his nature as 'a plain-
dealing villain' (I.iii.12–13, 30) his villainy could hardly be
effective, but this bravado is specious; the good characters get no
further than finding him tart and taciturn (Beatrice; II.i.3, 8) or
'very melancholy' (Hero; II.i.5). They are readily deceived until

1. *Sunday Telegraph*, 11 April 1976.
2. He evidently was played thus in the great Irving/Ellen Terry production
of 1882. The *Saturday Review* (21 October 1882) reported that 'a character
hitherto almost neglected in the stage versions of the play, on his side takes his
proper place as one of Shakespeare's truest and least obvious villains. His
motives are complex, and do not loudly assert themselves. [They do, of course,
to the audience, but that is not the point: so do Iago's, without reducing his
impact: Ed.] He is plausible, and he is sinister.' Don John's 'increasingly
saturnine' aspect in the 1958 Stratford-upon-Avon production (the part was
taken by Richard Johnson) had an 'unexpected success' (*Leamington Spa Courier*,
29 August), and whenever he appeared the *Daily Telegraph*'s critic felt 'very
much "the cool of the evening" ', which sounds decidedly right (27 August).
Ian Richardson's impressive Don John in 1961 was 'grey-visaged and furiously
fighting a speech-impediment' (*Leamington Spa Courier*, 7 April), with a
'neurosis of romantic self-pity' (*The Times*, 5 April); an effective realization,
surely.
3. The sequence of moods in II.i, ii, and iii is particularly definitive in
contrasting Don John and his environment. On Don John's self-approving
churlishness (e.g. at I.iii.25–35) L. C. Knights comments in *Further Explorations*
(1965), p. 168: 'A good many things are plain from this—Don John's
exacerbated sense of superiority . . ., his particular kind of "melancholy", and
his affectation of a blunt, no-nonsense manner. Clearly he is related to Richard
of Gloucester, and to Iago. Their common characteristic is an egotism that
clenches itself hard against the claims of sympathy, and that is unwilling to
change . . . . It is, in short, the opposite of a character that is "open" to others
and to the real demands of the present. That is all we know about Don John
and all we are required to know. . . . He is simply a perversely "melancholy"
man.'

after the church scene Benedick belatedly observes that his spirits 'toil in frame of villainies' (IV.i.189). In Elizabethan plays such impercipience is normal; the Machiavel works undetected, save by his cronies, until his schemes have taken effect. Don Pedro's circle certainly proves vulnerable to Don John's cunning, but it is soon redeemed by wit, love, and forgiveness (not extending to him, true; but the threatened 'brave punishments' do not sound as grim as he deserves). Shakespeare could hardly have done more to present Don John as an alien whose contagion, however powerful, is soon expelled and will not return.

Yet while the contagion lasts it is devastating, and it moves the play somewhat (though not, ultimately, much) towards the dark shades of the problem plays. A source of the play's power, in both serious and comic plots, is its sense of love's dangers. As in *The Merchant of Venice*, the happiness finally attained is the more precious for the perils undergone. In the Hero–Claudio plot these cause real pain, most poignant in Hero herself but evident also in Beatrice, Leonato, and Antonio, and reportedly felt by Claudio himself. The comic plot, too, is not without its dangers: if Beatrice can be waspish, this results from the wounds of past contests with Benedick, who, himself invulnerable, has played her false (II.i.261–4). Her surrender is moving (III.i.107–16), yet even near the end her love and Benedick's play riskily with fire.

(iii) Don Pedro's error

To return, though, to the serious plot: is there, perhaps, some 'spirit of Aragon'—Don John's, finding an ally in Don Pedro's— against which Claudio's and Leonato's defencelessness proves Messina to be a flawed world? Leonato may be forgiven for so frantic a reaction to so unexpected a shock as he suffers; his rhetoric is anguished. But what of Don Pedro and Claudio? Are they tarred with Don John's brush?

Don Pedro behaves honourably within his conventions, however mistakenly. He believes that Hero has been detected in utter disgrace. If his retorts to Leonato and to Hero herself bite like a lash (IV.i.63–5, 87), Hero's supposed conduct is indefensible. His rejoinders to the angry Leonato and Antonio are embarrassedly considerate (V.i.50, 102–5), though his subsequent jesting at Benedick is odious. Too used, perhaps, to princely pre-eminence to be fully sensitive, he is at fault here, though presumably the scene is meant much less to expose heartlessness in him and Claudio than to be a dramatic intensifica-

tion of their error immediately before the splendid coup of
Dogberry's entry. In general, Don Pedro is considerate and
helpful, first among equals, left at the end a trifle 'sad', alone
unmarried of all the comedy principals.

(iv) The problem of Claudio

A graver problem arises over Claudio, Swinburne's 'pitiful fellow',
Andrew Lang's 'hateful young cub', Ridley's 'miserable
specimen', and Harbage's 'least amiable lover in Shakespeare',
the exoneration and indeed rewarding of whom at the end is held
to outrage all good feelings.[1] He is doubtless meant for a brave,
inexperienced youth, shocked out of romantic devotion by an
unsuspected and cunning enemy and, himself a wounded victim,
not overblameworthy for his appalling error, and so not dis-
qualified for future happiness. Yet to convey this needs sensitive
skill.

Shakespeare surely meant the creditable in him decidedly to
outweigh the discreditable (though what he meant would not
signify had he in fact achieved the opposite—which is not
the case). No performance, therefore, does Claudio justice which
takes him as 'this languid dandy who . . . remains superciliously
detached from first to last [and] denounces Hero to enjoy the
effect rather than from any real indignation'.[2] Before ever he
enters we hear of him as valiant in Don Pedro's war: 'all the
glory' of Don John's defeat is his, as Don John himself admits. He
is very young ('the figure of a lamb'), elegant ('the most exquisite
Claudio'), well born ('right noble'), and, though shy in society,
yet intimate with the experienced Benedick. On entering he is
silent: Beatrice and Benedick make all the running. But left with
Benedick, and later with Don Pedro, he enquires after the 'modest
young lady' for whom his 'liking' has grown into 'soft and delicate
desires'. 'If my passion change not shortly' and 'That I love her,
I feel' (I.i.202, 211) may sound lukewarm but are rather the
diffidence of immaturity which deserves indulgence. This is all
shy and well bred, and warrants his church protestations that he
showed 'Bashful sincerity and comely love' and 'never tempted
[Hero] with word too large'.

True, he is no Romeo: Benedick's satire on his amorous

1. Algernon Swinburne, *A Study of Shakespeare* (1880), p. 152; Andrew Lang,
Harper's Magazine, September 1891, p. 452; M. R. Ridley, *Shakespeare's Plays:
A Commentary* (1936), p. 106; Alfred Harbage, *As They Liked It* (1947), p. 192.
2. *The Times*, 9 April 1976.

extravagances one takes with a large pinch of salt (II.iii. 12–21). But by contrast with the boisterous older friend the modest younger one could do pleasingly enough. His circumspect courtship proceeds not from a calculating nature but from the expected social diplomacies; conducted via the Prince it obeys the proprieties which well-to-do Elizabethans thought the wise order of things. Arranged marriages, post-romantic taste is apt to think, have little to do with love—and indeed in *As You Like It* (III.v. 79–80) Shakespeare himself has the sentimental Phebe quoting Marlowe on spontaneous attraction:

> Dead shepherd, now I find thy saw of might;
> 'Whoever lov'd, that lov'd not at first sight?'

Yet societies practising this custom, like those of Elizabethan England, nineteenth-century France, or modern India, deny its lovelessness. Compared with the passion of Romeo and Juliet the devotion of Claudio and Hero is temperate, yet Claudio's shy tribute of broken silence (II.i. 288–9) is touchingly sincere (as is Proteus's similar sentiment in *The Two Gentlemen of Verona* (II.ii. 16–17)—'What, gone without a word? / Ay, so true love should do; it cannot speak'). Hero, moved by love to the point of plotting gaily to inveigle Beatrice into it also, is charmed with the match, and she pays her heartfelt tribute to her 'dear Claudio' as outranking even Benedick as 'the only man in Italy' (III.i. 92–3). Beatrice, though laughingly reminding Hero that she has the right to say 'Father, as it please me', endorses the value of the union. No question should arise that, even granted the social diplomacies which go to its achieving, the betrothal is truly affectionate and, if at all at odds with romantic tradition, at odds only in its care for propriety.

Claudio, however, is vulnerable. A few words from Don John convince him that his trusted Prince has played him false, and with the generalizing habit which inexperience mistakes for wisdom he concludes that such falsehood is 'an accident of hourly proof': 'Farewell, therefore, Hero!' Since Benedick is equally deluded, and indeed is bold enough to accuse Don Pedro, Claudio's credulity is less remarkable than his acquiescence. Yet, young and diffident, he yields before Don Pedro's prestige; that, like the 'poor hurt fowl' of Benedick's sympathy, he should shrink into himself is understandable. Love's feeling, Berowne had recently proclaimed in *Love's Labour's Lost* (IV.iii. 333–4), 'is more soft and sensible / Than are the tender horns of cockled snails', and this describes Claudio's hurt.

Nothing warrants objection before Don John's intervention in
III. ii. Once Claudio's jealousy of Don Pedro is dispelled, his
union with Hero proceeds with a gentle ritual of courtesy. If his
shyness makes unlikely his professed impatience for an instant
wedding, we note that what he desires is that love should 'have
all his rites' (II. i. 335). This sounds like 'rights', and the audience
doubtless thinks of consummation, but Shakespeare's word
suggests ceremonious proprieties rather than physical passions.[1]
To the tricking of Benedick, Claudio contributes resourcefully, his
success in love keying his spirits up. That Don John's plot is
shortly to detonate heightens the dramatic expectancy; that when
it does so Claudio and Don Pedro are so readily deluded is
startling. There follows the assault on Hero which to many
irretrievably condemns them, Claudio in particular. The play,
it is easy to feel, never really recovers.

Certainly the ground on which Claudio's defenders stand looks
shaky. Within thirty lines of hearing Hero traduced by a man they
should mistrust, he and Don Pedro virtually concede that the
case will be proven. Don John is admittedly skilful; he offers a
challenge to witness and judge—'If you dare not trust that you
see, confess not that you know' (III. ii. 108–9). But instead of being
angrily incredulous Claudio vows, if convinced, publicly to shame
Hero, and in church, having lulled his hearers with apparent
courtesies, he does so. The stress he and Don Pedro lay on their
damaged honours sounds like a prime concern for prestige. Later,
shaken by encountering Leonato and Antonio, Claudio spars
with Benedick in tones of petulance, bravado, and cocky mirth
(v. i. 110–81). The audience may well join with Beatrice in
wishing Benedick to run him through.

But Claudio's defenders are not helpless. By Elizabethan (and
later) convention a hypocrite like Don John was in the nature of
things believed by his victims; hypocrisy, vice disguising itself as
virtue, was the devil's mask, and impenetrable except to those in
the know (here, Don John's cronies). The experienced and
honourable Don Pedro is equally deceived. The window escapade
on which all depends must be taken as wholly convincing—one
reason why Shakespeare discreetly keeps it offstage. In addition,
Borachio 'confesse[s] the vile encounters they have had / A
thousand times in secret'; so Hero's guilt seems patent. As for
the honours that depend on her virtue, these are not mere

---

1. Except in northern and south-western speech the 'gh' in such words was
not sounded after the fifteenth century: H. Kökeritz, *Shakespeare's Pronunciation*
(1953), p. 306.

formulae of social 'face': they are the honours of deserved reputation, in Hero's case her whole integrity, in Don Pedro's and Claudio's the whole sense of honourable dealing and being honourably dealt with. Such honours include prestige but go beyond it to the public recognition of probity.

But need Claudio's accusation be so public and fierce? Humanly speaking, no. Theatrically speaking (like Hal's rejection of Falstaff in *2 Henry IV*), yes. Don Pedro and Claudio are to be led into the committal of error so deep that the discovery of truth is their education in humility and understanding. Since this happens in comedy, neither the tragic shock (alleviated for the audience by the Watch's prior discovery) nor the redemptive process compares in power with that in, say, *The Winter's Tale*, and Claudio's redemption is effected without undue difficulty.

(v) The redemptive process

But the process needs more examination than it often receives. The course of Claudio's and Don Pedro's error runs through several stages. First there is the Machiavellian deception to which they succumb; second, the belief in Hero's guilt on evidence that seems irrefutable; third, the outburst in church of supposedly justified anger; fourth, the embarrassed encounter with Leonato and Antonio, and the lamentable jesting with Benedick; fifth, the realization of Don John's villainy, running 'like iron' or 'poison' through the blood (v.i.239–40); and sixth, the expiation at the tomb. During this process we are meant to feel, not sympathy for Claudio, despite his reported tears (iv.i.154), since all sympathy is with Hero, but the depth and pain of his delusion, and we watch with exasperated dismay while he and Don Pedro flounder deeper and deeper into the morass, aware though we are that when they are in deepest they will be faced with the recognition and shame of what they have done and offered the saving means to remedy it. Having been tricked into damnation by Don John, they are to have and take the chance of repentance and redemption. In the last stage of v.i Shakespeare gives his actors very little material for expressing this fundamental change, yet perhaps enough, if their lines are spoken with heartfelt sincerity (helped, too, by Leonato's full forgiveness). Then comes the tomb scene.

(vi) The tomb scene

This, too, unless attentively considered, may seem too slight to validate Claudio's spiritual expiation; we look for such convincing penitence as Leontes shows in *The Winter's Tale* or Alonso in *The Tempest*. Instead, the matter is completed in thirty-three formal lines. Yet in fact we get far more (or should, in a right production), a compressed symbolic ritual of remorse and regeneration, done as it were in dramatic shorthand. The process is far more condensed than that of Leontes' remorse and regeneration, but it is analogous to it, as Hero's 'death' and 'rebirth' are to Hermione's. Hero's 'life that died with shame' now 'Lives in death with glorious fame' and will annually be celebrated as so doing, since the deluded darkness under which Claudio and Don Pedro erred is now dispelled by the light of her known innocence. The effects about to be described are all in the text, not inter-polated, and should receive full weight. The numinous impressive-ness of the monument, the silent black-robed procession with tapers flickering in the darkness, the elegiac verses (on the deeply felt delivery of which much depends), the grave music and slow dirge to which the mourners circle the tomb, the sense of midnight, of attending spirits, and of withdrawal from the normal world into an enclosed space for the gravity of fully 'uttered' death and spiritual reconstitution—all this, legitimately present in the scene, warrants its acceptance not as a superficial formal rite but as a fundamental turning-point. At its end, night yields to 'gentle day' dappling the east, mourning blackness will change to the 'other weeds' of wedding, and past wrongs will be eclipsed by approaching Hymen's 'luckier issue'. Brief but powerful in meaning, the tomb scene corresponds to Shakespeare's other worlds of withdrawal and purified return like the Forest of Arden, the mountains of Wales, or Prospero's island.

(vii) The final phase

Messina's world has to learn through comic or tragic trial the worth of feelings true and deep as against feelings assumed—'assumed' in the double sense of 'disguisedly adopted' (as with Beatrice and Benedick) or of 'accepted without insight' (as with Claudio's early 'love', a naive idealism not grounded on ex-perience). Don John, of course, learns nothing. Love is learned as a giving in trust, not as a polite routine or, with Beatrice and Benedick, a trial of supremacy. In both plots the play has three phases: the recognition of love, but not its grounded certainty; the stresses of trial; and the resolution, with love's confirmation.[1]

1. These points owe debts to J. R. Mulryne's *Shakespeare: 'Much Ado About Nothing'* (1965), particularly pp. 14, 44, 48.

To understand all is not always to pardon all. But to understand that Claudio is hurt to whatever depths his adolescent nature holds, and that except for this shock and his unhappy reaction the play makes him out a brave, courteously diffident young man, gives the actor a chance. His praises of Hero, soft-toned though they are, are not those of a self-satisfied prig. Having mourned at the tomb, and submitted all choice to Leonato, he qualifies for reunion with the 'reborn' Hero. In prejudiced blindness to her true nature he has rejected her; enlightened, in humble and penitent trust, he accepts her supposed substitute. This is a truer and more human presentation than that of the heartless hanger-on of privileged triflers. His companions, generous about each other, and normally considerate of each other's well-being, are by no means 'coldly frivolous' but are genial members of a cheerful world, happily at home in their festive leisure, too lively in wits to be romantically bemused, too good at heart to be unfeeling.

That is the world of Messina, with Don John its total contrary. He stands for an ill will quite foreign to it: Beatrice and Benedick stand for a strong-sinewed good will quite integral to it. In between, Don Pedro and Claudio, while clearly of the Beatrice–Benedick persuasion, prove for a while vulnerable, too outraged in their sense of virtue to probe deeply enough or to react humanely, yet, as Claudio claims (for both of them, in effect), sinning only through mistaking.

8. FORM AND STRUCTURE

Consideration of the play's form and structure may start from the same point as that of its style: all is so fresh as to seem spontaneous and inevitable, yet nothing is casual or automatic. As with the style, formality interplays with freedom. Scenes of decorum and etiquette—the proprieties of hospitality and courtship, the patterns of masquing and music, the suspension of action while Balthasar sings, the ritual at the tomb, the symmetrical conjoining of both sets of lovers, and the concluding figures of the dance— these form the ceremonies against which the freebooting wit and the Machiavellian cunning exert themselves. As the social rituals contrast with wit or malice a double sense arises, of established form and of spontaneity, in vital tensions. As with the style's formalities and freedoms, the spectator or reader is always half-conscious, yet never too conscious, of the unobtrusive yet exhilarated skill with which Shakespeare controls his plot. Such organic aptness is the mark of high art.

What a full account of a Shakespeare play's form would include is interestingly described thus: it is to comprise

> the play viewed as a scenic build-up in which the action of the text is only one element, but where also positioning, grouping, movement, costumes, properties, use of silence or sound or music, have to be taken into account, ... and ... the change of verse and prose and the infinite varieties of style. ... The structural power ... is behind the musical balance of the play as a whole, no less than in the tact and delicate understanding in the treatment of the source material, as [Shakespeare] now adds new characters, now changes the story to create the harmony he wants.[1]

Inescapably noticeable are the interactions of the serious plot (Claudio and Hero), the comic plot (Benedick and Beatrice), and the auxiliary plot (Dogberry and Verges). Since the sources are innocent of comic elements one can only, as so often, salute Shakespeare's inventive, amplifying, and harmonizing skill. Swinburne hardly exaggerated in saying that 'For absolute power of composition, for faultless balance and blameless rectitude of design, there is unquestionably no creation of his hand that will bear comparison with *Much Ado About Nothing*.'[2] The serious plot alone might have afforded a full drama; it did so for the anonymous author of *The Partiall Law* (*c.* 1615–30), who focused his play on two major events, the window-entering, and the challenge to the accuser.[3] Had Shakespeare so limited his theme, however, the result might have been hardly ampler than *The Two Noble Kinsmen*, which he and Fletcher put together from Chaucer's *The Knight's Tale*, and what has gripped audiences from the play's earliest days has been the fascination of Beatrice and Benedick.

1. Henning Krabbe, 'Elements in Shakespeare's Construction', read at the Stratford-upon-Avon International Shakespeare Conference, 1978.

2. *A Study of Shakespeare* (1880), p. 152.

3. This play, which Bertram Dobell published in 1908 from a manuscript he dated 1615–30, is a straight version of Ariosto's story of Ariodante, Genevra, Polynesso, and Dalinda, though the names become, respectively, Bellamour (incognito Prince of Cyprus), Florabell (the King of Corsica's daughter), Philocres (Prince of Majorca), and Lucina (Florabell's companion). The main plot difference is that, of the two champions who turn up incognito to defend the accused Florabell (Genevra) against Philocres (Polynesso), one is Bellamour (Ariodante) in disguise, and the other, piquantly, is Florabell herself, donning armour to fight in her own defence, and impersonated while she does so by her disguised maid Fiducia. The fight is undertaken by Bellamour who, predictably, wins. The lovers are reunited, and the vanquished Philocres, claiming immunity as a prince from retribution, quits the scene.

Yet one need not conclude that Shakespeare took merely a perfunctory interest in Claudio and Hero. The theme of love disturbed by treachery, disloyalty, or misconception attracted him from the time of *The Two Gentlemen of Verona* to that of *Cymbeline* and *The Winter's Tale*, and in *Much Ado*, as Don John's schemes take effect, Shakespeare shows great skill in heightening expectations, guarding against incredulity, interweaving comic reassurances with tragic apprehensions, and, throughout the church scene and its aftermath, evolving events with wonderful impetus and significance. Even if one rejects, as one should, the apoplectic denunciations of Claudio quoted on p. 54, the fact that they can be provoked bears witness to the scene's intensity. If Beatrice and Benedick are, on the whole, the characters who predominate, that is because they have extraordinary appeal, not because Claudio and Hero have little. For even in such an unobtrusive pair he is dramatically interested (contrary to much critical opinion), and although the serious plot's salience, unrivalled in the sources, has except during the church scene to yield to the vitality of Beatrice and Benedick, it involves much power and earnestness of feeling. To stress the brief, passing references to Hero as heiress, and to judge Claudio mercenary, is to misread the whole tenor of the play (as *The Merchant of Venice* is misread when Bassanio is taken for a sheer fortune-hunter). It is an unquestioned datum of Shakespeare's world of comedy that brides and bridegrooms are to be affluent. There is nothing mercenary about this; it is not 'opposed to the romantic tradition' but in fact an integral part of it, in virtually all traditional comedy. Claudio and Hero may be short on romantic fervour, but no one should doubt that they are—gently, earnestly—in love.

Starting as the two major plots do by alternating twin (though contrasting) themes in the spirit of affluent gaiety, their themes interweave harmoniously up to the middle of III. ii. Concurrently, Don John's hostile strategies give the young lovers' story a dramatic potential it would not otherwise have.[1] After that point, until the crisis is over, the two main plots take on a very different relationship. Hitherto they have gaily interacted. Henceforth, and until reconciled in the solution, they polarize. As Don John's accusations bite, one feels an intense desire to see how Beatrice's and Benedick's germinating union will bear upon the

1. Hudson (*Life*, vol. I, p. 319) observes that, had Hero's and Claudio's course of true love run smooth, 'its voice, even if audible, would have been hardly worth hearing'.

Claudio–Hero crisis. The result is the climactic moment of the play, with Beatrice's cry of 'Kill Claudio', and Benedick's choice, facing the loss of either his old friends or his new-found beloved, against friendship and for love. The plots' early and late accord, and interim polarization, form a strong dramatic rhythm.

The notion that two disjunct stories split the play is quite misguided. Harmoniously related as serious and comic themes are in the first and last phases, drastically opposed in between, they always belong together, as either analogous or antithetical counterparts of each other. Both plots have heroes (the comic plot a heroine also) attitudinizing over their senses of honour and self-esteem. If Claudio and Hero are mild and immature young lovers manoeuvred together by social diplomacies, Benedick and Beatrice are vigorous and mature professed anti-lovers held apart by independence of spirit and then manoeuvred into the union they inwardly desire. Both couples offer (in contrasted ways) reactions against extravagant romanticism. In a sense (though this should not be overschematized) Benedick and Claudio are inversely parallel—Benedick hubristic in comic error, Claudio in tragic (and both meet a nemesis); Benedick rashly confident in renouncing love and Beatrice, Claudio equally so in renouncing love and Hero; Benedick irrepressible in social aplomb, Claudio shy and tentative, yet both friends and comrades-in-arms under Don Pedro, and both as the play ends able (if they wish) to reflect with gathered wisdom on the errors of comic or tragic delusion through which each has been brought to happiness. Of Beatrice and Hero something similar is true: the former is sparkling and self-possessed, the latter quiet and gentle (though not spiritless); Beatrice takes initiatives, Hero submits; none the less they are loving cousins, both bound for final happiness. About this there is no schematic rigidity; all evolves naturally; yet it holds the play together with a decisive if unobtrusive pattern. Analogies and antitheses abound.

Both plots are activated by eavesdroppings and the consequent 'notings', true or false, which provoke the 'ado'. Don Pedro's proxy wooing for Claudio results in interpretations or misinterpretations from everyone but himself. Beatrice and Benedick are lured into hearing home truths about themselves and cheerful falsehoods about each other. Borachio's window talk with Margaret is the trap of error into which Don Pedro and Claudio fall. Conrade and Borachio are overheard by the Watch who, besides discovering 'the most dangerous piece of lechery that ever was known in the commonwealth', 'flat burglary as ever was committed', make much ado about the mysterious Deformed. Both plots are galvanized by hoaxes; Don Pedro's 'amiable hoax' unites Beatrice and Benedick, Don John's 'malicious hoax' divides Hero and Claudio, and the Friar's 'benign hoax' paves the way for recovery.[1] Another word for 'hoax' might be 'masquerade', the disguised strategies so often employed.[2]

Structurally, the Beatrice–Benedick plot is the perfect means of occupying the time between Claudio's and Hero's betrothal and the day of wedding. Within it, the gullings of the two rivals are beautifully parallel and yet beautifully varied—parallel in the strategies employed, in common images of snaring and catching, in common reactions and surrender, and in the charming sympathy each party discovers for the other's supposed sufferings, yet varied in the different lengths of the gullings (Benedick has to hear a full repertoire of witty fabrications, Beatrice a much shorter one of character truths), and in the substitution of verse for prose and of Beatrice's tenderness for Benedick's bounce. Both before and after his deception Benedick is given full soliloquies of witty prose; Beatrice, after hers, confines herself (yet with a touching surge of feeling) to a truncated sonnet of romantic surrender. The comic symmetries, the comic variations, between the two gullings are exquisitely satisfying.

As for the structural value of the Watch, that needs no insisting upon. Introduced as soon as Don John has intervened, guarding Leonato's door for the 'great coil tonight', shrewd enough to 'comprehend', even before the church scene, 'a couple of as arrant knaves as any in Messina', but led by a commander so successfully tedious as to conceal their findings until after the crisis, they are deployed in the story with an impeccable sense of timing as to both the process of discovery and the guidance of our dramatic responses: we respond to the church scene assured that the truth will out, however tardily. Dogberry, moreover, deserves our inestimable gratitude for his genius for the absurd which, as in IV. ii and at the end of V. i, dissolves tensions into hilarity.

The play's form involves not only Shakespeare's interlocking of plot lines but his control over emotion. During the church scene, without sacrificing any dramatic strength (Claudio's deluded anger, Hero's distress, Leonato's anguish, and Beatrice's power of feeling are fully given), he heartens us with the prior discovery of Don John's plot, buoys us up with recollection of the

---

1. Paul and Miriam Mueschke, 'Illusion and Metamorphosis in *Much Ado About Nothing*', *ShQ* XVIII (1967), p. 58.
2. Francis Fergusson, *Shakespeare: the Pattern in the Carpet* (1970), p. 140.

gaiety recently prevailing and presumably to be regained, and, never having shown in Hero any depth of passion, harrows us less with her suffering than he startles us with Claudio's histrionics.[1] So the scene, intense though it is, is shrewdly controlled to suit the play's over-all modelling: though a drastic offset to what has preceded, unprecedented in its impact, and a shock to the feelings, it is framed (like the similarly functioning trial scene in *The Merchant of Venice*) by the assurance of happiness soon to be renewed.

The church scene is handled so strongly as to give it a different nature from the rest. Still, throughout the play a fine flexibility prevails. Formal scenes interplay with free-running ones, good-natured courtesy alternates with witty bravura and calculated venom, 'the solemnity of Love is relieved by the generosity of Laughter, and the irresponsibility of Laughter by the seriousness of Love'.[2] Such stimulating variations occur throughout, and to remark on them is to state the obvious, but since the ingenuity of the plot mechanics is oftener noticed than this tonal interplay it is worth mentioning.

Another aspect of form is the play's social coherence, its firm contours of place, time, and company. These are much clearer than in the more evidently 'romantic' comedies and tragi-comedies. *Much Ado* is businesslike. In respect of time, there are dozens of references (not quite all consistent) to hours and days for plans and arrangements. And in respect of place, all the participants are familiar acquaintances in familiar surroundings. Don Pedro, Claudio, Benedick and Leonato may assemble respectively from Aragon, Florence, Padua, and Messina, yet they are intimates. Don Pedro has stayed before with Leonato, Claudio and Benedick have campaigned with Don Pedro, Claudio has an uncle in Messina and has already 'liked' Hero, Benedick has 'set up his bills here' and challenged Cupid, and his 'merry war' with Beatrice is a matter of common knowledge (including some mysterious unexplained affair: II.i.261–4). By marrying cousins, Claudio and Benedick themselves become cousins. In a society so intimately interrelated the church crisis shocks like the tearing of a handsome fabric.

The plot is tightly concerned with ploys affecting the group. Nothing is irrelevant to the strands with which it binds them. The dialogue, fittingly for a social courtship or for comic hubris resolved in comic nemesis, ranges always over ground familiar to

1. These points are from Grace Trenery's original Arden edn, pp. xxii–xxiii.
2. G. S. Gordon, *Shakespearian Comedy and Other Studies* (1944), p. 49.

the participants. The jests about the savage bull, and the avowed bachelor becoming the married man (I.i.229, 241–8), are gleefully recalled (v.i.178–81, v.iv.42). Benedick's offer to replace with drink any blood he might lose with love (I.i.231–2) is taken up in Don Pedro's 'There's no true drop of blood in him to be truly touched with love' (III.ii.17–18). The qualities Beatrice has already revealed are vividly recalled in Hero's characterization of her (III.i). Ursula's praise of Benedick as 'foremost in report through Italy' (III.i.97) chimes with Beatrice's reported sigh that he is 'the properest man in Italy' (v.i.169–70). As Benedick admits his present love he gaily recalls his past intransigence (II.iii.227–35); and he does not forget in his final high spirits to remind Claudio 'I did think to have beaten thee' (v.iv.108). This is a close-knit company, 'noting' its members, storing up for jest or strategy anything that may provide ammunition, and holding it readily available.

One large qualification, however, needs admitting. Not every strand is tightly tied up; some strands are not tied up at all. Small inconsistencies left in haste are of no account, admittedly. Nothing further is heard of Leonato's wife mentioned in the first Quarto entry direction, or of Claudio's 'uncle here in Messina', or why Benedick hails from Padua, or how he had earlier contested with Cupid and Beatrice, or when it was that she gave him a double heart for his single one, or why the variant over-hearings of Don Pedro's talk with Claudio seem to arise from different occasions, or who Leonato's 'cousin' and Antonio's 'son' may be. Why does Don John set off for 'the great supper' (I.iii.67) but never reach it (II.i.1)? What becomes of the music Don Pedro proposes for 'tomorrow night . . . at the Lady Hero's chamber-window' (II.iii.85–7)? (Its presence would have ruined Don John's plot.) Such loose ends spring from Shakespeare's invention, which scatters ideas he never takes up.

More troublesome is the problem of how the chamber-window intrigue was managed, and what Margaret was up to. The temptation need not be resisted to quote Lewis Carroll on the subject, long though his exposition is. Writing to Ellen Terry he posed it thus:

Why in the world did not Hero (or at any rate Beatrice on her behalf) prove an 'alibi' in answer to the charge? It seems certain that she did *not* sleep in her room that night; for how could Margaret venture to open a window and talk from it, with her mistress asleep in the room? It would be sure to wake her.

Besides, Borachio says, after promising that Margaret shall speak with him out of Hero's chamber-window, 'I will so fashion the matter that Hero shall be absent'. (How he could possibly manage any such thing is another difficulty, but I pass over that.) Well, granting that Hero has slept in some other room that night, why didn't she say so? When Claudio asked her,

> What man was he talk'd with you yesternight
> Out at your window betwixt twelve and one?

why didn't she reply,

> I talk'd with no man at that hour, my lord,
> Nor was I in my chamber yesternight,
> But in another, far from it remote?

And this she could, of course, prove by the evidence of the housemaids, who must have known that she occupied another room that night.

But even if Hero might be supposed to be so distracted as not to remember where she had slept the night before, or even whether she had slept anywhere, surely Beatrice had her wits about her; and when an arrangement was made, by which she was to lose, for one night, her twelve-months' bedfellow, is it conceivable that she didn't know *where* Hero passed the night? Why didn't she reply:

> But, good my lord, sweet Hero slept not there;
> She had another chamber for the nonce.
> 'Twas sure some counterfeit that did present
> Her person at the window, ap'd her voice,
> Her mien, her manners, and hath thus deceiv'd
> My good Lord Pedro and his company?

With all these excellent materials for proving an 'alibi' it is incomprehensible that no-one should think of it. If only there had been a barrister friend present to cross-examine Beatrice! 'Now, ma'am, attend to me, please, and speak up so that the jury can hear you. Where did you sleep last night? Where did Hero sleep? Will you swear that she slept in her own room? Will you swear that you do not know *where* she slept?' I feel inclined to quote old Mr Weller and to say to Beatrice at the end of the play, 'Oh, Samivel, Samivel, vy wornt there a halibi?'[1]

---

1. Letter to Ellen Terry, quoted in George Gordon, *Shakespearian Comedy*, pp. 24–5.

Hero's and Beatrice's lack of rebuttal one must attribute to shocked bewilderment. As for Margaret, one can only say that, firstly, how Borachio plotted his exploit is left an offstage mystery; secondly, that Shakespeare follows Ariosto and Spenser in making the accomplice unaware of her action's real bearing; thirdly, that the window episode is shrewdly kept out of sight and Margaret away from the church; fourthly, that as we never see anything of Margaret save in scenes of innocent mirth we cannot think her wicked;[1] and fifthly, that Shakespeare performs sleight-of-hand tricks to juggle her fault away without ever explaining it. The play simply does not turn our thoughts to what Margaret is or should be feeling; her state of mind would be a distracting complication, so he veils it from us. When Leonato asks about her guilt, Borachio defends her as 'always . . . just and virtuous' (v.i.296). No sooner has Leonato again hinted at enquiry than she enters as gay as can be (v.ii.1). Finally all we learn is that she 'was in some fault for this, / Although against her will' (v.iv.4–5), and with no sign of displeasure Beatrice recalls her share, along with Hero and Ursula, in the arbour scene (v.iv.78). The audience, Shakespeare realized, needed reassurance; he gave it his word that Margaret was to be forgiven whatever folly she had committed, and with that we must rest content.

The general close-knitness, then, does not account for everything. There are passing references to times, events, and persons, outside the play's confines, which relate it to a wider world and tell against claustrophobia. There are plot elements left for speculation, but speculation which sets in only in the leisure of the study and can hardly reach any other conclusion than that Shakespeare was not too concerned about casual detail, and sometimes was cavalier about detail by no means casual. With these qualifications, the point is still valid that *Much Ado About Nothing*, a play of ceremonies and strategies, is, for Shakespeare, more than usually intent on the interlinking of its parts, for social verisimilitude and the coherence of its intrigues. Of it, more than of most of the others, one can say that he 'interrelates part to part and every part to the whole', and that 'no speech exists in a vacuum'.[2]

---

1. See II.i, III.i, III.iv, v.ii. The third of these is on the wedding morning itself, immediately after her night's escapade, yet clearly no sense of misdoing has entered her head. The fourth is immediately after Borachio has confessed the truth, when, if guilt-stricken, she should be appalled and contrite, yet in her risqué bantering of Benedick she shows no cognizance that anything has been wrong or that she has been involved.

2. H. T. Price, *Construction in Shakespeare* (1951), pp. 2, 41.

9. CRITICAL RÉSUMÉ

The play's main aspects have already been presented, but the evidence for a coherent assessment has inevitably been dispersed. This résumé offers little new but it gathers together material hitherto scattered, risking repetition for the sake of unity.

In general, Shakespeare's romantic comedies present a courtly or pastoral world in which the action, however fanciful and entertaining, exists mainly for the moods and manoeuvres of lyrical courtship. To this generalization exceptions like *The Comedy of Errors*, *The Taming of the Shrew*, and *The Merry Wives of Windsor* offer themselves (though these are not really romantic comedies) but the account is prevalently true of the rest, from *The Two Gentlemen of Verona* to *Twelfth Night*. As Lysander observes in *A Midsummer Night's Dream*, the course of true love never did run smooth, and in the romantic comedies, though seldom in real jeopardy, it has amusing or touching impediments to surmount. But the interest is normally less in the strategies of plot than in the humanity of the characters, the sequence of their emotions, the interplay of comic levels, and the delights of lyrical elaboration. Neither time nor business presses: poetry is the prevailing language, leisurely, delicate, appealing in image and sentiment.

Much Ado About Nothing is partly similar, partly different. It is similar in sharing the world of affluent leisure and general good nature; happiness, it assumes, is the intended lot of the good. Yet it differs in manner from most of the others; its schemings and sallies of wit demand the head rather than the heart, and prose rather than poetry. It differs also in impact. To say that an impact is what it decidedly makes, in the comic gusto of Beatrice and Benedick or the tragic shock of the church scene, is to point out a difference from the easygoing tenor generally typical of the rest (though its force of plot is shared by *The Taming of the Shrew* and *The Merchant of Venice*). It is unusually tight-knit, a pattern of intrigue-devisings interrelated and intently pursued, its events not saunteringly consecutive but purposeful and co-ordinated.[1] Composed about 1598, when Shakespeare was fully mature in dramatic skill, it is written with great assurance and adroitness as to plot structure, and great confidence in the focusing of dialogue.

Though not precisely realistic, that is, factually faithful to

---

1. *A Midsummer Night's Dream*, though less tight-knit, also ingeniously interlocks its plot elements; cf. H. F. Brooks's New Arden edn, Introduction, pp. xciv–cii.

ordinary conditions, the sense of life as real is prevalent, within the frame of the elegant and delightful. Leonato's household is convincingly rendered in those aspects which conduce to hospitality and enjoyment, with its servants and musicians, its accommodations, its 'busy time' of banqueting and dancing, and its orchard's pleached alleys and bowers. Though there is much less domestic detail than in, say, *The Merry Wives of Windsor* or Jonson's *Every Man In His Humour* or the city comedies of Dekker and Massinger (the level is that of the reception room and banqueting hall), there is entirely enough to support the idea of the kindly host welcoming friends, the goodnatured Prince and his companions, on a festive visit. Their concern is for courtesies, for wit and repartee, for courtship and an expected wedding, and for intrigues benevolent or otherwise.

The plot elements are closely interdependent—romance comedy, wit comedy, plebeian comedy, and malevolent intrusion. The participants are not loosely assembled by hazard but fit like pieces of a jigsaw. The Prince's circle are familiar acquaintances; even Don John, however alien in nature, is courteously accepted. Beatrice and Benedick belong irrevocably together but are also integral parts of the receiving and the visiting parties. Dogberry and Verges are virtually part of Leonato's household, 'honest neighbours' charged to guard his premises during the 'great coil' of the wedding preparations. Not only are all parties linked by unforced contiguity, they are all active in each other's fortunes, purposefully contributing to the excitements of manoeuvre.

Critics blind to the skill of the play's organization have thought it both unbalanced in allowing the (ostensibly main) Claudio–Hero plot to be less compulsive than the (ostensibly minor) Benedick–Beatrice one, and also disconcerting in the severity of the church scene after the general lightheartedness prevailing hitherto. As to the former criticism, it is true that Claudio and Hero play second fiddle to Benedick and Beatrice, the play's outstanding interest and the one for which it is primarily known. Until Don John intervenes, Claudio's love affair, though charming, is uneventful; its only prominent event (but how prominent when it comes!) is being saved up for the church crisis. Yet Shakespeare returned repeatedly in his plays to the theme of love betrayed, and if in its earlier stage Claudio's and Hero's affair is too placid, in its later it is almost too stormy. Shakespeare, one guesses, relished the dramatic contrast between its two phases. As for the latter criticism, that the church crisis is a very uncomfortable partner for the rest of the play, the answer must depend on how far Don Pedro's and Claudio's behaviour can be accommodated within a coherent view of the whole. If it cannot be so accommodated, the criticism stands; if, with all its shock-effect, it can be seen as part of a total modelling, darkness which heightens the value of light, illness the healing of which enhances the joy of health, the criticism falls. The matter is discussed below (pp. 72–4).

The characters are all, as has been suggested, functionally related—Don Pedro the presider over both plots, Don John the precipitant of both (all but finally splitting Claudio and Hero, all but finally uniting Benedick and Beatrice). Benedick and Claudio are intimate friends, contrasted in temperament, experience, and the nature of their love affairs, yet with common as well as opposite traits, both fellow-soldiers with Don Pedro, both clearly destined for matrimony (in however differing ways), both tricked by intrigue, both meeting the crises of their fortunes in the church scene, and both at the end, after such opposition between them as threatens fatality, united as cousins by marriage. Beatrice and Hero likewise, bosom friends and cousins, to be yet more nearly conjoined by simultaneous weddings, are paired by contrasted and by common traits, differing as they do in nature and experience, yet both of them young, beautiful, honourable, and good hearted, and both, like their prospective husbands, reaching contrasted climaxes of their fortunes in church. As for Beatrice and Benedick, they are opposed yet akin in their autonomies, as clearly partners, even if rivals, as any two comedy characters could be. This functional alliance of each part with every other combines with the sense of social reality to make *Much Ado* more a social than a romantic comedy.

Things are kept always practically in hand, and mind. Characters discuss their own and each other's natures as relevant to the social whole, not so much their inward individual feelings (because of Claudio's and Hero's reticence, and Benedick's and Beatrice's self-possession, the play is short of these as compared with most of the comedies) as the impact they make on the others or the relationship they have with them—Claudio's shy need of an intermediary, Don John's tartness and melancholy, Beatrice's 'pleasant-spirited' warmth and Benedick's bouncing briskness, and of course the qualities these two display in their campaign against each other, a campaign which is clearly of long continuance, as is Don Pedro's friendship with Leonato and the rest. Characters seek each other's help in social predicaments, they receive courteous or mocking rejoinders, they advise or plot for or against each other, they guide or misguide one another by plausible facts. They arrange manoeuvres, appoint times and places, and apply their wits to managing events. To some extent, of course, this is so in all dramatic plotting; things have to happen. But here 'plotting' is specifically apt, both in the basic sense of ensuring a sequence of events and in the narrower one of devising plans to achieve ends. Though different in spirit from Restoration comedy, *Much Ado* in the texture of its design foreshadows it.

The dialogue confirms the sense of alert intelligences knowing what moves to make, not content (as the exiled lords of *As You Like It* are said to be) to 'fleet the time carelessly as they did in the golden world' but eager to prove fertile in consciously directed pursuits. Deriving in general terms from the traditions of courtesy books, wit contests, and Lylyan artifices, it is unfailingly alert, in courteous, witty, or humorous prose which aims always at being telling and spirited. Hardly a phrase fails in piquancy; each one balances, amends, or outdoes its precursor; yet the result is never strained except, passingly, in the early rudenesses of Beatrice and Benedick. What saves it, to revert to Coleridge's happy description (cf. p. 27) is that 'exuberance of hilarity which . . . distribute[s] a portion of gladness to the surrounding air'. When courteous, the speeches interchange their decorum like figures in a dance (a dance improvisation, deft and free, rather than a routine); when aggressive (comically so with Beatrice and Benedick, maliciously so with Don John), they suggest the self-assertive dexterity of a fencing match. In other words, whilst in most of Shakespeare's comedies the plots, moods, and dialogue are informal, liberating, and happily loose-limbed, in *Much Ado* they are shrewdly directed, wittily controlled, and almost gymnastically agile.

Characters may delude themselves or others but until freed from delusion they are confident in their own intelligences. Not for them the trusting resignation of *Twelfth Night*'s Viola:

> O Time, thou must untangle this, not I;
> It is too hard a knot for me t'untie. (II. ii. 38–9)

Much Ado is not an intellectual play in any sense of propounding ideologies, yet it is one in which, assured of their skills in strategy, the characters use their minds, not floating on the fortuitous evolution of situations but organizing the future, or thinking to organize it. Hero, it is true, is understandably at a loss in the church scene, but even she has taken lively initiatives in the tricking of Beatrice; gentle though she is, in a good cause she is a spirited user of her wits. Claudio, at first diffident and dependent on Don Pedro, also proves happily resourceful in measuring his powers of invention against Benedick's, and then unhappily masterful in denouncing Hero. Don Pedro and Don John are both, in their different ways, shrewd manipulators. Dogberry has no doubt that he has wits enough to drive any malefactor to a 'non-come'. As for Beatrice and Benedick, it needs no saying that the merry war is waged between the play's two most active minds, for whom a sentence without a point—barbed, gracious, or fantastic—is a sentence lost, and for whom witty strategies are the essence of life. Since the play's sphere is that of strategic challenge, little room remains for the lyrical enrichments so central to most of the other comedies; the chief stress is on prose, on quickness of idea and the confident exercise of acuteness, though it should be added that, except when speakers aim to score off each other (Beatrice off Benedick and vice versa, their companions off both of them, and Don John off the rest), the tone is less one of competitive wit than of generous and affectionate appreciation.

The prose, consequently, is extraordinarily vivacious. It is lively in rhythm, expressive for the voice (the courtesy, the wit, or the malevolence is meant to be heard), never heavy-footed, flaccid, or haphazard. It is happily self-conscious but unaffected. As for the verse, it provides a refreshing change of mode, lucidly courteous in Claudio's exchanges with Don Pedro, picturesque and animated as Beatrice is being tricked, and, during the church scene and its successors, expressive over a wide range of effects from single-line concentrations which rivet the attention, to passionate harangues far outgoing the expected range of comedy.

This brings up the major question of the church scene itself. So disturbing is its affront to decent feelings, both in the readiness with which Don Pedro and Claudio succumb to Don John and in the impetuosity with which Claudio hurls his accusations at Hero, that very hostile views are often taken of Claudio himself, not infrequently of Don Pedro too, and occasionally (in the sociologically earnest mood of some modern critics) of Messina's ruling class in general; these views have been surveyed in the sections of the play's modern stage history (pp. 45 ff.) and on the world of Messina (pp. 50 ff.). The sense, which basically we can and should share, that the play's near-tragic crisis must not be reduced in impact by the exuberance prevailing elsewhere has provoked some raised critical eyebrows at the supposed heartlessness of Don Pedro's entourage, and, whether one agrees or disagrees about this, the treatment of Hero points to the one great crux—can the spirit of the church scene be accommodated within any unified interpretation of the play?

Shakespeare has presented the scene with exceptional force (analysed in the section on form and structure, pp. 63 ff.). He has made it the dramatic high peak, like *The Merchant of Venice*'s trial scene (also by a significant parallel the first scene of that play's fourth Act). He startles us into a fuller enquiry as to the natures of those responsible than is usual in comedy (again recalling *The Merchant of Venice*). But he presents it to demonstrate not what a callous and self-centred prig Claudio is, or what a prestige-conscious autocrat the Prince, but what evil effects malignancy can produce by deluding honourable but unsuspicious victims into error. In far more tragic fashion that theme appears later at the heart of *Othello*—and Othello himself has his detractors who judge him self-dramatizing and immature. The crucial fact in such cases is the old convention—conviction, even—that the hypocrite-villain is actually opaque to those against whom he schemes, who are therefore not to be thought overcredulous even though readily deceived. When in *Paradise Lost* (III.682–9) Uriel is deceived by Satan, Milton writes that

> neither man nor angel can discern
> Hypocrisy, the only evil that walks
> Invisible, except to God alone,
> By His permissive will, through Heav'n and Earth,
> And oft though wisdom wake, suspicion sleeps
> At wisdom's gate, and to simplicity
> Resigns her charge, while goodness thinks no ill
> Where no ill seems.

The church scene by no means represents Don Pedro and Claudio as relishing their *coup de théâtre*, as has been alleged. In bitter mood they perform what they think an act of stern justice. Yet however justified they feel, their procedure is a shock. To say, in effect, 'You have sensationally disgraced our love and trust: we shall sensationally square the account' is dramatically strong but humanly lamentable, and their behaviour in v.i is unfeeling.

The fact is that, having been led by Don John's 'evidence' into a misjudgement the responsibility for which lies with his wickedness, not with their credulity, they are led further by the impetus of its consequences into grave faults of conduct which need correction not only as to fact (that is, as to Hero's innocence) but as to their spiritual natures—whence the scene at the tomb, of repentance, humility, forgiveness, and restoration. In this whole phase the play offers Claudio's nature in three successive lights: first, in the church crisis, as shocked into almost hysterical anger by conduct which, if true, would be the worst of treacheries towards trusting love; second, in its aftermath, as thrown off balance into adolescent arrogance; and third, on Borachio's confession, as thunderstruck by realization of his error, prepared for any 'vengeance' or 'penance' Leonato may impose, reduced to tears by Leonato's 'overkindness', and humbly penitent—a mood which the tomb scene (v. iii), if given all due gravity, will render as earnest and genuine. The play is now hurrying to its end, and the redemptive phases are presented in dramatic short-hand: the redeemed Claudio of the last scene looks much the same as the lively youth we have known earlier, though no doubt he will in future avoid any such mistakes. *Much Ado*, after all, is a comedy, not a sermon. As in *The Merchant of Venice*, its sunlight world suffers the darkness of a near-tragic storm, only to emerge again into the light; and, as in *The Merchant of Venice* again, in the interests of happiness the conclusion virtually forgets that the storm ever blew up. For the moralist, Claudio may well be let off too lightly; yet if the penitence at the tomb has been properly performed he has made spiritual amends.

The play is, on balance, one of the 'happy comedies', and not an admonition against heartlessness. Yet 'happy', with its sense of a contented or laughing serenity, is not precisely the word. *Much Ado* is less notably tender or warmhearted than *A Midsummer Night's Dream* or *As You Like It* or *Twelfth Night*. All these have enough of poignancy to touch the heart, and enough of charm to raise the spirit. *Much Ado* affects one differently. Some critics have thought it discomfiting, hard-edged in its confrontations whether of wit or of malice, and even to those more sympathetic it shows little of the romantic (as distinguished from the good-hearted), if by that one means the generous effusion of idealizing sentiment. True, it begins, continues through half its course, and ends, in friendly courtesies and high spirits, and its characters (save for Don John's group) enjoy their world and each other; despite the initial edginess of Beatrice and Benedick audiences have always found these two wholly reassuring, and no play with a Dogberry in it could in its over-all effect be other than cheering. Yet all this is in spirit rather different from romantic happiness. There certainly presides over most of the action too much of kindliness and play to stretch the nerves (which is why the nerve-stretching in church is so violent a surprise) and one hardly doubts that ultimately all will go well; so, for most of the time, enjoyment is the prevalent mood, enjoyment among the acting agents, and among the attending audience. Yet it is enjoyment with an edgy thrill, a sort of tightrope watching; we are intent, alert—'noting', in fact. The participants, whether good- or ill-natured, show a lively concern to catch others out; they walk, as it were, among benevolent or malevolent minefields. Within the general air of enjoyment there is a tingling vitality, even a sense of hazard; this is not an easygoing world but a lively, challenging one, where to be outmanoeuvred is to incur penalty.

In the end, of course, Shakespeare dispels any doubt that all tensions are annulled in love, joy, and harmony. He resolves the whole sense of contest, comic or otherwise, in the swirl of the final celebratory dance, with all that that means symbolically to the Elizabethan mind;[1] from this, Don John, the man with no music in himself, one fit for treasons, stratagems, and spoils, is of course absent, as, earlier, he had stood aside from the banquet and the masked ball. Music and dance are the arts of measure and concord, and these not in worldly terms only but in heavenly also: marriage is their counterpart in the relationship of sex. The ending is designed to assure us that, however tricky the causes of the preceding 'ado', in a world which so values the good head and the good heart all must be well that ends well.

10. THE TEXT

(i) The Quarto

The 1600 Quarto is the authority for the text.[2] It shows every sign of having been set up from Shakespeare's manuscript, which

1. Sections xx, xxi, and xxii of Sir Thomas Elyot's *The Governour* (1531) (particularly xxi—'Wherefore in the good order of dancing a man and a woman danceth together', by which 'may be signified matrimony' and 'which betokeneth concord') contain a classic account of the symbolic significance of dancing. In 'East Coker' (*Four Quartets*) T. S. Eliot gave the passage modern currency.

2. Seventeen copies are known (H. C. Bartlett and A. W. Pollard, *A Census of Shakespeare's Plays in Quarto*, revised, 1939, pp. 74–5). Four are seriously defective. Charlton Hinman's collation in his *Much Ado* facsimile (Clarendon Press Shakespeare Quarto facsimiles, 1971, pp. vi–viii) of twelve others (the thirteenth being not available) revealed only five variant words, all self-evident corrections of mere slips: see collation at iii.i.111, iii.ii.87, iii.ii.92, iii.iii.124, iii.iv.1. The other variants are small punctuation or spelling changes. Uncorrected copies of Q have *Bero* for *Hero* at iv.i.86, and the occurrence in F of *Bero* at iii.iv.7, 10, and 16 (see collation) shows that a specimen with that error was its copy-text.

seemingly presented few real problems and from which the compositor, following copy generally legible and orderly, produced a reasonably satisfactory result, though as Charlton Hinman observes in his Clarendon Press Shakespeare Quarto facsimile edition (1971), 'There is reason . . . to believe that the text is less faithfully represented in Q than it might have been' (p. xvi). This is because the compositor, who can be identified by certain typographical idiosyncrasies, worked on other texts from which it is evident that he was liable to make small verbal errors. In the absence of a surviving copy-text few of these can now be identified since 'it is characteristic of this man's work that it usually makes sense, and so is not *obviously* corrupt' (p. xvii). But with that proviso, the compositor did his work competently enough. Now and then he set prose as verse or verse as prose;[1] now and then some confusion or illegibility posed him (or his editorial successors) a problem—a major one with the baffling 'And sorrow, wagge,' at v.i. 16,[2] and a few minor ones.[3] At one point (Sig. G1ʳ) he had to increase the lines on his page from the normal 37 to 39 and to squeeze into five lines of prose seven lines of verse (iv.i. 143–5, 155–8). This could have arisen from faulty calculation of text-lengths if he were setting by formes,[4] or from

1. For prose as verse see collation at i.iii. 37–9. For verse as prose, see collation at v.i. 325–6, v.ii. 25–8, v.iii. 22–3, and (for special reasons—see n. 4 below and p. 77, n. 1), iv.i. 143–5 and 155–8.

2. If the compositor unreflectingly set what he thought he saw, this was no problem for him. For editors it is a serious one.

3. At ii.i. 78 Q's '*Balthaser, or dumb Iohn*' is clearly wrong; the ludicrous '*dumb*' suggests illegibility. See collation and note. At iii.iii. 168–9 the 'neuer' of Q's '*Conr* Masters, neuer speake' must be the first word of the Watch's interruption. Likewise at iv.ii. 65–6 Q's 'Let them be in the hands of Coxcombe' must conflate two speeches; see collation.

4. The question whether Q was set by formes or seriatim fortunately has no bearing on the actual readings of Q's text. Charlton Hinman's analysis of Q (see p. 75, n. 2 above), pp. xiii–xv, makes the point that only one compositor was involved, so that one reason for setting by formes (to let more than one compositor work simultaneously) did not exist; but that the large number of capital Bs (mostly italic) needed for the speech-prefixes and other namings of Beatrice, Benedick, Borachio, and Balthasar had to be found by re-use of type from already printed pages in a way which points to forme-setting; and that the squeezing and the two extra lines on Sig. G1ʳ strongly suggest the same process: this is exactly how an unexpected surplus of text owing to a miscalculation would need particular measures.

Yet other typographical evidence, he concludes, virtually proves that the text was 'for the most part set by consecutive pages (seriatim) not by formes' (p. xv). The best informed view (i.e. his own) is that sheet G was set by formes, but not the rest. Similar mixed methods have been detected in the 1600 *A Midsummer Night's Dream*: see New Arden edn, p. xxvi, n. 1.

accidental textual omission not spotted until the following pages had been set up, but then calling for remedy.[1]

In general Q is a good text, set to all appearances from Shakespeare's 'foul papers'—that is, his last complete draft before polishing had removed such irregularities as the speed of composition had occasioned.[2] The evidence lies in abundant signs that, as Heminge and Condell testified in prefacing the First Folio, 'His mind and hand went together', and that what Q reflects is his original invention little revised as to inconsistencies or to ideas varying as the play evolved. Several stage-directions reflect flexible intentions, mentioning, for instance, characters who never appear in the scene in question or indeed ever. '*Balthasar*' (i.i.87 S.D.) is retained by editors as an appropriate part of Don Pedro's entourage, though in this scene he says nothing; but '*Iohn the bastard*' (i.i.188 S.D.) and '*Iohn and Borachio, and Conrade*' (ii.i.195 S.D.) are impossible. '*Innogen his wife*' (i.e. Leonato's; i.i S.D.) and '*his wife*' (ii.i S.D.) reflect an unrealized intention, though this phantom survived until Theobald's edition banished her in 1733. Her inclusion in Q has been thought evidence that Shakespeare was revising an 'old play', but the evidence is unconvincing and it is clear that originally he meant Hero to have a mother (Juliet had had one, as had Fenicia in Bandello's source-story, a mother instrumental in reviving the heroine from her death-like swoon) but then found no use for her. Leonato's '*kinsman*' in Q (ii.i S.D.) has no function unless intended as Antonio's son, said at i.ii.1–3 to be busy about music (and perhaps identical with Balthasar?) or as the 'friend' or 'cousin' addressed at i.ii.23–4.

As well as these entry directions which do not correspond with the text, or do so ambiguously, others show authorial imprecision. Besides '*and a kinsman*' (ii.i S.D.) these are '*and three or foure with tapers*' (v.iii S.D.), and '*and two or three other*' (v.iv.33). ('*Enter Balthaser with musicke*' at ii.iii.42, following upon '*Enter Prince, Leonato, Claudio, Musicke*' at l. 36, may be thus explained, but it may instead be a book-keeper's insertion: see fourth paragraph below.) Entry and exit directions are sometimes missing. There are no entry directions in ii.i for Margaret, Ursula, and Borachio,

1. If the compositor's eye jumped from the concluding 'mine' of iv.i.134 to that of l. 138, omitting four lines, these would need fitting in; similarly if he skipped the Benedick/Beatrice exchange at ll. 143–6 in favour of that immediately following.

2. This definition amalgamates those of Fredson Bowers, in *On Editing Shakespeare and the Elizabethan Dramatists* (1955), p. 13, and Stanley Wells, in 'Editorial Treatment of Foul-Paper Texts', *RES*, n.s., xxxi (1980), p. 1.

though they all speak (Borachio may be concealed under Q's eccentric direction for '*Balthaser, or dumb Iohn*' at l. 78: see the note at that point), or at III.v.49 for the Messenger, IV.ii S.D. for Conrade and the Watch, or v.iv S.D. for Beatrice, though surely she belongs to the party. Some of the exit directions are omitted, presumably as being self-evident.

In the heat of composition characters receive variable appellations, or descriptive tags or generic names, in entry directions and speech-prefixes, as in '*Hero his daughter*' and '*Beatrice his neece*' (I.i S.D., II.i S.D.), '*sir Iohn the bastard, and Conrade his companion*' (I.iii S.D.), and '*Dogbery and his compartner*' (III.iii S.D.). The '*Towne clearke*' of IV.ii S.D. speaks as '*Sexton*'.

There is an interesting feature of Q's nomenclature. On characters' early appearances, when they need identifying, names are mostly personal (*Leonato, Pedro, Claudio, Hero, Beatrice, Benedick, Iohn*, and so on). On later appearances, particularly if they have, as it were, a generic condition, Shakespeare thinks of and prefers to specify some of them by social function (*Prince, Constable, Headborough*) or morality trait (*Bastard*), and to do this regularly. In Q, for instance, Don Pedro speaks as *Pedro* (or variants) until *Prince* supervenes at II.i.307. After that, except for a single *Pedro* at II.i.326, he speaks throughout as *Prince* (or variants). Don John speaks as *Iohn* before III.ii.71, when *Bastard* appears, and this, with variants, continues thenceforward with the single exception of *Iohn* at IV.i.95. He is '*(the) Bastard*' in several stage-directions (I.i.87, I.iii, III.ii.70, IV.i: his entry at I.i.188 is an error). In the text, however, he is not so described until, after the church crisis, he is so by Benedick (IV.i.188): up to that late point the audience remains uninformed about a significant fact of his nature which doubtless Shakespeare, having often so specified his bastardy in non-dialogue references, assumed had already been conveyed. Friar Francis, so addressed on his first appearance (IV.i.1), is *Fran.* when he first speaks (IV.i.4) but thereafter *Frier*, throughout IV.i and v.iv. As for Antonio, Q hardly allows him personal identity at all. He is spasmodically named (II.i.103, 104, 106, 110; v.i.91, 100) but elsewhere is '*an old man brother to Leonato*' (I.ii S.D.) or merely '*old man*' (v.iv S.D.), speaking as '*Old*'; or '*his brother*' (v.i S.D.; v.i.252 S.D.), speaking as '*Brother*' or '*Bro.*'. Merely functional characters like the messengers or the Sexton can hardly hope to be named, but, one would think, Leonato's brother qualified for more recognition.

The most striking name variants occur over Dogberry and Verges. Here particularly Shakespeare thought in terms other than their names. Dogberry is actually so addressed only once, when Verges speaks to him at III.iii.7 (his first appearance—the audience needs to know who he is). In this initial scene's stage-directions and speech-prefixes also he is '*Dogbery*' (or abbreviations). Later, however, he is 'Master Constable' or 'honest neighbour' when spoken to, and '*Constable*' or '*Const. Dog.*' or variants of these in III.v's entry and speech-directions (except for '*Dogb.*' and '*Dogbery*' once each), and '*Const.*' throughout v.i. In IV.ii he is predominantly '*Kemp*' (the actor's name) or variants of this, '*Andrew*' (=Merry Andrew, Clown) and '*Constable*' once each: in this scene Conrade, though not included in the entry direction, speaks as '*Con.*', so doubtless for differentiation Shakespeare here thought of the comic actor rather than the constabulary function. Verges appears as '*his* [Dogberry's] *compartner*' (III.iii S.D.), and Dogberry and he together are '*the Constable, and the Headborough*' (III.v S.D.), '*the Constables*' (IV.ii S.D.), and '*Constables*' (v.i.201 S.D.). In speech-prefixes he is '*Headb.*' (or '*Head.*') as well as '*Verges*'. In IV.ii he is '*Cowley*' or '*Couley*' (the actor's name), and as '*Couley*' he is given one of Conrade's speeches (IV.ii.70), the prefix doubtless being a misreading of '*Con.*' or '*Conr.*'. At l. 48 he speaks as '*Const.*'.

There seem to have been minor adjustments by a book-keeper, perhaps attempts to tidy up the manuscript before the prompt-book was prepared, though if so they were very haphazard. The speech-prefixes '*Const. Dog.*' (or variants) at III.v.2, 6, 9, 15, 18, 23, 32, 41, and 43 do not look likely from Shakespeare—the awkward duplication is not like him—and are probably intended for clarification, if Shakespeare had repeatedly written merely an indeterminate '*Const.*'. At II.iii.42, '*Enter Balthaser with musicke*', duplicating the '*Musicke*' entry at l. 36, is probably an attempt to introduce Balthasar immediately before Don Pedro refers to his 'song'. (It may, alternatively, be Shakespeare's second thought, but there seems no reason why, having called for '*Musicke*' at l. 36, he should not leave it at that.) At III.i S.D. '*Margaret, and Vrsley*', following upon '*Enter Hero and two Gentlewomen*', also looks like an attempt at specificity, the names being gathered from the following lines of text, as the form *Vrsley* shows.[1] But the book-keeper's interventions were very unmethodical; they did not even

---

1. E. K. Chambers (*William Shakespeare*, vol. 1, p. 386) surmises that the book-keeper rather than Shakespeare might have written the *Kemp/Cowley* speech-prefixes for Dogberry and Verges in IV.ii, if Shakespeare had merely indicated them as *Con. 1* and *Con. 2*, so failing adequately to distinguish them from *Con[rade]*. But would the book-keeper have varied the prefixes so oddly?

extend to the rectifying of 'don Peter' at I.i. I and 8, though this should have struck anyone with a knowledge of the text. Many other details, too, need amending. All in all, 'If ever there was a text printed from foul papers that still needed a good deal of correction to fit them for use in the theatre, it is Q.'[1]

Q's own punctuation is light, as seems usually to have been Shakespeare's own practice. (His addition to the manuscript of *Sir Thomas More* is only sketchily punctuated.) While punctuation in print was normally the compositor's responsibility, and doubtless was so here, the effect in *Much Ado* is often felicitous enough to suggest that Q's compositor was intelligently interpreting Shakespeare's intentions. In the prose scenes particularly the rapid sequence of clauses and phrases, fluently evolving on successive commas, can be strikingly appropriate (for instance in rendering Dogberry's self-important volubility). The flurry of ejaculations at IV.ii. 77–83 (from 'I am a wise fellow' to 'about him') gains its air of indignant expostulation largely from Q's light punctuation, retained in this edition. Sometimes Q's use of a comma instead of a heavier stop lets a clause relate both backwards and forwards with a lively shuttle of idea, as at II.iii. 100–2—'By my troth my Lord, I cannot tell what to thinke of it, but that she loues him with an inraged affection, it is past the infinite of thought'. Earlier editions tend to impede the flow by inserting heavier stops after 'thinke of it' or 'affection', but in this and similar cases Q's lighter pointing, wherever it does not offend modern usage, is retained in the present edition as reflecting the excited flurry of notions.[2] However much or little Q's punctuation is actually Shakespeare's, it often serves his dramatic purposes expressively, and when it does so it is worth preserving.

(ii) The Folio[3]

That F was printed from a copy of Q, somewhat marked up, is evident. Both versions show many common typographical features

---

1. W. W. Greg, *The Shakespeare First Folio* (1955), p. 279.

2. For further ambivalent syntax resulting from light stopping see I.i. 185–7 ('Go to . . . Sundays') and III.iii. 169–70. For fluent commas see III.iv. 74–86, where Q is followed faithfully save for heavier stops replacing its commas after 'holy-thistle' (l. 75), 'man' (l. 82), and 'grudging' (l. 84).

3. Charlton Hinman's collation of First Folio copies found only three type variants in different specimens, none of which altered a word (*The Printing and Proof-Reading of the First Folio of Shakespeare*, 1963, vol. I, pp. 258–9). To refer to 'the' Folio text is therefore legitimate.

and common errors.[1] Theoretically, such common features and errors might come from a transcript of Shakespeare's draft, F being based on that transcript and Q on the draft. But in practice such a degree of fidelity in minute particulars is inconceivable and the many details common to the two texts prove incontestably that F derives from Q. An important consequence is that when a common error is suspected F's concurrence in the reading confers no stronger authority than belongs to Q alone. An editor, therefore, is more justified in emending, if he believes a reading wrong, than he would be if the two texts had passed through different channels of derivation. Actually, Q's text is too good to require much emendation.[2]

F differs from Q in the following respects:

(*a*) stage-direction changes seeming to reflect playhouse practice, though many more would have been apparent had F consistently followed a prompt-book;
(*b*) commonsense stage-direction changes not necessarily involving playhouse origin;
(*c*) erroneous stage-direction changes;
(*d*) insertion of Act divisions, though scenes are not indicated after *Actus primus, Scena prima*;

1. Common errors are numerous. A full list would be very long, and a few examples must stand for all: e.g. Peter (=Pedro), I.i.1 and 8; stuffing wel, (=stuffing, well), I.i.54; Benedict, I.i.81; cannot (=can), III.ii.26; *Couley* (=*Conrade*), IV.ii.70; And sorrow, wagge, V.i.16 (see collation and note); likt (=like), V.i.115; *Leon.* (=*Bene.*), V.iv.97. Common typographical features are still more numerous, and again a few examples must stand for all: e.g. common setting of I.iii.37–9 as ostensible verse; division of III.i.104 at 'you' into two short lines; identical brackets in the corrected Q and F enclosing 'I thinke ... heart' at III.ii.86–7; identical punctuation of 'her, then' at III.ii.103; common setting of IV.i.143–5 and 155–8 as prose (resulting from Q's need to squeeze into Sig.G1r more text than would conveniently go in); V.i.325–6 and V.ii.25–8 given as prose; virtually identical eccentric speech-prefixes for Dogberry and Verges in IV.ii; premature exit directions for Leonato and Antonio at V.i.108 instead of 109; identical attribution of V.iii.22–3, printed as a single line, to *Lo.* Passages as long as, for instance, II.i.287–98 are typographically identical in virtually every particular in both texts.
2. Apart from 'And sorrow, wagge,' the main amendments needed are merely the following: alternative speech-prefixes for QF's *Bene.* at II.i.92, 95, 97; 'can' for 'cannot' at III.ii.26; 'princes left for dead,' for 'princesse (left for dead,)' at IV.i.202 (though QF's reading is not certainly wrong); verse for QF's prose at V.i.325–6 and V.ii.25–8; *Bene.* for *Leon.* at V.iv.97; and correction of some speech-prefixes, misattributed speeches, mislineation, and stage-directions. Most of the corrections are self-evident.

(*e*) omission, or addition, of some dozens of individual words, and omission also of five short passages, i.i. 289–90, iii.ii. 31–4, iv.i. 19, iv.ii. 16–19, and v.iv. 33.
(*f*) many minor textual variations.

The following illustrations exemplify these points:

(*a*) For '*Musicke*' of Q's stage-direction at ii.iii. 36 F reads '*and Iacke Wilson*', that being the performer's name. F consequently removes Q's duplicated direction, '*Enter Balthaser with musicke*' at l. 42. While it follows Q's odd '*or dumb Iohn*' (ii.i. 78 S.D.) it adds '*Maskers with a drum*', doubtless indicating stage practice. Further specific provision of music occurs at ii.i. 144 (in this edition shifted to l. 140), where Q's '*Dance exeunt*' becomes '*Exeunt. | Musicke for the dance.*'. Whereas Q brings on Leonato and Hero (at ii.i. 195) with Don Pedro and—oddly—Don John, Borachio, and Conrade, F postpones their entry to l. 245, to accompany Claudio and Beatrice, and rightly omits Don John and his men. Q gives ii.iii. 182 to '*Claudio*', F to '*Leon.*'; this may be a change in practice, or a slip. F also gives iii.ii. 49 to '*Prin.*' instead of to Q's '*Bene.*', correcting a clear error. At v.i. 252 S.D., for Q's '*Enter Leonato, his brother, and the Sexton.*', F has only '*Enter Leonato.*', stage practice perhaps having revealed that the Sexton serves no purpose (though his arrival is mentioned in the preceding speech). Antonio speaks only l. 323.
(*b*) F omits '*Iohn and Borachio, and Conrade*' (ii.i. 195 S.D.) and has Beatrice on at iii.i. 23 instead of 25, and at v.ii. 40 instead of 42. It gives exits where Q omits them for Don Pedro, Claudio, and Leonato at ii.iii. 211, for Hero and Ursula at iii.i. 106, for Don Pedro, Don John, and Claudio at iii.ii. 123, and for Dogberry and Verges at iii.iii. 92 S.D. and v.i. 322 (for 321). It turns '*exit*' into '*Exeunt*' at i.iii. 70 and v.ii. 96. And, perhaps thinking Q's '*and two or three other*' at v.iv. 33 S.D. too informal, it alters this to '*with attendants*'.
(*c*) Its omission of Q's '*his brother, and the Sexton*' at v.i. 252 S.D., where the Sexton (announced in l. 252) and Antonio should enter, may be erroneous or, as suggested in (*a*) above, a reflection of stage practice. F brings Benedick on at v.i. 107 instead of 109, and Ursula at v.ii. 85 instead of 87. These are insignificant changes but rather curious; in the case of the latter, there seems no reason why anyone with Q's page before his eyes should shift the perfectly clear placing of Ursula's entry, and, in the case of the former, F's compositor set Benedick's entry as if it

were the first item standing at the top of Sig. H2ᵛ, as soon as he turned the page, whereas it occurs in Q in its obviously appropriate place two lines lower.

(*d*) F's Act divisions are sensible enough, and they must be retained for familiarity of reference. But a somewhat more logical and shapely scheme was suggested by James Spedding in *The Gentleman's Magazine* (June 1850) and reprinted in the New Shakspere Society's Transactions (1877–9, pp. 20–4).[1]

(*e*) The omission or addition of individual words can be attributed to inadvertence; none is significant. Of the five longer omissions three likewise seem mere accidents of the composing room. But those at III. ii. 31–4 and IV. ii. 16–19 are more noteworthy, and the commentary discusses them. The former passage was probably sacrificed so as not to offend foreign representatives at court, and the latter either in deference to a general wish to avoid profanity or in obedience to the 1606 statute against it, though many references to God survive in F and any censorious blue pencil must have been negligently wielded.

(*f*) Dover Wilson's New Cambridge edition (pp. 89–107, 154–7) contains a thorough comparison of Q and F variants, excluding stage-directions, punctuation changes, and indifferent spellings. It reckons that of 140 variants, most of them small verbal omissions, additions, transpositions, and different words resulting from letters dropped or added, only seventeen represent improvements, and that these are all within the powers of a sensible editor or compositor (p. 90), as, for instance, with the rhyme replacement of Q's 'dead' by F's '*dombe*' at v. iii. 10.

The conclusion must be that the copy of Q used for F received only cursory comparison with the prompt-book, and a modest amount of unauthoritative amendment (some of it acceptable, some not). As W. W. Greg observed,

> We may safely assume that it was with a manuscript prompt-book that a copy of Q was compared before being handed to the printer, but the comparison can have been no more than superficial, since only a few of the alterations needed in the

1. Spedding's first Act would comprise merely I. i, after which a break in the action would allow for the apparent further conversations between Don Pedro and Claudio reported in I. ii and iii. Spedding's Act II would run from I. ii to II. ii, at which point the Hero–Claudio and Beatrice–Benedick plots are both on the verge of crises. His Act III would comprise II. iii to III. iii, containing the entrapping of Benedick, Beatrice, Claudio, Borachio, and Conrade. His Act IV would cover the whole marriage business, from III. iv to the end of Act IV. His Act V would therefore coincide with F's.

directions were actually made, most of the irregularities and incongruities of Q being passed over without notice.[1]

(iii)   Editorial procedures

The collation records (a) significant differences between Q and F; (b) readings, including stage-directions and speech-prefixes, adopted from editions later than F; (c) punctuation changes significantly affecting sense or syntax; (d) certain readings from editions later than F which, though not adopted, are worth noting: these include suggested locations. It generally ignores unambiguous alternative spellings, and typographical details not affecting the sense. F's splitting of Q's verse lines is noted only when the reason is not merely F's narrow column width. The lemmas are given in modernized form, though the subsequent citations are in original spelling; when necessary the original reading follows in brackets. 'Subst.' (= substantially) means that the reading is as given save for immaterial differences. A collation reading such as 'I.i.1, 8. Pedro] QF (Peter) subst., Rowe.' means that QF substantially have the word as bracketed, Rowe has it as in the text.

When alternative spellings exist the form chosen is the prevalent modern one (e.g. 'tenor' for QF's 'tenure': IV.i.167). 'And' (= if) is not changed to 'an'.

Stage-directions and speech-prefixes additional to those in QF are square-bracketed, as are scene numbers after the first scene (F's 'Actus primus, Scena prima'). In the verse, -ed marks the syllabic past verb-ending, 'd the non-syllabic, except for -ied forms ('married', 'belied', and the like): here an apostrophe would look odd, and the -ed is sounded or silent as metre requires. ('Shall be lamented, pitied, and excus'd' at IV.i.216 represents all three varieties.) Modern forms of elision are followed rather than Elizabethan (e.g. 'pamper'd' at IV.i.60 for QF's 'pampred'). Past endings are elided when metre requires, even when QF do not elide. In prose the -ed is sounded or silent according to modern usage; it is spelt in full, as are other past forms, despite QF's frequent elisions (e.g. 'stuffed', 'stolen', 'shortened', 'entered', and the like, for QF's 'stuft', 'stolne', 'shortned', 'entred').

1. *The Shakespeare First Folio* (1955), p. 281.

MUCH ADO ABOUT NOTHING

DRAMATIS PERSONÆ

DON PEDRO, *Prince of Aragon.*
DON JOHN, *his bastard brother.*
CLAUDIO, *a young lord of Florence.*
BENEDICK, *a young lord of Padua.*
LEONATO, *Governor of Messina.*
ANTONIO, *his brother.*
BALTHASAR, *a singer, attendant on Don Pedro.*
CONRADE, ⎫
BORACHIO, ⎬ *followers of Don John.*
FRIAR FRANCIS.
DOGBERRY, *master constable.*
VERGES, *a headborough.*
First watchman.
Second watchman.
A sexton.
A boy.
A lord.
HERO, *daughter to Leonato.*
BEATRICE, *niece to Leonato.*
MARGARET, ⎫
URSULA, ⎬ *gentlewomen attending on Hero.*

Messengers, Musicians, Watchmen, Attendants, etc.

SCENE: *Messina.*

Dramatis Personæ] Rowe's was the first edition (1709) to list the characters, substantially as above, but including 'Innogen, *Wife to Leonato*'. She was dropped from Theobald's edition (1733).

Don Pedro] A variation of Bandello's 'il Re Piero di Ragona' (in Belleforest, 'le Roy Pierre d'Aragon'): given in QF I. i. 1 and 8 as 'Don Peter'.

Don John] 'In 1458 a bastard prince of the house of Aragon, named John, assumed the crown of Sicily' (Warwick). The coincidence of details is doubtless fortuitous.

Claudio] 'Sir Timbreo de Cardona' in Bandello.

Benedick] from 'Benedictus', he who is blessed.

Leonato] 'Messer Lionato de' Lionati' in Bandello.

Borachio] from Spanish *borracho*, drunkard; cf. '*Bourrachon*: m. A tipler, quaffer, tossepot, whip-canne; also, a little *Bourrachoe*' (Cotgrave). In Tourneur's *The Atheist's Tragedy* (1611) it is the name of the wicked D'Amville's accomplice.

Dogberry] the fruit of the wild cornel or dogwood, a common shrub; found

87

as a surname in a charter (Harl. 76 c. 13) of Richard II's reign (Halliwell).

Verges] i.e. *verjuice*, the acid juice of unripe fruit, formerly used in cookery and medicine. The name occurs in a satirical rhyme, 'Uppon old Father Varges, a misserable usurer'—'Here lies father Varges/Who died to save charges' (MS. Ashmolean 38). Verges seems by no means as acidulous as the name suggests.

Hero] 'Fenicia' in Bandello. That, because the Hero of Marlowe's *Hero and Leander* passionately kills herself when Leander drowns, 'a certain irony' is implied in the naming of *Much Ado*'s submissive heroine (Riverside, p. 328) is quite improbable. Hero is not viewed ironically, nor should she be. If the name derives from the Greek legend, this must be on the grounds of her being the devoted lover. 'Leander's Hero could not be more loyal than Claudio's Hero is finally proved to be' (M. Mahood, *Shakespeare's Wordplay*, p. 177).

Beatrice] from 'Beatrix', she who blesses: in Elizabethan pronunciation *Bettris* or *Betteris*. Pronounced this latter way, with a short vowel in *Bet*, it pairs better with *Benedick* than *Be-a-trice* does.

MUCH ADO ABOUT NOTHING

ACT I

[SCENE I]

Enter LEONATO *Governor of Messina,* HERO *his daughter, and* BEATRICE *his niece, with a* Messenger.

Leon. I learn in this letter that Don Pedro of Aragon comes this night to Messina.

Mess. He is very near by this, he was not three leagues off when I left him.

Leon. How many gentlemen have you lost in this action? 5

Mess. But few of any sort, and none of name.

ACT I

Scene 1

ACT I SCENE 1] F (*Actus primus, Scena prima.*); not in Q. [*Location*] *A Court before* Leonato's *House.* Pope; *Leonato's orchard.* Boas; *not in* QF. S.D. *Messina,*] Theobald; *Messina, Innogen his wife,* QF. 1, 8. Pedro] QF (*Peter*) *subst.,* Rowe.

Stage-directions and scene- and speech-headings additional to those of Q or F are enclosed in square brackets. Stage-directions in Q or F within speeches are enclosed in round brackets.

Location] Shakespeare specifies no locations. This edition confines its suggestions to the commentary. Here the scene is presumably an open space, forecourt, garden, or the like, before Leonato's house: for that of Claudio's talk with Don Pedro see Appendix IV.

1. *Pedro*] Corrected by Rowe (1709) from QF's 'Peter' (found also in l. 8), Shakespeare probably at first intending to anglicize Bandello's 'Piero' and then, since the Prince is Aragonese, settling for the Spanish form.

6. *sort*] Here and in l. 31 this may = 'high rank' or else merely 'kind'. Halliwell gives three quotations to show it used in the former sense—'a gentleman of *sort*' (*Every Man Out of His Humour,* III. vi. 59: Jonson, H. & S., III. 510), 'lords and ladies of great *sort*' (*Ballad of Jane Shore*), and 'many a man of *sort*' (Chapman, *Odyssey,* xvi. 637). One may add 'such men of *sort* and suit' (*Meas.,* IV. iv. 14) and, from *Ram Alley,* IV. i (Hazlitt's *Dodsley,* x. 343), '*Beard.* She shall be bail'd./ . . . / Her husband is a gentleman of *sort./ Serjeant.* A gentleman of *sort*! Why, what care I?' Yet *any sort* implies the wider sense of 'any kind' by contrast with *none of name.*

Leon. A victory is twice itself when the achiever brings
home full numbers. I find here that Don Pedro
hath bestowed much honour on a young Florentine
called Claudio.   10

Mess. Much deserved on his part, and equally remembered by Don Pedro. He hath borne himself beyond the promise of his age, doing, in the figure of
a lamb, the feats of a lion: he hath indeed better
bettered expectation than you must expect of me to   15
tell you how.

Leon. He hath an uncle here in Messina will be very
much glad of it.

Mess. I have already delivered him letters, and there
appears much joy in him, even so much that joy   20
could not show itself modest enough without a
badge of bitterness.

Leon. Did he break out into tears?

Mess. In great measure.

Leon. A kind overflow of kindness: there are no faces   25
truer than those that are so washed. How much
better is it to weep at joy than to joy at weeping!

Beat. I pray you, is Signior Mountanto returned from
the wars or no?

Mess. I know none of that name, lady, there was none   30
such in the army of any sort.

Leon. What is he that you ask for, niece?

Hero. My cousin means Signior Benedick of Padua.

9. *bestowed much honour*] Claudio is
introduced in terms of high and
deserved praise.

11–12. *remembered*] recognized, rewarded.

13–14. *figure . . . lion*] The cross-
alliteration is an ornament of the
Messenger's euphuistic style, to which
Leonato replies similarly.

17. *uncle*] Not otherwise mentioned.
Like other casual allusions it creates
the impression of an offstage social
context.

22. *badge*] 'A mark of service worn
by the retainers of a nobleman; hence
. . . a mark of inferiority and . . . an

expression of modesty' (Wright).

25. *kind . . . kindness*] *kind*=natural,
instinctive, true to nature; as often.
Hamlet's 'more than kin, and less
than *kind*' (I.ii.65) is the most familiar
play on the word.

28. *Mountanto*] fencer, duellist; from
montanto or *montant*, a fencing term for
an upright blow or thrust; cf. 'I would
teach . . . your *Punto*, . . . your *Passada*,
your *Montanto*' (*Every Man in His
Humour*, IV.vii.76–9: Jonson, H. & S.,
I.377): also *Wiv.*, II.iii.25–7—'to see
thee pass thy punto, thy stock, . . . thy
montant'.

Mess. O, he's returned, and as pleasant as ever he was.

Beat. He set up his bills here in Messina and challenged   35
Cupid at the flight; and my uncle's fool, reading the
challenge, subscribed for Cupid, and challenged
him at the bird-bolt. I pray you, how many hath he
killed and eaten in these wars? But how many hath
he killed? For indeed I promised to eat all of his   40
killing.

Leon. Faith, niece, you tax Signior Benedick too much,
but he'll be meet with you, I doubt it not.

Mess. He hath done good service, lady, in these wars.

Beat. You had musty victual, and he hath holp to eat it: 45
he is a very valiant trencher-man; he hath an
excellent stomach.

---

38. bird-bolt] *QF* (Burbolt), *Theobald 1726, Pope 2.*   45. victual] *Q* (vittaile),
F (victuall).   eat] *Q; ease F.*   46. he is] *Q; he's F.*

34. *pleasant*] entertaining.

35. *bills*] placards, for advertisement; cf. Nashe, *Have With You to Saffron Walden* (McKerrow, III. 121)—'setting vp *bills*, like a Bear-ward or Fencer, what fights we shall haue and what weapon she will meete me at'.

36. *flight*] either the *flight*-arrow, a light, well-feathered arrow for long distance, or *flight* shooting, in which such arrows were used.

38. *bird-bolt*] a short blunt arrow. The word seems here to have a double significance: (*i*) the weapon allowed to fools as safer than the long-distance arrow; cf. 'A fool's bolt is soon shot', and Marston's *What You Will*, Induction (*Plays*, ed. Wood, II. 232)—'Some boundlesse ignorance should on sudden shoote/His grosse knob'd *burbolt*'; (*ii*) the arrow commonly attributed to Cupid. Cf. John Cock's *The City Gallant* (Hazlitt's *Dodsley*, XI. 200)—'Now the boy with the *bird-bolt* be praised!', and *LLL*, IV. iii. 19–21—'Proceed, sweet Cupid, thou hast thumped him with thy *bird-bolt* under the left pap'. Beatrice seems to mean that Benedick, thinking himself 'loved of all ladies' though 'a professed tyrant to their sex', challenged Cupid

at the god's own pastime of shooting at hearts, whereupon the fool accepted on Cupid's behalf but substituted the bird-bolt for the flight-arrow, doing so (*i*) to imply that he himself could replace Cupid at wielding Cupid's own weapon; (*ii*) to pose as being himself more Benedick's counterpart than Cupid was; and (*iii*) to deride Benedick's pretensions as a lady-killer.

39. *killed and eaten*] Cf. Cotgrave—'*Mangeur de charrettes ferrées*: A notable kill-cow, monstrous huff-snuff, terrible swaggerer: one that will kill all he meets, and eat all he kills'. A similar ferocious suggestion occurs in Sir John Davies's Epigram 37 (*The Scourge of Folly*, p. 11; *Works*, ed. Grosart, II)—'Bomelio braggs how many he hath beaten,/And then hee looks as if he had them eaten'.

40–1. *to eat all of his killing*] Proverbial (suggesting there will be none); cf. *H5*, III. vii. 89– '*Rambures.* He longs to eat the English./*Constable.* I think he will *eat all he kills*'.

43. *meet*] even.

46. *trencher-man*] man of hearty appetite (*trencher* from old French *trenchoir*, wooden platter).

47. *stomach*] For the same double

Mess. And a good soldier too, lady.

Beat. And a good soldier to a lady; but what is he to a
lord?   50

Mess. A lord to a lord, a man to a man, stuffed with all
honourable virtues.

Beat. It is so indeed, he is no less than a stuffed man; but
for the stuffing—well, we are all mortal.

Leon. You must not, sir, mistake my niece. There is a   55
kind of merry war betwixt Signior Benedick and
her: they never meet but there's a skirmish of wit
between them.

Beat. Alas, he gets nothing by that. In our last conflict
four of his five wits went halting off, and now is the   60
whole man governed with one: so that if he have
wit enough to keep himself warm, let him bear it for
a difference between himself and his horse, for it is
all the wealth that he hath left, to be known a
reasonable creature. Who is his companion now?   65
He hath every month a new sworn brother.

Mess. Is't possible?

Beat. Very easily possible: he wears his faith but as the

---

54. stuffing—well,] *Theobald (anticipated by Davenant's 'The Law Against Lovers' in Davenant's 'Works', 1673, I. i, p. 274); stuffing wel, QF subst.*

sense see II.iii.247: Benedick's appetite for *valiant* performance (cf. *H5*,
IV.iii.35—'He that hath no *stomach* to
this fight') is that merely of gour-
mandizing.

51–2. *stuffed . . . virtues*] Not necessarily derogatory; cf. *Rom.*, III.v.183—
'*Stuff'd*, as they say, with honourable
parts'; and *Wint.*, II.i.184–5—'whom
you know/Of *stuff'd* sufficiency'.

60. *five wits*] common wit, imagination, fantasy, estimation, memory;
often used synonymously with the five
senses; cf. Chaucer, *Persones Tale*,
§207—'thy *fyve wittes*, as sight, hieryng,
smellyng, savoring, and touching'
(similarly §959). But in *Everyman* the
character *Five Wits* represents the
faculties of the mind, not the body,

and Shakespeare's Sonnet cxli differ-
entiates them—'But my *five wits* nor
my five senses can/Dissuade one
foolish heart from serving thee'. These
mental, not the bodily, faculties, are
doubtless what Beatrice has in mind.

62. *wit . . . warm*] Proverbial; Tilley
K10.

63. *difference*] heraldic distinguishing
mark, 'usually indicating that one
belongs to a younger branch of the
family' (Kittredge).

64–5. *all . . . creature*] i.e. his only
mark of superiority, to show he has
something of human reason.

66. *sworn brother*] brother in-arms, in
medieval chivalry bound to help his
fellow in all fortunes: cf. *H5*, II.i.11—
'We'll be all *sworn brothers* to France'

fashion of his hat, it ever changes with the next
block.   70
Mess. I see, lady, the gentleman is not in your books.
Beat. No; and he were, I would burn my study. But I
pray you, who is his companion? Is there no young
squarer now that will make a voyage with him to
the devil?   75
Mess. He is most in the company of the right noble
Claudio.
Beat. O Lord, he will hang upon him like a disease; he
is sooner caught than the pestilence, and the taker
runs presently mad. God help the noble Claudio!   80
If he have caught the Benedick, it will cost him a
thousand pound ere a be cured.
Mess. I will hold friends with you, lady.
Beat. Do, good friend.
Leon. You will never run mad, niece.   85
Beat. No, not till a hot January.
Mess. Don Pedro is approached.

---

81. Benedick] *QF1* (Benedict), *F2*.   82. a] *Q*; he *F*.   85. You will never]
Q; You'l ne're *F*.

70. *block*] mould upon which the
hat is shaped. So in Dekker's *Seven
Deadly Sinnes of London* (*Works*, ed.
Grosart, II.60)—'the *blocke* for his
heade alters faster then the Feltmaker
can fitte him'.

71. *in your books*] Proverbial: Tilley
B534; = in favour with you, or,
possibly, in the list of your followers.
The phrase's origin is uncertain;
several explanations are possible. (*i*)
Servants were entered in the books of
their employers; (*ii*) Members of a
college were (and are) in or on the
books of their institution; (*iii*) Names
in the heraldic register were 'in the
books'—cf. *Shr.*, II.i.221, 'A herald,
Kate? O, put me *in thy books*!'; (*iv*) A
host would keep a visiting book to
record his guests; (*v*) A tradesman
would keep credit-worthy customers

'in his books', and others 'out of his
books'.

72. *and*] if (as often subsequently).

74. *squarer*] brawler, 'squaring' for a
fight.

80. *presently*] immediately. The
growth of the modern sense (=soon)
'was so imperceptible' that examples
before *c.* 1650 'are doubtful' (*OED*).

80–1. *mad . . . Benedick*] NCS points
out that a *benedict* or *benet* was a Roman
Catholic priestly order qualified to
exorcise evil spirits (*OED*, Benedict,
Benet). That it actually meant some
kind of madness seems unlikely, but
the association with madness may
have sparked off the idea of *catching
the Benedick*.

85. *You . . . niece*] referring to
Beatrice's remark at l. 80.

Enter DON PEDRO, CLAUDIO, BENEDICK, BALTHASAR, *and*
[DON] JOHN *the Bastard.*

D. Pedro. Good Signior Leonato, are you come to meet
your trouble? The fashion of the world is to avoid
cost, and you encounter it.   90

Leon. Never came trouble to my house in the likeness of
your Grace, for trouble being gone, comfort should
remain; but when you depart from me, sorrow
abides, and happiness takes his leave.

D. Pedro. You embrace your charge too willingly. I   95
think this is your daughter.

Leon. Her mother hath many times told me so.

Bene. Were you in doubt, sir, that you asked her?

Leon. Signior Benedick, no, for then were you a child.

D. Pedro. You have it full, Benedick; we may guess by   100
this what you are, being a man. Truly the lady
fathers herself. Be happy, lady, for you are like an
honourable father.

Bene. If Signior Leonato be her father, she would not
have his head on her shoulders for all Messina, as   105
like him as she is.   [*Don Pedro and Leonato talk aside.*]

Beat. I wonder that you will still be talking, Signior

---

87. S.D. *Don John*] Rowe; *Iohn QF*.   88. *D. Pedro*] *QF* (*Pedro*), *Capell* (*D. Pe.*)
(*so throughout scene*).   are you] *Q*; you are *F*.   98. sir] *Q*; *not in F.*
106. S.D.] *This edn; not in QF.*

87. S.D. *the Bastard*] Not until IV.i.
188, after his last appearance, is Don
John's bastardy spoken of, but
throughout it forms part of the tenor of
his character; cf. Bacon, *Of Envy*—
'Deformed Persons, Eunuchs, and
Old Men and *Bastards* are *Envious*:
For he that cannot possibly mend his
owne case, will doe what he can to
impaire others'.

88–90. *are you . . . encounter it*] Tilley
T532 notes as proverbial 'He that
seeks trouble never misses it'.

95. *charge*] expense and trouble.

99.] Leonato's speech implies that

Benedick is a womanizer, despite his
protestations ('truly I love none'), but
no real weight need be given to such
impromptu ripostes.

102. *fathers herself*] proves who her
father is by resembling him.

105. *his head on her shoulders*] i.e. she
may be like him, but she would not
wish the likeness to extend to a head of
white hair.

107–9.] This is the first passage of
arms recorded, though clearly not the
first to occur. The Beatrice–Benedick
plot 'gets going before the "main"
plot . . . and this sex-antagonism in a

Benedick: nobody marks you.

Bene. What, my dear Lady Disdain! Are you yet living?

Beat. Is it possible disdain should die, while she hath   110
such meet food to feed it as Signior Benedick?
Courtesy itself must convert to disdain, if you come
in her presence.

Bene. Then is courtesy a turncoat. But it is certain I am
loved of all ladies, only you excepted; and I would   115
I could find in my heart that I had not a hard heart,
for truly I love none.

Beat. A dear happiness to women, they would else have
been troubled with a pernicious suitor. I thank God
and my cold blood, I am of your humour for that; I   120
had rather hear my dog bark at a crow than a man
swear he loves me.

Bene. God keep your ladyship still in that mind, so
some gentleman or other shall scape a predestinate
scratched face.   125

Beat. Scratching could not make it worse, and 'twere
such a face as yours were.

Bene. Well, you are a rare parrot-teacher.

Beat. A bird of my tongue is better than a beast of yours.

Bene. I would my horse had the speed of your tongue,   130
and so good a continuer. But keep your way, a
God's name, I have done.

fencing match between experts with
sharp swords is musically "the first
subject'" (Rossiter, p. 73).

108. *nobody marks you*] 'This indicates
the beginning of the conversation
between Don Pedro and Leonato
which ends at l. [135]' (Kittredge).

109. *Lady Disdain*] This trait (she
is *disdainful* also at II. i. 119 and III. i. 34)
implies some standing resentment be-
hind what develops as the tart exchanges below, resulting from some
not always 'merry' war; cf. the indications of hurt feelings at II. i. 193 ('the
base, though bitter, disposition') and
II. i. 261–4.

118. *dear happiness*] precious stroke of

good fortune.

124. *predestinate*] Many verbs with
stems ending in *d* or *t* form participles
which may drop the final *d*; cf. III. ii.
1–2 ('consummate'). See Abbott §342.

127. *as yours were*] One would expect
as yours or *as yours is*. *Were* arises presumably because the subjunctive
implications of *'twere* pull the verb out
of the indicative mood.

128. *rare parrot-teacher*] outstanding
repeater of empty phrases.

129.] i.e. a creature that can speak
(such as a parrot and I) is better than
a dumb one (such as a horse and you).

131. *continuer*] horse with good
staying power.

Beat. You always end with a jade's trick, I know you of
        old.

D. Pedro. That is the sum of all, Leonato. [*Turning to the*   135
        company.] Signior Claudio and Signior Benedick, my
        dear friend Leonato hath invited you all. I tell him
        we shall stay here at the least a month, and he
        heartily prays some occasion may detain us longer:
        I dare swear he is no hypocrite, but prays from his   140
        heart.

Leon. If you swear, my lord, you shall not be forsworn.
        [*To Don John.*] Let me bid you welcome, my lord,
        being reconciled to the Prince your brother: I owe
        you all duty.   145

D. John. I thank you: I am not of many words, but I
        thank you.

Leon. Please it your Grace lead on?

D. Pedro. Your hand, Leonato, we will go together.

                    Exeunt all but Benedick and Claudio.

Claud. Benedick, didst thou note the daughter of Signior   150
        Leonato?

Bene. I noted her not, but I looked on her.

Claud. Is she not a modest young lady?

Bene. Do you question me as an honest man should do,
        for my simple true judgement, or would you have   155
        me speak after my custom, as being a professed
        tyrant to their sex?

Claud. No, I pray thee speak in sober judgement.

---

135. That] *Q ;* This *F.*   all, Leonato.] *Collier 2;* all: Leonato, *QF subst.*
135–6. S.D.] *This edn; not in QF.*   143. S.D.] *Hanmer (after l. 145); not in QF.*
146. *D. John.*] *QF (Iohn), Capell (D.Jo.).*   149. S.D. *all but*] *Q (Manent), F
(Manet), Rowe.*

133. *jade's trick*] trick as of a frac-
tious horse. The trick Beatrice has
in mind may be that of slipping the
neck out of the collar (as Benedick
eludes the contest), as in *Every Man in
His Humour,* III. iv. 10–12 (Jonson, H.
& S., III. 351), where, to Cob's 'And
you offer to ride me with your collar,
or halter either, I may hap shew you a
jades trick, sir', Cash replies, 'O, you'll
slip your head out of the collar?'

140–1. *no hypocrite . . . heart*] A
possible allusion to the hypocrites of
Matthew, xv. 7, who worshipped God
but whose hearts were far from him.

152. *noted her not*] took no special
note of her.

154–7.] A self-exposure which explains Benedick's readiness to fall into
the trap later. His strictures on
women arise not from conviction but
from the fun of diverting his friends.

Bene. Why, i' faith, methinks she's too low for a high
    praise, too brown for a fair praise, and too little for   160
    a great praise: only this commendation I can afford
    her, that were she other than she is, she were un-
    handsome, and being no other but as she is, I do
    not like her.

Claud. Thou thinkest I am in sport: I pray thee tell me   165
    truly how thou lik'st her.

Bene. Would you buy her, that you inquire after her?

Claud. Can the world buy such a jewel?

Bene. Yea, and a case to put it into. But speak you this
    with a sad brow, or do you play the flouting Jack,   170
    to tell us Cupid is a good hare-finder, and Vulcan
    a rare carpenter? Come, in what key shall a man
    take you to go in the song?

Claud. In mine eye, she is the sweetest lady that ever I
    looked on.   175

Bene. I can see yet without spectacles, and I see no such
    matter: there's her cousin, and she were not pos-
    sessed with a fury, exceeds her as much in beauty as
    the first of May doth the last of December. But I
    hope you have no intent to turn husband, have you?   180

Claud. I would scarce trust myself, though I had sworn
    the contrary, if Hero would be my wife.

Bene. Is't come to this? In faith, hath not the world one
    man but he will wear his cap with suspicion? Shall

170. *sad*] serious.

flouting Jack] mocking rascal: *jack*
was a common term of contempt. See
v. i. 91; also Marlowe, *Edward II*, i. iv.
412 (*Works*, ed. Bowers, II. 35)—'I
have not seene a dapper *jack* so briske'.
Puttenham's *Arte of English Poesie*
illustrates 'the broad floute'—'when
we deride by plaine and flat contradiction, as he that saw a dwarfe go in
the streete said to his companion . . .
See yonder gyant: and to a Negro or
woman blackemoore, in good sooth ye
are a faire one, we may call it the
broad floute'. To call blind Cupid *a
good hare-finder*, or the blacksmith
Vulcan *a rare carpenter*, is a broad

flout; Benedick means, 'Do you speak
mockingly of Hero, praising qualities
she does not possess?'

171. *hare-finder*] 'To detect a hare in
brown fallow or russet bracken needs
sharp and practised eyes' (Madden).

173. *go in the song*] be in tune with
you.

184. *wear . . . suspicion*] The well-
worn Elizabethan jest about the
imaginary horns worn by husbands of
faithless wives. Painter's *Pallace of
Pleasure*, Novel 51, last para., proclaims, 'Al they that weare hornes, be
pardoned to weare their *capps* vpon
their heads'.

I never see a bachelor of threescore again? Go to,   185
i' faith, and thou wilt needs thrust thy neck into a
yoke, wear the print of it and sigh away Sundays.
Look, Don Pedro is returned to seek you.

Enter DON PEDRO.

D. Pedro. What secret hath held you here, that you fol-
lowed not to Leonato's?   190
Bene. I would your Grace would constrain me to tell.
D. Pedro. I charge thee on thy allegiance.
Bene. You hear, Count Claudio: I can be secret as a
dumb man, I would have you think so; but on my
allegiance, mark you this, on my allegiance—he is   195
in love. With who? Now that is your Grace's part.
Mark how short his answer is: with Hero, Leonato's
short daughter.
Claud. If this were so, so were it uttered.
Bene. Like the old tale, my lord: 'It is not so, nor 'twas   200
not so: but indeed, God forbid it should be so!'
Claud. If my passion change not shortly, God forbid it
should be otherwise.

188. S.D.] *Hanmer subst.; Enter don Pedro, Iohn the bastard.* QF.

187. *sigh away Sundays*] find Sundays
tedious (presumably because, with the
encumbrance of a wife, they prove
tiresome rather than enjoyable). There
may be a glance at attempts made
under Elizabeth to restrict Sunday
amusements, for long a scandal to the
grave-minded. Joseph Strutt's *Sports
and Pastimes of the People of England* (ed.
W. Hone, 1830, p. lvi) refers to (*i*) an
edict in the 22nd year of her reign
banishing 'all heathenish players and
interludes . . . uppon Sabbath days' in
London; (*ii*) the general prohibition
of Sunday pastimes following on a
disaster at Paris Garden in January
1583, when eight spectators at a
Sunday bear-baiting were killed and
many injured ('a freendlie warning to
all such as more delight themselves in
the crueltie of beasts . . . than in the
works of mercie, which . . . ought to be

the sabboth daies exercise': Holinshed,
IV. 504). Such restrictions were only
spasmodically enforced, but might
well reduce Sunday merriment.

188. S.D.] The original stage-
direction (see collation) is clearly
faulty, since Don John first hears of
Claudio's intended marriage when
told by Borachio in scene iii below.

196. *With who*] *Who* for *whom* occurs
often; cf. '*Who* have you offended,
. . . ?' at v.i. 221, and Abbott § 274.

199.] Irked by Benedick's flippancy,
and unsure of Don Pedro's approval,
Claudio sounds sulky—'Supposing
this to be the case, I admit I said so',
or, perhaps, 'had I really confided
such a secret to him, yet he would
have blabbed it so'.

200. *the old tale*] see Appendix
V. i.

202–3.] Inauspicious words, but due

D. Pedro. Amen, if you love her, for the lady is very well
    worthy.   205
Claud. You speak this to fetch me in, my lord.
D. Pedro. By my troth, I speak my thought.
Claud. And in faith, my lord, I spoke mine.
Bene. And by my two faiths and troths, my lord, I spoke
    mine.   210
Claud. That I love her, I feel.
D. Pedro. That she is worthy, I know.
Bene. That I neither feel how she should be loved, nor
    know how she should be worthy, is the opinion that
    fire cannot melt out of me; I will die in it at the   215
    stake.
D. Pedro. Thou wast ever an obstinate heretic in the
    despite of beauty.
Claud. And never could maintain his part, but in the
    force of his will.   220
Bene. That a woman conceived me, I thank her: that she
    brought me up, I likewise give her most humble
    thanks: but that I will have a recheat winded in my
    forehead, or hang my bugle in an invisible baldrick,

209. spoke] *Q;* speake *F.*

rather to embarrassment than to
doubts of his constancy.

206. *fetch me in*] lead me on, cause
me to give myself away.

209. *my two . . . troths*] i.e. those to
both Don Pedro and Claudio. The
two nouns are here almost synonymous.

217–18. *in the despite of beauty*] in
scorning beauty (contrary to the
orthodox faith).

219–20. *in the force of his will*] Heresy
was wilful and obstinate adherence to
heterodox views; cf. Milton, *Of True
Religion* (*Works*, ed. J. Mitford, 1851,
v. 109)—'Heresie is in the *will* and
choice profestly against Scripture'.

221–8.] 'Benedick speaks with mock
solemnity, as if he were reciting his
heretical confession of faith' (Kittredge).

223. *recheat*] a horn call to direct

hounds at the start and finish of a hunt
and on certain occasions during it.
There were many different kinds. A
handsome illustrated chart, headed
'The Antient Hunting Notes', prefixed to Nicholas Cox's *The Gentleman's Recreation* (1676) gives 'A
Recheat when the Hounds Hunt a right
Game', 'The Double *Recheat*', 'The
Treble or S^r. Hewets *Recheat*', 'A New
Warbling *Recheat*', 'The Royal *Recheat*', 'A Running *Recheat* with very
quick Time', and 'A *Recheat* or Farewell at Parting', all with notation for
the calls.

224. *baldrick*] leather belt over the
shoulder and across the breast, holding
the forester's horn. Some contrast is
suggested between the *recheat* and the
invisible baldrick, though both imply
horns (of the cuckold). Benedick may
mean he will not be pursued with

all women shall pardon me. Because I will not do   225
them the wrong to mistrust any, I will do myself the
right to trust none: and the fine is, for the which I
may go the finer, I will live a bachelor.

D. Pedro. I shall see thee, ere I die, look pale with love.

Bene. With anger, with sickness, or with hunger, my   230
lord, not with love: prove that ever I lose more
blood with love than I will get again with drinking,
pick out mine eyes with a ballad-maker's pen, and
hang me up at the door of a brothel-house for the
sign of blind Cupid.   235

D. Pedro. Well, if ever thou dost fall from this faith, thou
wilt prove a notable argument.

Bene. If I do, hang me in a bottle like a cat and shoot at
me, and he that hits me, let him be clapped on the
shoulder and called Adam.   240

---

233. ballad] *Q;* Ballet *F.*

public scorn (horn calls of cuckoldry),
nor conceal his 'horn' furtively.

227. *fine*] conclusion.

228. *the finer*] more finely apparelled
(being spared the expense of a wife).

231–2. *lose more blood*] with sighing. A heavy sigh is still super-
stitiously thought to draw blood from
the heart; cf. *MND*, iii.ii.97—'With
sighs of love, that costs the fresh
blood dear'.

232. *with drinking*] 'Good wine
makes good blood' was proverbial;
Tilley W461.

233. *ballad-maker's pen*] i.e. one
dedicated to love and lovers, as in
AYL, ii.vii.148–9—'A woeful ballad/
Made to his mistress' eyebrow'—and
so, in Benedick's estimation, an
ignominious object.

234–5. *hang . . . Cupid*] A passage
from Edward Coke's *The Third Part of
the Institutes of the Laws of England*
(1644: cap. xcviii) illustrates Benedick's words: 'King H[enry] 8 sup-
pressed all the Stews or *Brothel-houses*
. . . on the Bankside in Southwark. . . .

Before the reigne of H. 7. there were
eighteen of these infamous houses, and
H. 7. for a time forbad them; but
afterwards twelve only were permitted,
and had *signs* painted on their wals;
as a Boares head, the Crosse keyes, the
Gun, the Castle, the Crane, the Car-
dinals hat, the Bell, the Swan, &c.'

237. *argument*] subject for discussion.

238. *bottle*] wicker basket; cf. *Oth.*,
ii.iii.140—'twiggen bottle'.

like a cat] Steevens '93 quotes from a
pamphlet, *Warres, or the Peace is
Broken*: 'arrows flew faster than they
did at a catte in a basket, when Prince
Arthur, or the Duke of Shorditch,
strucke up the drumme in the field'.
This does not indicate whether or not
the target was alive; he produces
other quotations in which it was artificial.

240. *Adam*] Probably an allusion to
Adam Bell, who with Clym of the
Clough and William of Cloudesley
made up a famous trio of archers; cf.
English and Scottish Ballads, ed. F. J.
Child (1860), v.124.

D. Pedro. Well, as time shall try. 'In time the savage
   bull doth bear the yoke.'

Bene. The savage bull may; but if ever the sensible
   Benedick bear it, pluck off the bull's horns and set
   them in my forehead, and let me be vilely painted,   245
   and in such great letters as they write, 'Here is good
   horse to hire,' let them signify under my sign, 'Here
   you may see Benedick, the married man.'

Claud. If this should ever happen, thou wouldst be horn-
   mad.   250

D. Pedro. Nay, if Cupid have not spent all his quiver in
   Venice, thou wilt quake for this shortly.

Bene. I look for an earthquake too, then.

D. Pedro. Well, you will temporize with the hours. In
   the meantime, good Signior Benedick, repair to   255
   Leonato's, commend me to him, and tell him I will
   not fail him at supper; for indeed he hath made
   great preparation.

Bene. I have almost matter enough in me for such an
   embassage; and so I commit you—   260

260. you—] *QF* (you.), *Theobald.*

241. *as time shall try*] Proverbial;
Tilley T336—'Time tries all things'.

241-2.] From Kyd's *The Spanish
Tragedy*, II.i.3—'In time the sauuage
Bull sustaines the yoake' (*Works*, ed.
Boas, p. 21), taken in turn from
Thomas Watson's *Ecatompathia* (1582),
Sonnet 47—'In time the Bull is
brought to weare the yoake'; in fact,
proverbial—Tilley T303. There are
antecedents in Italian literature and
in Ovid, *Tristia*, IV.vi.1, and *Ars
Amatoria*, i.471.

249-50. *horn-mad*] raving mad (a
proverbial phrase; Tilley H628), as in
Wiv., III.v.133-4, and Dekker's *Old
Fortunatus*, I.ii.120 (*Works*, ed. Bowers,
I.129)—'I am mad, . . . horne-mad'.

251-2. *quiver . . . quake*] The pun,
one suspects, is intentional.

252. *Venice*] Famed for courtesans.
'The name of a Cortezan of *Venice* is
famoused over all Christendome . . .

As for the number of these Venetian
Cortezans it is very great. . . . A most
ungodly thing without doubt that
there should be a tolleration of such
licentious wantons in so glorious, so
potent, so renowned a city' (Thos.
Coryat, *Coryat's Crudities*, 1905, I.401-
402).

254. *temporize with the hours*] come to
terms, or, perhaps, become temperate,
amenable, in time.

260-4. *commit . . . Benedick*] Tags
from conventional letter-endings.
Archbishop Whitgift finishes to Lord
Burghley, 'Thus remayning your
Lordships most assueredlie, I *committ
you to the tuition of Almightie God.* Frome
Lambeth, the 21 of March, 1585', and
Sir Thomas Bodley to Mr Cotton,
'*From my house.* June 6. Yrs to use in
any occasion, Tho. Bodley' (*Original
Letters*, ed. Henry Ellis, Camden
Society, 1843, pp. 44, 103).

Claud. To the tuition of God. From my house, if I had
    it—

D. Pedro. The sixth of July. Your loving friend, Bene-
    dick.

Bene. Nay, mock not, mock not; the body of your dis-   265
    course is sometime guarded with fragments, and the
    guards are but slightly basted on neither. Ere you
    flout old ends any further, examine your con-
    science; and so I leave you.   *Exit.*

Claud. My liege, your Highness now may do me good.   270

D. Pedro. My love is thine to teach: teach it but how,
    And thou shalt see how apt it is to learn
    Any hard lesson that may do thee good.

Claud. Hath Leonato any son, my lord?

D. Pedro. No child but Hero, she's his only heir.   275
    Dost thou affect her, Claudio?

Claud.   O my lord,
    When you went onward on this ended action,
    I look'd upon her with a soldier's eye,
    That lik'd, but had a rougher task in hand
    Than to drive liking to the name of love: 280
    But now I am return'd, and that war-thoughts
    Have left their places vacant, in their rooms
    Come thronging soft and delicate desires,

---

262. it—] *QF* (it.), *Theobald.*

266. *guarded*] = (*i*) ornamented; (*ii*) protected. For (*i*) see Dekker, *The Shoemaker's Holiday*, II.iii.95 (*Works*, ed. Bowers, I.42)—'I haue sent for a *garded* gown, and a damask Cassock'—and lines of Samuel Rowland's, quoted in *The Four Knaves*, Introduction (Percy Society Paper IX, 1844, p. xi)—'No lesse than crimson velvet did him grace/All *garded* and *re-garded* with gold lace'.

267. *basted*] loosely sewn.

267–9. *Ere . . . conscience*] Tilley F107 quotes as proverbial 'He that will blame another must be blameless himself'.

268. *old ends*] old tags (including the conventional letter-endings Claudio

and Don Pedro have bandied about).

271.] Prose changes to verse for the change of tone.

274.] To assume that Claudio asks this from mercenary motives is to misjudge the 'soft and delicate desires' which he feels he must disclose only by indirection. His inquiry, anyway, could hardly be more tentative.

276. *affect*] love, as in Webster, *Appius and Virginia*, I.iii.31–3 (*Works*, ed. Lucas, III. 161)—'Clodius laughes not/To think you love, but that you are so hopelesse/Not to presume to injoy whom you *affect*.'

280. *liking . . . love*] Similarly Sidney, *Astrophel and Stella*, Sonnet 2, l. 5—'I saw, & *lik'd*: I *lik'd*. but *loved* not'.

All prompting me how fair young Hero is,
Saying I lik'd her ere I went to wars.   285
D. Pedro. Thou wilt be like a lover presently,
And tire the hearer with a book of words.
If thou dost love fair Hero, cherish it,
And I will break with her, and with her father,
And thou shalt have her. Was't not to this end   290
That thou began'st to twist so fine a story?
Claud. How sweetly you do minister to love
That know love's grief by his complexion!
But lest my liking might too sudden seem,
I would have salv'd it with a longer treatise.   295
D. Pedro. What need the bridge much broader than the
        flood?
The fairest grant is the necessity.
Look what will serve is fit: 'tis once, thou lovest,
And I will fit thee with the remedy.
I know we shall have revelling tonight: 300
I will assume thy part in some disguise,
And tell fair Hero I am Claudio,
And in her bosom I'll unclasp my heart,
And take her hearing prisoner with the force
And strong encounter of my amorous tale: 305
Then after to her father will I break,
And the conclusion is, she shall be thine.
In practice let us put it presently.   *Exeunt.*

289–90. her, and with . . . have her.] *Q;* her: *F.*   292. you do] *Q;* doe you *F.*

286–305.] Walter Whiter's *A Specimen of a Commentary on Shakespeare* (1794; ed. A. Over, 1967, pp. 95–106) cites these lines among examples of recurrent image-clusters in Shakespeare, developing metaphors of the lover and the book, fairly bound, to be unclasped, perused for the story, and so on (cf. ll. 287, 291, 295, 303, 305). *Rom.,* I.iii.81–93, and *LLL,* IV.iii. 302–32, offer striking parallels.

286. *presently*] forthwith.

289. *break with*] broach the matter to.

295. *salv'd it*] softened it down more acceptably. *OED* cites '1635 Jackson *Creed* VIII.xviii.§2'—'Such . . . labour to *salve* the truth of the Propheticall prediction'.

297.] = Whatever meets the need is the fairest boon.

298. *Look what*] Whatever.

once] once for all, in a word; cf. Peele, *Old Wives' Tale,* ll. 471–2 (*Works,* ed. Prouty, III.403)—'Jack shall have his funerals, or some of them shall lie on Gods deare earth for it, thats *once*'.

[SCENE II]

Enter LEONATO *and an old man* [ANTONIO], *brother to Leonato*[, *meeting*].

Leon. How now, brother, where is my cousin, your son?
Hath he provided this music?
Ant. He is very busy about it. But brother, I can tell you
strange news that you yet dreamt not of.
Leon. Are they good?   5
Ant. As the event stamps them, but they have a good
cover; they show well outward. The Prince and
Count Claudio, walking in a thick-pleached alley in
mine orchard, were thus much overheard by a man
of mine: the Prince discovered to Claudio that he   10
loved my niece your daughter, and meant to
acknowledge it this night in a dance; and if he
found her accordant, he meant to take the present
time by the top and instantly break with you of it.
Leon. Hath the fellow any wit that told you this?   15
Ant. A good sharp fellow; I will send for him, and
question him yourself.
Leon. No, no, we will hold it as a dream till it appear
itself: but I will acquaint my daughter withal, that
she may be the better prepared for an answer, if   20

Scene II

SCENE II] *Capell; not in QF;* ACT II. *conj. Spedding.* [*Location*] *A Room in Leonato's House. Capell; not in QF.* S.D. *Antonio*] *Rowe; not in QF.* , *meeting*] *Camb.; not in QF.* 3. *Ant.*] *QF (Old.), Rowe (so throughout scene).* 4. *strange*] *Q; not in F.* 6. *event*] *F2;* euents *QF1.* 9. *mine*] *Q; my F.* much] *Q; not in F.*

Location] A room in Leonato's house.
1. *my cousin, your son*] probably the
'cousin' addressed in the last words of
this scene. At v.i.284 Antonio seems
to have no son at all—one of the oversights which on the stage pass un-
noticed. *Cousin* was used loosely for
near relationships.
5. *Are they*] *News* is often plural in
Elizabethan usage.

8. *thick-pleached*] of closely inter-
laced branches.
9. *mine orchard*] See Appendix IV.
13. *accordant*] agreeable, willing
(not elsewhere in Shakespeare).
13–14. *take . . . top*] Proverbial;
Tilley T311—'Take Time by the
forelock'.
18–19. *appear itself*] materialize,
present itself as a fact.

peradventure this be true. Go you and tell her of it.

[*Exit Antonio.*

Enter Antonio's Son, with a Musician, and Others.]

Cousins, you know what you have to do. [*To the Musician.*] O, I cry you mercy, friend, go you with me and I will use your skill. Good cousin, have a care this busy time.   *Exeunt.*   25

[SCENE III]

Enter DON JOHN the Bastard and CONRADE his companion.

Con. What the good-year, my lord, why are you thus out of measure sad?

D. John. There is no measure in the occasion that breeds, therefore the sadness is without limit.

Con. You should hear reason.   5

D. John. And when I have heard it, what blessing brings it?

Con. If not a present remedy, at least a patient sufferance.

D. John. I wonder that thou—being, as thou say'st thou   10
art, born under Saturn—goest about to apply a

21. S.D. *Exit . . . Musician,*] *Boas; not in QF.*   and Others.] *Kittredge; Several cross the Stage here. Theobald (after to do, l. 22).*

Scene III

SCENE III] *Capell; not in QF.*   [*Location*] *An Apartment in* Leonato's *House. Theobald; The Street. Hanmer; not in QF.*   S.D. Don] *Rowe; sir QF subst.* 3. *D. John.*] *QF (Iohn) subst., Capell (D. Jo.) (so throughout scene).*   6. brings] *Q; bringeth F.*   8. at least] *Q; yet F.*

21. S.D.] Some stage-directions are needed here. Antonio goes out and others enter, one being the *cousin* of l. 1, the *good cousin* of the last sentence.

23. *friend*] probably the musician whom the nephew was to provide.

Scene III

Location] A room in Leonato's house.

1. *What the good-year*] Whatever its origin, by Shakespeare's time this was a meaningless expletive (cf. 'What the

dickens'). *OED* comments that it might derive from early modern Dutch '*wat goedtjaar*', probably meaning '*what the good year*' as an exclamation, 'as I hope for a good year'.

8–9. *sufferance*] endurance; in v.i. 38, pain, suffering.

11. *born under Saturn*] saturnine, morose. Stephen Batman, *Uppon Bartholome* (1582), asserts that '*Saturnus . . . is an euill willed Planet, cold and drie, . . . And therefore a childe &*

moral medicine to a mortifying mischief. I cannot
hide what I am: I must be sad when I have cause,
and smile at no man's jests; eat when I have
stomach, and wait for no man's leisure; sleep when   15
I am drowsy, and tend on no man's business; laugh
when I am merry, and claw no man in his humour.

Con. Yea, but you must not make the full show of this
till you may do it without controlment. You have
of late stood out against your brother, and he hath   20
ta'en you newly into his grace, where it is impossible you should take true root but by the fair
weather that you make yourself. It is needful that
you frame the season for your own harvest.

D. John. I had rather be a canker in a hedge than a rose   25
in his grace, and it better fits my blood to be dis-
dained of all than to fashion a carriage to rob love
from any: in this, though I cannot be said to be a
flattering honest man, it must not be denied but I
am a plain-dealing villain. I am trusted with a   30
muzzle and enfranchised with a clog; therefore I
have decreed not to sing in my cage. If I had my
mouth I would bite; if I had my liberty I would
do my liking: in the meantime, let me be that I am,
and seek not to alter me.   35

---

22. true] *Q; not in F.*

other broodes that be conceiued &
come foorth vnder his Lordship, haue
full euill qualyties, . . . seldome gladde
or merrye, . . . for of their complection
melancholike humour hath maistrie'
(Folio 129 verso; quoted by Furness).
goest about] endeavourest.

12. *moral . . . mischief*] *moral medicine*
= medicine of philosophy; *mortifying
mischief* = deadly disease. The speech
is euphuistic in its sharp antitheses and
epigrammatic points. Similarly Lyly,
Euphues (*Works*, ed. Bond, 1.247)—'be
as earnest to seeke a *medicine*, as you
were eager to runne into a *mischiefe*'.
Shakespeare doubles the alliteration.

17. *claw*] flatter, cajole; literally,
scratch or stroke; cf. Cotgrave,

'*Gallonner*: To stroake, cherish, *claw*,
or clap on the back; to smooth'.

25. *canker*] wild rose. *OED* gives
'Canker †5. An inferior kind of rose;
the dog-rose'. Don John chooses to be
an outsider rather than to bloom in
the royal garden.

27. *fashion a carriage*] shape a
demeanour.

29. *it must . . . but*] Two constructions
confused: 'it must not be denied that'
and 'it must not be said but'. A double
negative results.

30–1. *trusted . . . clog*] 'He thinks
himself robbed of freedom when he is
not allowed to bite' (Hudson, *Life*,
1.323).

35. *seek . . . me*] 'An envious and un-

Con. Can you make no use of your discontent?

D. John. I make all use of it, for I use it only. Who comes
here?

Enter BORACHIO.

What news, Borachio?

Bora. I came yonder from a great supper. The Prince　40
your brother is royally entertained by Leonato; and
I can give you intelligence of an intended marriage.

D. John. Will it serve for any model to build mischief
on? What is he for a fool that betroths himself to
unquietness?　　45

Bora. Marry, it is your brother's right hand.

D. John. Who, the most exquisite Claudio?

Bora. Even he.

D. John. A proper squire! And who, and who? Which
way looks he?　　50

Bora. Marry, on Hero, the daughter and heir of Leonato.

D. John. A very forward March-chick! How came you
to this?

37. make] *Q;* will make *F.*　　37–9.] *as prose, Pope; as verse* (*?*), *QF* (*lines ending
only,/ . . . Borachio?*).　　38. S.D.] *QF* (*after l. 39*), *Capell.*　　46. brother's] *F;*
bothers *Q.*　　51. on] *F;* one *Q.*

social mind, too proud to give
pleasure, and too sullen to receive it,
always endeavours to hide its malignity from the world and from itself,
under the plainness of simple honesty,
or the dignity of haughty independence' (Johnson).

37. *I make . . . only*] I take all advantage of it; it is my sole resource (and
perhaps, Boas suggests, 'my familiar
company'; cf. *Mac.*, III.ii.9–10—'Of
sorriest fancies your companions
making,/*Using* those thoughts').

38. S.D. *Borachio*] See *Dramatis
Personæ*, note; cf. Middleton, *The
Spanish Gipsy*, I.i.2–8 (*Works*, ed.
Bullen, VI.118)—'Diego. Art mad?
Roderigo. Yes, not so much with wine;
. . . I am no *borachio*; . . . mine eye
mads me, not my cups.'

43–5.] 'It is notable that the misan-
thropic Don John really holds that

view of marriage [ll. 44–5] which
Benedick only "professes" especially
when the next scene opens with a formal contrast between the two men. . . .
Though Don John is provided with a
motive for thwarting Claudio [ll. 19–
21, 61–3], it is his general discontent
that is emphasized; his negative and
destructive attitude to love and
marriage comes out before Claudio's
name is mentioned' (Craik, p. 300).

43. *model*] ground plan (usually,
architect's design).

44. *What is he for*] A frequent formula of surprise, often contemptuous.

52. *forward March-chick*] This might
apply to either Hero or Claudio; if to
Hero, *forward* = 'precocious'; if to
Claudio, 'presumptuous'. Since
not even Don John is likely to think
Hero immodest, doubtless Claudio is
meant, an overweening youngster.

Bora. Being entertained for a perfumer, as I was
    smoking a musty room, comes me the Prince and   55
    Claudio, hand in hand in sad conference. I
    whipped me behind the arras, and there heard it
    agreed upon that the Prince should woo Hero for
    himself, and having obtained her, give her to Count
    Claudio.   60

D. John. Come, come, let us thither; this may prove
    food to my displeasure; that young start-up hath
    all the glory of my overthrow. If I can cross him any
    way, I bless myself every way. You are both sure,
    and will assist me?   65

Con. To the death, my lord.

D. John. Let us to the great supper; their cheer is the
    greater that I am subdued. Would the cook were
    o' my mind! Shall we go prove what's to be done?

Bora. We'll wait upon your lordship.   *Exeunt.*   70

---

57. me] *Q; not in F.*   65. me?] *F subst.;* me. *Q.*   69. o'] *Q* (a), *F* (of),
Theobald.   70. S.D.] *Q* (*exit*), *F.*

54–60.] On the various Claudio–
Don Pedro discussions see Appendix
IV.

54. *entertained for*] engaged as.

55. *smoking*] fumigating; cf. Burton,
Anatomy of Melancholy, Pt II, Sect. II,
Mem. III (Bohn edn, 1927, II. 76)—
'the smoke of Juniper . . . is in great
request with us at *Oxford*, to sweeten
our chambers'.

55–7. *comes me . . . whipped me*] The
ethical dative makes the language
both more vivid and more familiar.
Borachio echoes his master's mocking
tone.

56. *sad*] serious.

57. *arras*] tapestry hangings (named
from the French town where they
originated).

58–9. *for himself*] At II. i. 145 Don

John's 'Sure my brother is amorous on
Hero' suggests that, like others, he
thinks Pedro woos on his own account.
But since here he learns that Don Pedro
will 'give her to Count Claudio', by
'amorous on' he must, rather loosely,
mean not 'enamoured on' but 'acting
the lover to', 'about to vow love (on
Claudio's behalf) to'.

63–4. *cross . . . bless*] By a sardonic
quibble *cross* (= 'thwart') suggests
bless (by making the sign of the
cross).

64. *sure*] loyal.

68–9. *Would . . . mind*] In *The Jew of
Malta*, III. iv. vi, Barabas poisons a
conventful of nuns with a dish of rice.
Don John merely yearns towards a
comparable enterprise.

69. *prove*] try out, put to proof.

ACT II

[SCENE I]

Enter LEONATO, [ANTONIO] *his brother,* HERO *his daughter,
and* BEATRICE *his niece,* [MARGARET *and* URSULA].

Leon. Was not Count John here at supper?

Ant. I saw him not.

Beat. How tartly that gentleman looks! I never can see
    him but I am heart-burned an hour after.

Hero. He is of a very melancholy disposition.   5

Beat. He were an excellent man that were made just in
    the mid-way between him and Benedick: the one is

ACT II

Scene 1

ACT II] F (*Actus Secundus.*); *not in* Q.   SCENE 1] *Rowe; not in QF.*   [*Location*]
Leonato's *House. Pope; A hall in* Leonato's *house. Theobald; not in QF.*   S.D.
Antonio] *Rowe; not in QF.*   *Hero*] *Theobald; his wife, Hero QF;* Innogen, Hero
Rowe.   Margaret and Ursula] *Rowe; and a kinsman QF.*   2. Ant.] *QF* (*brother*)
subst. (*also ll. 18, 46*), *Rowe.*

Location] Presumably a hall in
Leonato's house, though the original
Cambridge editors placed it in the
garden, Don Pedro's closing 'Go in
with me' (l. 364) perhaps seeming to
suggest the open air. But Leonato's
'The revellers are entering, brother;
make good room' (ll. 77–8) indicates
an indoor scene.

S.D.] QF's entry-directions include
Leonato's '*wife*' (on which see 1.i.S.D.
note) and '*a kinsman*' of Leonato,
probably Antonio's 'son' (1.ii. 1). They
omit Margaret and Ursula, first introduced by Rowe; an alternative entry
point for them might be at l. 78—

see note at that point for S.D. *Others.*

1. *here at supper*] Since Don John
ended the previous scene with 'Let us
to the great supper' this comment on
his absence is one of several small inconsistencies. Shakespeare doubtless
felt that festivity was alien to his
nature and, overlooking what has just
gone before, made a point of his being
missing. At l. 159 Don John makes for
the banquet, perhaps the after-supper
refreshments, though he is never seen
enjoying himself. Presumably he
holds aloof from the celebrations of his
defeat.

6–7. *He were . . . Benedick*] 'Nobody

    too like an image and says nothing, and the other
    too like my lady's eldest son, evermore tattling.

Leon. Then half Signior Benedick's tongue in Count   10
    John's mouth, and half Count John's melancholy
    in Signior Benedick's face—

Beat. With a good leg and a good foot, uncle, and money
    enough in his purse, such a man would win any
    woman in the world—if a could get her good will.   15

Leon. By my troth, niece, thou wilt never get thee a
    husband, if thou be so shrewd of thy tongue.

Ant. In faith, she's too curst.

Beat. Too curst is more than curst: I shall lessen God's
    sending that way, for it is said, 'God sends a curst   20
    cow short horns', but to a cow too curst he sends
    none.

Leon. So, by being too curst, God will send you no horns.

Beat. Just, if he send me no husband, for the which
    blessing I am at him upon my knees every morning   25
    and evening. Lord, I could not endure a husband
    with a beard on his face! I had rather lie in the
    woollen.

Leon. You may light on a husband that hath no beard.

Beat. What should I do with him? Dress him in my   30
    apparel and make him my waiting-gentlewoman?
    He that hath a beard is more than a youth, and he
    that hath no beard is less than a man; and he that

---

15. a] *Q;* he *F.*   29. on] *Q;* vpon *F.*

---

has mentioned Benedick's name; she
is merely relating what is the thing
most present in her mind' (Mackenzie, p. 130).

  9. *my lady's eldest son*] i.e. spoilt, pert,
talkative.

  18. *curst*] perverse and ill-tempered.

  20–1. *God . . . horns*] = 'God limits
the power of the vicious to inflict
harm.' Proverbial; Tilley G217.

  24. *Just*] just so (as at v.i.161).

  no husband] no one to whom I may
prove unfaithful.

  27–8. *in the woollen*] Capell thought

that this meant to be buried in a
woollen shroud (as enforced by law in
1678). But Beatrice does not seem to
imply her death, and woollen shrouds
do not seem to have been usual in
Shakespeare's day. Steevens explained
it as meaning 'without sheets, in
rough blankets'. The idea probably is,
'If I must suffer discomfort, I'd prefer
scratchy blankets to a man's whis-
kers'. That a (smooth) sheet would be
the normal bedclothing is indicated
by II.iii.135–6.

is more than a youth is not for me; and he that is
less than a man I am not for him: therefore I will   35
even take sixpence in earnest of the bearward and
lead his apes into hell.
Leon. Well then, go you into hell?
Beat. No, but to the gate, and there will the Devil meet
me like an old cuckold with horns on his head, and   40
say, 'Get you to heaven, Beatrice, get you to heaven,
here's no place for you maids.' So deliver I up my
apes, and away to Saint Peter, for the heavens; he
shows me where the bachelors sit, and there live we
as merry as the day is long.   45
Ant. [*To Hero.*] Well, niece, I trust you will be ruled by
your father.

36. bearward] *QF1-2* (Berrord), *Knight;* bearherd *F3.*   38. hell?] *Hanmer;*
hell. *QF.*   43. Peter, for the heavens;] *Pope subst.;* Peter: for the heavens, *QF
subst.*   46. S.D.] *Rowe (after l. 47); not in QF.*

36. *in earnest*] as advance payment.
bearward] bear-keeper. Beatrice's
remark implies that he might keep
apes as well. QF's 'Berrord' indicates
the pronunciation but leaves unclear
whether it means 'bearherd' or 'bear-
ward'. In contemporary literature
bearward seems commoner; cf. Nashe
as quoted in 1.i.35, note; also the first
S.D. of *The Masque of Augurs* (Jonson,
H. & S., VII.629)—'Urson, *the
Bear-ward*'; Beaumont and Fletcher,
The Beggar's Bush, IV.v.41–2 (*Works*,
ed. Bowers, III.310)—'Higgen . . .
where's the Ape? *Prig.* Pox take him,/
A gowty *Beare-ward* stole him t'other
day'; *The Pedlar's Prophecie*, 1595
(Malone Society, 1914, l. 849)—
'When *Arthur* shall become a *Beare-
ward*'; and Stubbes, *Anatomie of Abuses*
(*Miscellaneous Tracts*, ed. J. P. Collier,
IV.178)—'I think the devill is the
maister of the game, *beareward* and all'.
37. *lead . . . hell*] Proverbial; Tilley
M37—'Old maids [or, Coy maids]
lead apes in hell'. Allusions abound; to
Halliwell's 23 references others may
be added; e.g. Peele, *The Arraignment
of Paris*, IV.ii.6 (*Works*, ed. Prouty,
III.99)—'All that be Dian's maids are

vowed to halter *apes in hell*'; *The
Returne from Parnassus*, ll. 917–18
(ed. J. B. Leishman, p. 179)—'take
heed that noe Ladies dye Vestals, and
leade aps in hell'. Most evidence
suggests that this fate was reserved for
virgins; but in *The Maid and the Palmer*
(F. J. Child, *English and Scottish
Ballads*, I.232) a woman who has
borne nine children is given a penance
by the palmer which includes 'to *lead
un ape in hell*' for seven years. Originally perhaps it was unmarried women
who were so doomed. The reason remains a mystery.
43–4. *Peter, for the heavens; he shows
me*] QF's reading ('Peter: for the
heauens, he shewes me . . .') has been
held to convey the sense 'as my share
of heaven, St Peter shows me . . .' But
this distorts the comic parallelism
('get you to heaven'/'away . . . for the
heavens'). 'Beatrice remembers . . .
"For when they shall rise from the
dead, they neither marry nor are
given in marriage: but are as the
angels which are in heaven" (*Mark
XII.25)*' (Kittredge).
45. *as merry . . . long*] Proverbial:
Tilley D57.

Beat. Yes, faith, it is my cousin's duty to make curtsy
and say, 'Father, as it please you': but yet for all
that, cousin, let him be a handsome fellow, or else   50
make another curtsy and say, 'Father, as it please
me'.

Leon. Well, niece, I hope to see you one day fitted with
a husband.

Beat. Not till God make men of some other metal than   55
earth. Would it not grieve a woman to be overmastered with a piece of valiant dust, to make an
account of her life to a clod of wayward marl? No,
uncle, I'll none: Adam's sons are my brethren, and
truly I hold it a sin to match in my kindred.   60

Leon. Daughter, remember what I told you: if the Prince
do solicit you in that kind, you know your answer.

Beat. The fault will be in the music, cousin, if you be not
wooed in good time. If the Prince be too important,
tell him there is measure in everything, and so dance   65
out the answer. For hear me, Hero: wooing, wedding, and repenting is as a Scotch jig, a measure,

49. Father] *Q ; not in F.*   57. an] *Q ; not in F.*

48. *Beat.*] Hero is given no chance
to reply to her uncle, or to her father
later (l. 63).

55. *metal*] material.

58. *marl*] clay, earth. Beatrice
alludes to God's making of Adam 'of
the dust of the ground' (Genesis II. 7)
or clay; cf. 'Adam's sons' (l. 59).

60. *in my kindred*] The Book of Common Prayer lists degrees of relationship within which marriage is for-
bidden.

62. *in that kind*] to that effect.
Leonato, like others, assumes that the
Prince will plead for himself.

63–6. *The fault . . . answer*] Puns, as
in the play upon *time* in *Tw.N.*, II. iii.
87–90—'*Malvolio.* Is there no respect
of . . . *time* in you?/*Sir Toby.* We did
keep *time*, sir, in our catches'. *Measure*
here = 'moderation', and also the
dance mentioned in the next sentence.
Answer = 'the repetition by one part

or instrument of a theme proposed by
another' (G. Grove, *Dictionary of
Music*, 5th ed., 1954, I, 163).

64. *important*] = 'importunate' (in
contrast to *in good time*), as in *Lr*,
IV. iv. 26—'My mourning and *important* tears')—and *All's W.*, III. vii. 21
—'his *important* blood'.

65. *measure in everything*] Proverbial;
Tilley M806—'There is measure in
all things'; implying also Tilley H196
—'Marry in haste and repent at
leisure.'

67. *jig*] a lively dance. For this and
the other dances mentioned, cf.
Middleton's *Women Beware Women*,
III. iii. 215–18 (*Works*, ed. Bullen,
VI. 317)—'Plain men dance the
measures, the *sinquapace* the gay;/ . . . /
Your drunkards the canaries; you[r]
whore and bawd the *jig*'.

measure] This could mean either a
dance figure (cf. *R2*, I. iii. 291—'a

and a cinque-pace: the first suit is hot and hasty
like a Scotch jig, and full as fantastical; the wedding mannerly-modest as a measure, full of state   70
and ancientry; and then comes repentance and,
with his bad legs, falls into the cinque-pace faster
and faster, till he sink into his grave.

Leon. Cousin, you apprehend passing shrewdly.

Beat. I have a good eye, uncle; I can see a church by   75
daylight.

Leon. The revellers are entering, brother; make good
room.   [*Leonato and the men of his company mask.*]

73. sink] *Q;* sinkes *F.*   78. S.D. *Leonato . . . mask.*] *Capell (Leonato and his Com-*
pany mask.); not in QF.

delightful *measure* or a dance') or a
stately dance itself—here, the latter,
as Beatrice's further words *full of state
and ancientry*, indicate.

68. *cinque-pace*] a capering dance, so
called from its five steps followed by a
sixth, this being a leap or 'sault
majeur'; cf. Sir John Davies, *Orchestra,*
stanza 67—'But for more diuers and
more pleasing show,/A swift and
wandring daunce she did inuent,/ . . .
/Fiue was the number of the Musickes
feete,/Which still the daunce did with
fiue paces meet'. As against the
'gay' spirit mentioned in the previous
note, Nashe's *Terrors of the Night*
implies that it was a stately affair—
'These louely youths and full of
fauour, hauing stalkt vp and downe
the iust measures of a *sinkapace'*
(*Works,* ed. McKerrow, 1.379). In
Nashe's jocular context this may be
ironical.

71. *ancientry*] elderly dignity, decorum.

72–3. *bad legs . . . grave*] William
Dauncey's *Ancient Scottish Melody*
(1838), p. 247, publishes a 'Sincopus'
tune from the Skene MS. in the
Faculty of Advocates Library,
Edinburgh. It contains running
quavers in its latter half but ends with
semibreves. Dauncey suggests (p.

300) that *bad legs* refers to the
'tottering fabric of the tune' (i.e. its
running nature after a squareish
start?), and that Beatrice's *faster and
faster* means the quaver runs, and
sinking into the grave the slow semibreves. It is likely, though, that
Beatrice's jests are less specific and
merely play on old age/wobbly legs/
dance capers/sinking apace.

74. *apprehend . . . shrewdly*] perceive
with unusual sharpness.

75–6.] 'Beatrice is now in the gayest
spirits, and in the very mood to
encounter her old enemy Benedick.
. . . In the dialogue that follows
between them the actress has the most
delightful scope for bringing out the
address, the graceful movement, the
abounding joyousness, which makes
Beatrice the paragon of her kind'
(Helen Faucit, Lady Martin, *On
Some of Shakespeare's Female Characters,*
p. 307).

78. S.D. *Leonato . . . mask*] It seems
from what follows that only the men
mask. Possibly Leonato, as host, and
Don John, as misanthrope, refrain;
but this is uncertain, and it is best to
conclude, as Antonio joins in the
masquerade, that all the men of both
groups, household and guests, are
wearing masks.

Enter Prince [DON] PEDRO, CLAUDIO, BENEDICK,
BALTHASAR, [BORACHIO,] DON JOHN, *and* Others,
masked, with a drum.

D. Pedro. Lady, will you walk a bout with your friend?
Hero. So you walk softly, and look sweetly, and say   80
nothing, I am yours for the walk; and especially
when I walk away.

78. S.D. *Don Pedro*] *Rowe; Pedro QF.*   *Benedick . . . Don John.*] *Capell subst.; and*
Benedicke, and Balthaser, or dumb Iohn. QF subst.   *and Others, masked*] F (*Maskers*),
Capell; not in Q.   *with a drum.*] *F; not in Q.*   79. a bout] *NCS;* about *QF.*
80. So you] *F;* So, you *Q.*

S.D. *Balthasar, Borachio, Don John*]
'*Balthaser, or dumb Iohn*' in QF (subst.)
indicates confusion, though the name
of Don John is clearly implied. E. K.
Chambers (*William Shakespeare*, 1930,
1. 386) suggested that a perhaps semi-
legible '*Balthaser, Bor[achio] don Iohn*'
might have produced the Q reading.
Though Borachio appears in this
scene, QF have no entry for him.
NCS excised Balthasar altogether,
believing that the MS. read '*B or dun
Iohn*' (i.e. '*Bor* [*achio*], *Don John*'), that
the *B* was expanded into '*Balthaser*'
and the intended '*Borachio*' omitted;
it took QF's speech-prefixes *Bene.*
(at ll. 92, 95, 97) and *Balth.* (at ll. 99,
102) to be faulty expansions of
'*Bo.*' (*Borachio*), and transferred all
these speeches to him, since later
Borachio proves to be 'in the favour of
Margaret' (II.ii.13) and so might here
be dancing with her. But it is unlikely
that Balthasar should appear er-
roneously twice (both in QF's entry
direction and in the speech-prefixes),
and the probability is that Shakespeare brought him in at l. 78 among
Don Pedro's friends, and meant Don
John and Borachio both to be alien
onlookers entering but not participating in the merriment. Alan Brissenden
points out that Balthasar, as Don
Pedro's musician, is equal in status to
Margaret, Hero's waiting-woman,
and fitter as her dancing partner than
is the friend of the unmusical, un-

dancing Don John ('*Much Ado About
Nothing* II.i.86–96 [i.e. 92–102]: the
case for Balthasar', *Notes and Queries*,
April 1979, p. 117).
S.D. *Others*] Margaret and Ursula,
soon to speak, are given no entry to
this scene in QF. From Rowe onwards
editors have introduced them at the
opening, but since they have nothing
to do hitherto an entrance here with
the 'Others' might be more appropriate; see Stanley Wells, 'Editorial
Treatment of Foul-Paper Texts', *RES*,
N.S., XXXI (1980), p. 6.
79.] 'Shakespeare here appears to
have had in mind a pavane and he
constructs the scene on its movements.
For this slow and elegant dance, the
couples are side by side with hands
linked at arm's length; the steps in-
volve turns back and forth, retreats
and advances, making it ideal for
highlighting dramatic conversation.
. . . The chief indication that it is this
kind of dance in *Much Ado About
Nothing* is Don Pedro's invitation to
Hero to "walk about" with him, for
the basic pavane movement is a
sliding, walking step' (Alan Brissenden, 'Shakespeare's Use of Dance', in
Shakespeare and Some Others, 1976, p.
38). Presumably when Beatrice and
Benedick start sparring (at l. 127)
they stop dancing.
a bout] QF's 'about' seems a likely
misreading of 'a bout', a term for a
division of a dance; cf. *Rom.*, I.v.14–15

D. Pedro. With me in your company?

Hero. I may say so, when I please.

D. Pedro. And when please you to say so?   85

Hero. When I like your favour, for God defend the lute
    should be like the case!

D. Pedro. My visor is Philemon's roof;
                Within the house is Jove.

Hero.   Why then your visor should be thatch'd.   90

D. Pedro.   Speak low, if you speak love.   [*They step aside.*]

Balth. Well, I would you did like me.

Marg. So would not I for your own sake, for I have
    many ill qualities.

Balth. Which is one?   95

Marg. I say my prayers aloud.

Balth. I love you the better; the hearers may cry Amen.

Marg. God match me with a good dancer!

Balth. Amen.

Marg. And God keep him out of my sight when the   100
    dance is done! Answer, clerk.

Balth. No more words; the clerk is answered. [*They step aside.*]

89. Jove] *Q* (Ioue); Loue *F.*   91. S.D.] *Hanmer (Drawing her aside to whisper)*;
not in *QF.*   92, 95, 97. Balth.] *Theobald; Bene. QF subst.; Bor. NCS.*   99,
102. Balth.] *QF; Bor. NCS.*   102. S.D.] *Kittredge subst.; parting different ways.
Capell; not in QF.*

—'Welcome, gentlemen! Ladies that
have their toes/Unplagu'd with corns
will have *a bout* with you'.

friend] 'Intentionally ambiguous:
friend often means lover' (Kittredge);
cf. *LLL*, v.ii. 405—'my *friend*' (=
beloved); and *Meas.*, i.iv. 29—'He
hath got his *friend* with child.'

86. *favour*] (*i*) face; cf. *Tw. N.*,
iii. iv. 312—'I know your *favour* [=
face] well'; (*ii*) looks; cf. iii. iii. 19, and
Bacon, *Essay* XLIII, 'Of Beauty'—'In
Beauty, that of *favour* is more then that
of Colour, and that of Decent and
Gracious Motion, more then that of
favour'.

defend] forbid (as French *défendre*).
OED observes that in '*God defend*' the
senses "prohibit" and "avert" seem to
unite'.

88–91.] These speeches comprise a
rhymed quatrain, the neat turn and
witty allusion enhancing the charm
and decorum. Their rhythmical form
matches that of the fourteen-syllable
verse of Arthur Golding's translation
of Ovid's *Metamorphoses*, the eighth
book of which tells of Baucis and
Philemon, an aged couple who enter-
tain Jupiter and Mercury, disguised as
mortals, in their cottage, '*thatched* all
with straw and fennish reede'. The
story was popular, and Shakespeare
again alludes to it in *AYL*, iii. iii. 7–8
—'O knowledge ill-inhabited, worse
than Jove in a *thatched* house!'

101. *Answer, clerk*] i.e. say 'Amen',
as the clerk does (or did) in church: so
in William Sampson's *The Vow-
Breaker* (ed. Hans Wallrath, Bang's

Urs. I know you well enough, you are Signior Antonio.

Ant. At a word, I am not.

Urs. I know you by the waggling of your head.   105

Ant. To tell you true, I counterfeit him.

Urs. You could never do him so ill-well, unless you were
    the very man. Here's his dry hand up and down:
    you are he, you are he.

Ant. At a word, I am not.   110

Urs. Come, come, do you think I do not know you by
    your excellent wit? Can virtue hide itself? Go to,
    mum, you are he: graces will appear, and there's an
    end.   [*They step aside.*]

Beat. Will you not tell me who told you so?   115

Bene. No, you shall pardon me.

Beat. Nor will you not tell me who you are?

Bene. Not now.

Beat. That I was disdainful, and that I had my good wit
    out of the 'Hundred Merry Tales'—well, this was   120
    Signior Benedick that said so.

Bene. What's he?

Beat. I am sure you know him well enough.

Bene. Not I, believe me.

Beat. Did he never make you laugh?   125

Bene. I pray you, what is he?

Beat. Why, he is the Prince's jester, a very dull fool;
    only his gift is in devising impossible slanders. None

---

114. S.D.] *Kittredge; mixing with the Company. Capell; not in QF.*

Materialien, 42, p. 10)—'Up with
your bag and baggage, and to Saint
Maries presently; the Priest stayes, the
Clarke whynes to say *Amen!*'

  108. *dry hand*] A sign of age; cf.
2H4, I. ii. 170—'Have you not a moist
eye? *a dry hand*? a yellow cheek?' (as
'characters of age').

  up and down] entirely, as in *Tit.*,
v. ii. 107—'*Up and down* she doth resemble thee'; perhaps literally, if
Ursula is stroking Antonio's hand.

  113. *mum*] silence.

  120. *Hundred Merry Tales*] A collection of crudely comic tales, of which

the only known copy is in the Royal
Library of the University of Göttingen.
Despite its crudities it cheered Queen
Elizabeth during distress in her last
year when 'she cannot attend to any
discourses of government and state,
but delighteth to heare some of the
100 merry tales' (Furness, p. 72,
quoting correspondence of 9 March
1603 in the Venetian Correspondence
of the State Paper Office). Beatrice's
pride in wit and sharpness is grossly
snubbed by such a comparison: see
Appendix V. iii.

  128. *only his gift*] his sole gift.

but libertines delight in him, and the commenda-
tion is not in his wit, but in his villainy; for he both   130
pleases men and angers them, and then they laugh
at him and beat him. I am sure he is in the fleet; I
would he had boarded me.

Bene. When I know the gentleman, I'll tell him what
you say.   135

Beat. Do, do, he'll but break a comparison or two on
me, which peradventure not marked, or not
laughed at, strikes him into melancholy, and then
there's a partridge wing saved, for the fool will eat
no supper that night. [*Music.*] We must follow the   140
leaders.

Bene. In every good thing.

Beat. Nay, if they lead to any ill, I will leave them at the
next turning.

> *Dance. Exeunt [all but Don John, Borachio, and Claudio].*

D. John. Sure my brother is amorous on Hero, and hath   145

---

131. pleases] *Q*; pleaseth *F*.   140. S.D.] *F* (*Musicke for the dance.*) (*after l. 144*),
Theobald; not in Q.   144. S.D. *Dance. Exeunt*] *Q*; *Exeunt.*/*Musicke for the dance. F.*
all . . . Claudio] *Theobald* (*Manent John, Borachio, and Claudio*); *not in QF.*
145. *D. John*] *QF* (*Iohn*), *Capell* (*D. Jo.*) (*so throughout scene*).

---

129. *libertines*] irresponsibles, frivolous in ideas and habits (not quite
the modern sense of immoralists).

130. *villainy*] i.e. 'wicked' sense of
fun (not so strong as moral wickedness).

131. *pleases . . . and angers*] entertains
(by his malice) and infuriates (by his
slanders).

133. *boarded*] tackled; cf. Sir Toby's
explanation of a similar term—'You
mistake, knight: "accost" is front her,
board her, woo her, assail her' (*Tw.N.*,
I.iii.52–4).

136. *break a comparison*] As tilters
break their lances; so in Lyly's *Campaspe*, II.i.56 (*Works*, ed. Bond, II.328)
—'*Psyllus*. Why, you were at mortall
iars./*Manus*. In faith no, we *brake a
bitter iest* one vppon another'.

comparison] gibing simile; cf. *LLL*,
v.ii.832—'Full of *comparisons* and

wounding flouts'. Beatrice herself,
Hero proclaims (III.i.59–67), is adept
at such comparisons.

139. *a partridge wing saved*] This looks
like sarcasm at Benedick's gluttony; a
'very valiant trencher-man' would eat
more than a partridge wing. But perhaps he was a gourmet rather than a
glutton. Francis Willughby's *Ornithology* (1678, II.168) testifies that 'As
the flesh of the Partridge . . . is very
delicate and grateful to the Palate, so
in like manner is it greatly commended. Palate-men, and such as have
skill in eating, do chiefly commend the
Partridges Wing, preferring it much
before the Leg'.

141. *leaders*] i.e. of the dance.

145. *Sure . . . Hero*] Some producers
have these words said so as to be overheard by Claudio (A. C. Sprague,
Shakespeare and the Actors, p. 13). But

withdrawn her father to break with him about it.
The ladies follow her, and but one visor remains.

Bora. And that is Claudio: I know him by his bearing.

D. John. Are not you Signior Benedick?

Claud. You know me well, I am he.   150

D. John. Signior, you are very near my brother in his
love. He is enamoured on Hero; I pray you, dis-
suade him from her, she is no equal for his birth. You
may do the part of an honest man in it.

Claud. How know you he loves her?   155

D. John. I heard him swear his affection.

Bora. So did I too, and he swore he would marry her
tonight.

D. John. Come, let us to the banquet.

Exeunt Don John and Borachio.

Claud. Thus answer I in name of Benedick,   160
But hear these ill news with the ears of Claudio.
'Tis certain so; the Prince woos for himself.
Friendship is constant in all other things
Save in the office and affairs of love:

---

159. S.D.] *QF (Exeunt: manet Clau.) subst., Rowe subst.*   162. woos] *Q (wooes);*
woes *F.*

Claudio is some way off (ll. 147–8)
and the stage-business would seem
awkward: moreover, Don John needs
to have the visor identified for him.
Amorous on Hero has been taken to
mean that, like others, Don John mistakes Don Pedro's intentions, but he
has heard the truth (i.iii.58–60) and
here he means 'courting Hero (on
Claudio's behalf)'.

157–8. *marry her tonight*] Abrupt
though this haste would be, it is
meant (along with the force of *swore*)
to precipitate Claudio into a sense of
hopeless crisis, which may explain the
lack of struggle in his reaction. The
case, he believes, is lost.

159. *banquet*] Probably the 'rere' or
'after' supper, a light repast or dessert
following the more formal meal, as in
Shr., v.ii.9–10—'My *banquet* is to
close our stomachs up/After our great

good cheer.' Since Don John seemingly missed the *supper* (l. 1), he is presumably making for the 'course of
sweetmeats, fruit, and wine served
either as a separate entertainment or
as a continuation of the principal
meal, but in the latter case usually in
a different room; a dessert' (*OED*,
Banquet 3).

160–70.] Claudio is regrettably
ready to believe himself betrayed, in a
foretaste of his later rejection of Hero,
but here, as then (when Don Pedro is
equally misled), Shakespeare somewhat exonerates him by showing
others (Benedick: l. 179) no less
deceived.

163–4.] A proverbial idea; Tilley
L549—'When love puts in, friendship
is gone.' 'The betrayal of lovers by
their false friends provided stock
literary material' (Craik, p. 301).

Therefore all hearts in love use their own tongues;   165
Let every eye negotiate for itself,
And trust no agent; for beauty is a witch
Against whose charms faith melteth into blood.
This is an accident of hourly proof,
Which I mistrusted not. Farewell, therefore, Hero!   170

Enter BENEDICK.

Bene. Count Claudio?
Claud. Yea, the same.
Bene. Come, will you go with me?
Claud. Whither?
Bene. Even to the next willow, about your own business,   175
          County. What fashion will you wear the garland
          of? About your neck, like an usurer's chain? Or
          under your arm, like a lieutenant's scarf? You must
          wear it one way, for the Prince hath got your Hero.
Claud. I wish him joy of her.   180
Bene. Why, that's spoken like an honest drover: so they

---

176. County] *Q subst.;* Count *F.*   177. of] *Q;* off *F.*   181. drover] *QF*
(Drouier), *Rowe 3.*

Shakespeare had treated this in *The
Two Gentlemen of Verona* and in
Helena's betrayal of Hermia's and
Lysander's confidence in *MND*,
I.i.208–51.
          165. *all hearts . . . use*] = let all
hearts . . . use.
          167–8. *beauty . . . blood*] i.e. before
beauty's bewitching spells, integrity
melts into desire.
          169. *accident . . . proof*] occurrence
proved true every hour.
          170. *mistrusted*] suspected.
          171. *Count Claudio?*] Claudio is still
masked but the others must have dis-
carded their visors; Benedick and Don
Pedro are readily recognized.
          175–6. *willow . . . garland*] 'To wear
the willow' was proverbial; Tilley
W403. The willow garland is the
emblem of the forsaken lover, un-
forgettably so since Desdemona's
song, 'Sing all a green willow must be
my garland' (*Oth.*, IV.iii.49).

          176. *County*] A not unusual form for
'count': e.g. *Mer. V.,* I.ii.40–'the
County Palatine'.
          177. *usurer's chain*] Such were worn
by wealthy merchants who were often
usurers. Chains, now worn only by
civic dignitaries on official occasions,
were in Elizabethan times a common
ornament to men of wealth and high
place. Gosson's *School of Abuse* (Shakespeare Society, 1841, p. 38) observes,
'If our gallantes of England might
carry no more linkes in their *chaynes*
. . . then they have fought feelds, their
necks should not bee very often
wreathed in golde'.
          178. *lieutenant's scarf*] A broad sash
worn diagonally over the shoulder and
under the arm marked a lieutenant's
rank.
          181. *honest drover*] friendly cattle-
dealer wishing the purchaser satis-
faction.

sell bullocks. But did you think the Prince would
have served you thus?

Claud. I pray you, leave me.

Bene. Ho, now you strike like the blind man! 'Twas the   185
boy that stole your meat, and you'll beat the post.

Claud. If it will not be, I'll leave you.   *Exit.*

Bene. Alas, poor hurt fowl, now will he creep into
sedges. But that my Lady Beatrice should know
me, and not know me! The Prince's fool! Ha, it   190
may be I go under that title because I am merry.
Yea, but so I am apt to do myself wrong. I am not
so reputed: it is the base, though bitter, disposition
of Beatrice that puts the world into her person, and
so gives me out. Well, I'll be revenged as I may.   195

Enter the Prince [DON PEDRO], HERO, LEONATO.

D. Pedro. Now, signior, where's the Count? Did you see
him?

Bene. Troth, my lord, I have played the part of Lady

195. S.D.] *Capell subst.; Enter the Prince, Hero, Leonato, Iohn and Borachio, and
Conrade. Q; Enter the Prince. F.*   196. *D. Pedro*] *QF (Pedro) (so to l. 302, also
l. 326), Capell (D. Pe.).*

185. *you strike . . . blind man*] See
Appendix V. ii.

188–9. *poor hurt fowl . . . sedges*] A
sensitive and sympathetic image.
Other perceptive bird-images occur
at III. i. 24 and 35–6.

193. *base, though bitter*] The unexpectedly strong epithets signalize
Benedick's hurt indignation. But why
though? Johnson conjectured, and
Steevens '93 read, 'the bitter', but
Q's reading may stand. Benedick
presumably means that Beatrice
basely reports him the Prince's fool,
whereas it is her bitter tongue that so
maligns him. Any bitterness in
Beatrice will be due to wounded
feelings resulting from past humilia-
tion: see her comments at ll. 261–4.

195. S.D.] Q certainly errs in
bringing on Don John, Borachio, and
Conrade. The next scene makes it
clear that they are missing when the

date of Hero's marriage is discussed.
It is less clear whether Leonato and
Hero enter here (as in Q) or at l. 245
(as in F). If here, it is odd that in their
presence Don Pedro and Benedick exchange badinage about the wooing of
Hero. Yet Benedick's *this young lady*
(ll. 201–2) implies that she is present.
(Were W. S. Walker right in proposing '*his*' for '*this*', one would sup-
pose her absent.) At l. 245 Beatrice's
entry (with Claudio) is the more
striking—after Benedick's diatribe
against her—than if Hero and Leonato accompany her too, and her 'I
have brought Count Claudio' (ll.
268–9) suggests that she and he have
entered without the others.

198–9. *Lady Fame*] Virgil's *Fama*
(*Aeneid,* iv. 181–90) has many eyes,
tongues, and ears, and in this sense
is report or gossip rather than re-
nown.

Fame. I found him here as melancholy as a lodge
in a warren. I told him, and I think I told him true,   200
that your Grace had got the good will of this young
lady, and I offered him my company to a willow-
tree, either to make him a garland, as being forsaken, or to bind him up a rod, as being worthy to
be whipped.   205

D. Pedro. To be whipped? What's his fault?

Bene. The flat transgression of a schoolboy, who, being
overjoyed with finding a bird's nest, shows it his
companion, and he steals it.

D. Pedro. Wilt thou make a trust a transgression? The   210
transgression is in the stealer.

Bene. Yet it had not been amiss the rod had been made,
and the garland too; for the garland he might have
worn himself, and the rod he might have bestowed
on you, who, as I take it, have stolen his bird's nest.   215

D. Pedro. I will but teach them to sing, and restore them
to the owner.

Bene. If their singing answer your saying, by my faith
you say honestly.

D. Pedro. The Lady Beatrice hath a quarrel to you: the   220
gentleman that danced with her told her she is
much wronged by you.

Bene. O, she misused me past the endurance of a block!

200. think I] *Q; thinke, F.*   201. good] *Q; not in F.*   204. up] *Q; not in F.*

199–200. *as melancholy . . . warren*]
The precise bearing of this simile is
uncertain, though some lonely (game-
keeper's?) hut may have struck
Shakespeare's mind with an air of
melancholy, confirmed possibly by
the forlorn tone of Isaiah 1. 7–8: 'Your
country is desolate, . . . and the
daughter of Zion is left as a cottage
in a vineyard, as a *lodge* in a garden
of cucumbers, as a besieged city.' A
warren was ground enclosed for breeding game, such as rabbits or hares,
and hares' flesh was proverbially
associated with melancholy—'Hare is
melancholy meat', Tilley H151; 'Hare,
a black meat, *melancholy*', Burton,

Anatomy of Melancholy, Pt 1, Sect. 11,
Mem. 11, Subs. 1 (Bohn edn, 1927,
1.250). But that such a train of ideas
was in Shakespeare's mind is pure
speculation.

207. *flat*] downright.

212–15.] Though suffering wounded
dignity after the masque ridicule,
Benedick also feels for Claudio and
makes his feeling clear to Don Pedro.

220. *to you*] = directed to you, or
against you.

222. *wronged by you*] injured by your
slanders.

223–45.] 'Spoken at high speed and
in a burlesque fury. [He] returns
again and again to the attack,

An oak but with one green leaf on it would have
answered her: my very visor began to assume life   225
and scold with her. She told me, not thinking I had
been myself, that I was the Prince's jester, that I
was duller than a great thaw, huddling jest upon
jest with such impossible conveyance upon me that
I stood like a man at a mark, with a whole army   230
shooting at me. She speaks poniards, and every
word stabs: if her breath were as terrible as her
terminations, there were no living near her, she
would infect to the North Star. I would not marry
her, though she were endowed with all that Adam   235
had left him before he transgressed. She would

227. jester,] *Q;* Iester, and *F.*   232. as her] *Q;* as *F.*

stopping momentarily to calm himself—"Come, talk not of her"—only
promptly to disobey his own in-
junction' (M. Crane, *Shakespeare's
Prose,* p. 195). 'In their skirmishes
[Beatrice] always gets the better of
[Benedick]. But he makes ample
amends when out of her presence,
trundling off jests in whole paragraphs
. . . . If his wit is slower, it is also
stronger than hers' (Hudson, *Life,*
1. 329).

228. *duller . . . thaw*] 'At such a time
[of thaw] in Shakespeare's day, the
roads were almost or quite impassable,
and . . . one could only stay at home
moping' (Kittredge).

229. *impossible conveyance*] inconceivable dexterity.

230. *man at a mark*] Probably the
man who stood near the butt to tell
archers how close to the mark they
were, as in Webster, *The White Devil,*
III. ii. 26–7 (*Works,* ed. Lucas, 1. 137)—
'I am *at the marke,* Sir, Ile give aime
to you/And tell you how neare you
shoote'. Strutt's *Sports and Pastimes* has
an illustration from a MS. of 1496
showing a man by the butt, directing
with outstretched arm the archers'
shots (ed. J. C. Fox, 1801, facing p. 42).

231. *speaks poniards*] A metaphor
(cf. 'to look daggers') which impressed
Massinger, who uses it twice: *The
Duke of Milan,* II. i. 377–8—'*euerie
word's a Poynard,*/And reaches to my
Heart', and *The Bondman,* I. iii. 265—
'I am sicke; the man/*Speakes ponyards,*
and diseases'. Similarly Webster in
The White Devil, IV. ii. 133 (*Works,* ed.
Lucas, 1. 157)—'I now *weepe poniardes,*
doe you see?'

233. *terminations*] terms to describe
me (Shakespeare's sole use, and
OED's sole example in this sense:
Termination. †8).

234–5. *I . . . her*] A hubristic vow,
inviting nemesis.

235–6. *all . . . transgressed*] Adam
transgressed God's command not to
eat the fruit of the tree of the knowledge of good and evil, and forfeited
his dominion over the rest of Creation
(Genesis II. 16–17, III. 1–23).

236–7. *She would . . . spit*] i.e. so outgoing Omphale in classical legend,
who forced the captive Hercules to
don woman's clothes and spin
among her maids (Ovid, *Fasti,*
ii. 317 ff., *Heroides,* ix. 55 ff.). The
turnspit was among the lowest of
servants.

have made Hercules have turned spit, yea, and
have cleft his club to make the fire too. Come, talk
not of her, you shall find her the infernal Ate in good
apparel. I would to God some scholar would con-   240
jure her, for certainly, while she is here, a man may
live as quiet in hell as in a sanctuary, and people
sin upon purpose, because they would go thither;
so indeed all disquiet, horror, and perturbation
follows her.   245

Enter CLAUDIO *and* BEATRICE.

D. Pedro. Look, here she comes.
Bene. Will your Grace command me any service to the
    world's end? I will go on the slightest errand now
    to the Antipodes that you can devise to send me on;
    I will fetch you a toothpicker now from the furthest   250

245. S.D.] *Q; Enter Claudio and Beatrice, Leonato, Hero. F.*

237. *have turned*] For duplication of
the perfect tense, see Abbott § 360.

239–40. *Ate . . . apparel*] Ate is the
eldest daughter of Zeus, and goddess
of discord, as in *Caes.*, III.i.271–3—
'*Ate* . . . come hot from hell,/Shall . . .
/Cry havoc'; and *John*, II.i.63 —'An
Ate stirring him to blood and strife'.
Beatrice, Benedick avers, is, like Ate,
devilish within and handsome without. In Spenser, as Duessa and Ate
ride together, 'in face/And outward
shew faire semblance they did beare;/
[Though] vnder maske of beautie and
good grace,/Vile treason and fowle
falshood hidden were,/That mote to
none but to the warie wise appeare'
(*Faerie Queene*, IV.i.17). In Homer she
is strong and fleet-footed, eluding the
lame and ugly Prayers which strive
to plead for mercy (*Iliad*, ix.502ff.),
and one would assume her, as Zeus'
eldest daughter, to be beautiful—she
is bright-haired and delicate of foot
(ibid. xix. 91–126).

240–5. *I would . . . her*] = Would
that, like an evil spirit, she might be

conjured back to hell, which in her
absence has been a quiet sanctuary,
so that people prefer being sent there
to enduring her presence here.

240. *scholar*] Latin was accepted as
the language of the spirit world. Only
scholars, therefore, could deliver
exorcisms; cf. *Ham.*, I.i.42—'Thou
art a *scholar*; speak to it, Horatio'; and
Beaumont and Fletcher, *The Night
Walker*, II.i (*Works*, ed. Glover and
Waller, VII.329)—'Lets call the butler up, for he speaks Latine,/And that
will daunt the devil'.

250. *toothpicker*] *Toothpicks* were
often thought a sign of affectation, as
in Chapman and Shirley, *The Ball*,
I.i. (Chapman's *Plays*, ed. R. H.
Shepherd, 1874, p. 488)—'Here
comes the thing [i.e. the dandified
Freshwater]./With what formality he
treads, and talks,/And manageth a
toothpick like a statesman!'; Earle in
Microcosmographie, 'A Gallant'—'His
Pick-tooth beares a great part in his
discourse'; and Overbury in *Characters*—'A Courtier'—'If you finde him

inch of Asia; bring you the length of Prester John's
foot; fetch you a hair off the great Cham's beard;
do you any embassage to the Pygmies, rather than
hold three words' conference with this harpy. You
have no employment for me?   255

D. Pedro. None, but to desire your good company.

Bene. O God, sir, here's a dish I love not! I cannot endure my Lady Tongue.   *Exit.*

D. Pedro. Come, lady, come, you have lost the heart of
Signior Benedick.   260

Beat. Indeed, my lord, he lent it me awhile, and I gave
him use for it, a double heart for his single one.

258. my] *Q;* this *F.*   262. his] *Q;* a *F.*

not heere, you shall in *Paules,* with a
pick-tooth in his hat, a cape cloke, and
a long stocking'.

251. *Prester John*] a Christian ruler,
sometimes identified with the king of
Abyssinia, emperor and priest of a
fabulously rich kingdom in the East.
For discussion of his origin see Henry
Yule's translation of *The Book of Ser
Marco Polo* (3rd edn, Henri Cordier,
1921, I.231–7, note). *Prester* or
Presbyter John appealed strongly to the
imagination of medieval Europe.
Marco Polo refers to him briefly and
to his death in battle against Chingis
Kaan (1.238–45). Mandeville gives
full details about his land, 'full gode
& ryche, but not so riche as is the lond
of the *grete CHANE*' (*Travels,* ed. P.
Hamelius, EETS, chap. xxxi, p. 179).
Purchas in his *Pilgrimage* (1617 edn)
tells how '*Priest Iohn*' was thought to
rule the Tartars (p. 834), though later
subject to 'the Great *Can*' (p. 835).
Cf. Dekker, *Old Fortunatus,* 1.ii.197–
200 (*Works,* ed. Bowers, 1.131)—'Ile
trauell to the Turkish Emperour:/
And then ile reuell it with *Prester John,*
/Or banquet with great *Cham* of
Tartarie,/And trie what frolicke Court
the Soulden keepes'.

252. *great Cham*] the title given to
the Khans or emperors of the Mon-
gols, more especially to Kublai,

seventh of the line. Marco Polo tells
much about 'Cublay Kaan, the
Great Kaan' and his power, wealth, and
palace in Cambaluc (ed. cit., 1.331 ff.).
Mandeville describes the splendour of
his kingdom, so marvellous that a man
'shall not trowe it lightly'—which is
true enough (*Travels,* ed. cit., chaps
xxiv–xxvii).

252. *beard*] In Dekker's *The Shoemaker's Holiday,* v.v.22–3 (*Works,* ed.
Bowers, 1.84) Simon Eyre, referring
to his own beard, says, 'Tamar *Cham's
beard* was a rubbing-brush too't'.

253. *Pygmies*] In Homer these are a
tiny race at war with the Cranes and
constantly defeated. They appear
often in later literature and both
Marco Polo and Mandeville describe
them. Various medieval travellers
fell in with some such diminutive
people.

261–4.] No more light can be
thrown on this episode than the lines
themselves give. They are part of the
evidence of former Beatrice–Benedick
dealings which may explain any
'bitter disposition' in Beatrice. She
seems to mean that he professed for a
while that his heart was hers; when
she returned him double affection he
proved false.

262. *use*] interest.

Marry, once before he won it of me with false dice,
therefore your Grace may well say I have lost it.

D. Pedro. You have put him down, lady, you have put   265
him down.

Beat. So I would not he should do me, my lord, lest I
should prove the mother of fools. I have brought
Count Claudio, whom you sent me to seek.

D. Pedro. Why, how now, Count? Wherefore are you   270
sad?

Claud. Not sad, my lord.

D. Pedro. How then? Sick?

Claud. Neither, my lord.

Beat. The Count is neither sad, nor sick, nor merry, nor   275
well; but civil Count, civil as an orange, and something of that jealous complexion.

D. Pedro. I' faith, lady, I think your blazon to be true,
though I'll be sworn, if he be so, his conceit is false.
Here, Claudio, I have wooed in thy name, and fair   280
Hero is won. I have broke with her father, and his
good will obtained. Name the day of marriage, and
God give thee joy!

Leon. Count, take of me my daughter, and with her my
fortunes; his Grace hath made the match, and all   285
grace say Amen to it.

Beat. Speak, Count, 'tis your cue.

277. that] *Q; a F.*

276. *civil*] sober in behaviour; with a pun on Seville. 'A "civil" (not "Seville") orange was the usual orthography of the time' (Dyce). Shakespeare's word-play is antici-pated by Nashe's *Strange Newes, Of the Intercepting Certaine Letters*, 1592 (ed. McKerrow, I. 329)—'For the order of my life, it is as *ciuil* as a *ciuil* orange'.

277. *jealous complexion*] Yellow was the accepted token of jealousy, envy, and suspicion, probably because of melancholy associated with jaundice; Greene's *Quippe for an Vpstart Courtier* (*Works*, ed. Grosart, XI. 213) calls the yellow daffodil 'a flowre fit for gelous

Dottrels, who through the bewty of their honest wiues grow suspitious'.

278. *blazon*] description; from the technical sense, the heraldic setting forth of armorial bearings.

279. *conceit*] conception, idea.

280–93.] These speeches show a strikingly courteous poise.

285–6. *all grace say Amen*] God con-firm it.

287–8. *Speak . . . joy*] In Lyly's *Endimion*, v. iii. 208–11, on Endimion's prompting, Cynthia unites Semele and Eumenides. To Semele she says, 'are you content . . . to take *Eumenides*? Why speake you not? Not a word?'

Claud. Silence is the perfectest herald of joy; I were but
    little happy, if I could say how much. Lady, as you
    are mine, I am yours; I give away myself for you   290
    and dote upon the exchange.
Beat. Speak, cousin, or, if you cannot, stop his mouth
    with a kiss, and let not him speak neither.
D. Pedro. In faith, lady, you have a merry heart.
Beat. Yea, my lord, I thank it, poor fool, it keeps on the   295
    windy side of care. My cousin tells him in his ear
    that he is in her heart.
Claud. And so she doth, cousin.
Beat. Good Lord, for alliance! Thus goes everyone to
    the world but I, and I am sunburnt. I may sit in a   300
    corner and cry 'Heigh-ho for a husband!'
D. Pedro. Lady Beatrice, I will get you one.
Beat. I would rather have one of your father's getting.
    Hath your Grace ne'er a brother like you? Your

---

297. her] *Q*; my *F*.   301. 'Heigh . . . husband!'] *Staunton*; heigh . . . husband. *QF*.

It is left to Endimion to answer,
'Silence, Madame, consents: that is
most true' (*Works*, ed. Bond, III. 77).
Tilley L165 gives as proverbial
'Whom we love best to them we can
say least'.

    295–6. *the windy side*] the windward
side, so having the advantage over
care, to take the wind out of care's
sails.

    296–7. *My cousin . . . heart*] A cue for
stage-action.

    299. *Good . . . alliance*] Either, or
both, (*i*) amused recognition that she
will acquire a new cousin in Claudio;
or (*ii*) mock reflection on the popular
habit of marrying.

    299–300. *goes . . . to the world*] enters
the married state. It may derive from
Luke xx. 34—'The children of this
world marry wives, and are given in
marriage'; or Genesis xix. 31 (Bishops'
Bible) where marriage is said to be
'after the manner of all the *world*'
(Noble, p. 29).

    300. *sunburnt*] Elizabethan ladies

cherished fair skin; cf. *Troil.*, I. iii. 282
—'The Grecian dames are *sunburnt*,
and not worth/The splinter of a lance'.
In Webster's *The White Devil*, v. iii.
269–71 (*Works*, ed. Lucas, I. 179),
the Moorish Zanche hopes to win
marriage with a gift of stolen money;
she alludes to Jeremiah xiii. 23—'Can
the Ethiopian change his skin?'—and
says of her wealth, 'It is a dowry/Me
thinkes, should make that *sunburnt*
proverbe false,/And wash the Ethiop
white'. The Song of Solomon i. 6 is
clear about the sun's ill effects—
'Look not upon me, because I am
black, because the sun hath looked
upon me'.

    301. *Heigh-ho for a husband*] Prover-
bial: Tilley H833; cf. Burton, *Ana-*
tomy of Melancholy, Pt III, Sect. II,
Mem. v, Subs. III (Bohn edn, 1927,
III. 250–1)— '*Heigh-ho for a husband*,
cries she, a bad husband, nay, the
worst that ever was, is better than
none'.

    303. *getting*] begetting.

  father got excellent husbands, if a maid could come 305
  by them.
D. Pedro. Will you have me, lady?
Beat. No, my lord, unless I might have another for work-
  ing days: your Grace is too costly to wear every day.
  But I beseech your Grace pardon me, I was born 310
  to speak all mirth and no matter.
D. Pedro. Your silence most offends me, and to be merry
  best becomes you, for out o' question, you were
  born in a merry hour.
Beat. No, sure, my lord, my mother cried, but then there 315
  was a star danced, and under that was I born.
  Cousins, God give you joy!
Leon. Niece, will you look to those things I told you of?
Beat. I cry you mercy, uncle. By your Grace's pardon. *Exit.*
D. Pedro. By my troth, a pleasant-spirited lady. 320
Leon. There's little of the melancholy element in her, my
  lord; she is never sad but when she sleeps, and not
  ever sad then; for I have heard my daughter say
  she hath often dreamt of unhappiness and waked
  herself with laughing. 325
D. Pedro. She cannot endure to hear tell of a husband.

307. *D. Pedro.*] *QF (Prince) (so subst. to scene end, except l. 326, Pedro), Rowe (Pedro),
Capell (D. Pe.).* 313. o'] *Q (a), Camb.; of F.*

311. *no matter*] nothing sensible.

316. *a star danced*] Beatrice accounts
for her disposition, like Conrade
(I.iii.II) and Benedick (v.ii.39–40), by
half-mocking reference to astrono-
mical influence. Her words recall the
old belief that the sun danced on
Easter Day.

319.] Beatrice apologizes first to her
uncle for forgetfulness, then to the
Prince for withdrawing.

320.] '"By my troth, a pleasant-
spirited lady", says Don Pedro. The
actress . . . should remember that
testimonial. Beatrice's repartee . . .
can easily be made to sound malicious
and vulgar. It should be spoken as the
slightest raillery, with mirth in the

voice and charm in the manner'
(Ellen Terry, *Four Lectures on Shakespeare*, 1932, pp. 83 4).

321. *melancholy element*] Temperament was held to depend on the mixture of the four bodily humours, blood,
phlegm, choler, and melancholy,
corresponding respectively to the four
elements, air, water, fire, and earth.
Melancholy, like earth, was dry and
cold; it was engendered by the black
bile. In the perfect temperament all
elements or humours combined
ideally; cf. *Caes.*, v.v.73–4—'the ele-
ments/So mix'd in him, that Nature
might stand up/And say to all the
world, "This was a man".'

323. *ever*] always.

Leon. O, by no means, she mocks all her wooers out of
  suit.

D. Pedro. She were an excellent wife for Benedick.

Leon. O Lord, my lord, if they were but a week married,   330
  they would talk themselves mad.

D. Pedro. County Claudio, when mean you to go to
  church?

Claud. Tomorrow, my lord: time goes on crutches till
  love have all his rites.   335

Leon. Not till Monday, my dear son, which is hence a
  just seven-night, and a time too brief, too, to have
  all things answer my mind.

D. Pedro. Come, you shake the head at so long a breathing, but I warrant thee, Claudio, the time shall not   340
  go dully by us. I will, in the interim, undertake one
  of Hercules' labours, which is, to bring Signior
  Benedick and the Lady Beatrice into a mountain of
  affection th'one with th'other. I would fain have it
  a match, and I doubt not but to fashion it, if you   345
  three will but minister such assistance as I shall give
  you direction.

Leon. My lord, I am for you, though it cost me ten
  nights' watchings.

Claud. And I, my lord.   350

D. Pedro. And you too, gentle Hero?

Hero. I will do any modest office, my lord, to help my
  cousin to a good husband.

D. Pedro. And Benedick is not the unhopefullest husband that I know. Thus far can I praise him: he is   355
  of a noble strain, of approved valour, and confirmed honesty. I will teach you how to humour

---

332. County] *Q* (Countie); Counte *F.*   338. my] *Q; not in F.*

327–8. *out of suit*] out of courtship
(punning on *love suit* and *legal suit*):
i.e. she *nonsuits* her wooers.

339–40.   *breathing*]   interval,
breathing-space.

349. *watchings*] lyings awake; the
word does not necessarily imply being
on the watch.

356. *strain*] Probably = 'disposition'
(cf. *Lr*, v.iii.41—'Sir, you have
show'd today your valiant *strain*');
possibly = 'stock', 'lineage', but Don
Pedro's praises seem meant for
Benedick's own qualities.

approved] proven; as also at iv.i.44.

357. *honesty*] honourableness.

your cousin that she shall fall in love with Benedick;
and I, [*to Leonato and Claudio*] with your two helps,
will so practise on Benedick that, in despite of his   360
quick wit and his queasy stomach, he shall fall in
love with Beatrice. If we can do this, Cupid is no
longer an archer; his glory shall be ours, for we are
the only love-gods. Go in with me, and I will tell you
my drift.   *Exeunt.*   365

[SCENE II]

Enter [Don] John *and* Borachio.

D. John. It is so, the Count Claudio shall marry the
    daughter of Leonato.
Bora. Yea, my lord, but I can cross it.
D. John. Any bar, any cross, any impediment will be
    medicinable to me. I am sick in displeasure to him,   5
    and whatsoever comes athwart his affection ranges
    evenly with mine. How canst thou cross this
    marriage?
Bora. Not honestly, my lord, but so covertly that no dis-
    honesty shall appear in me.   10
D. John. Show me briefly how.
Bora. I think I told your lordship, a year since, how
    much I am in the favour of Margaret, the waiting-
    gentlewoman to Hero.

359. S.D.] *Kittredge; not in QF.*   365. S.D.] *QF (exit) subst , Rowe.*

Scene II

Scene ii.] *Capell; not in QF.*   [*Location*] *Another Apartment in* Leonato's
House. *Theobald; not in QF.*   S.D. Don] *Rowe; not in QF.*   1. D. John] *QF*
(Iohn) *subst., Capell (D. Jo.) (so throughout scene).*

Scene II

360. *practise on*] craftily work upon.
Practise often implied cunning: here,
though there is a hint of this, the
sense is benevolent.

361. *queasy stomach*] *queasy* = over-
fastidious, easily upset; *stomach*, used
figuratively, is equivalent to 'disposition', 'pride'.

Location] Another apartment in
Leonato's house.

5. *medicinable*] medicinal, healing.
6. *affection*] inclination, cf. *LLL*,
v. i. 75–6—'Sir, it is the King's most
sweet pleasure and *affection* to con-
gratulate the Princess'.

D. John. I remember.   15

Bora. I can, at any unseasonable instant of the night,
    appoint her to look out at her lady's chamber-
    window.

D. John. What life is in that, to be the death of this
    marriage?   20

Bora. The poison of that lies in you to temper. Go you
    to the Prince your brother; spare not to tell him
    that he hath wronged his honour in marrying the
    renowned Claudio—whose estimation do you
    mightily hold up—to a contaminated stale, such a   25
    one as Hero.

D. John. What proof shall I make of that?

Bora. Proof enough to misuse the Prince, to vex Claudio,
    to undo Hero, and kill Leonato. Look you for any
    other issue?   30

D. John. Only to despite them I will endeavour any-
    thing.

Bora. Go then, find me a meet hour to draw Don Pedro
    and the Count Claudio alone: tell them that you
    know that Hero loves me; intend a kind of zeal both   35
    to the Prince and Claudio—as in love of your
    brother's honour, who hath made this match, and
    his friend's reputation, who is thus like to be
    cozened with the semblance of a maid—that you
    have discovered thus. They will scarcely believe   40
    this without trial: offer them instances, which shall
    bear no less likelihood than to see me at her
    chamber-window, hear me call Margaret Hero,

33. Don] *Q* (don); on *F.*   36. in] *Q;* in a *F.*

21. *temper*] mix, compound.

24. *estimation*] worth, or repute:
both senses are implied.

25. *contaminated stale*] polluted wanton. *OED* quotes this to illustrate one
of the meanings derived from *stale*
(= decoy bird).

28. *misuse . . . vex*] delude . . . distress
(a stronger sense than the modern
'vex').

31. *despite*] wreak malice on—

Shakespeare's only use of the word as
a verb; cf. Anon., *The Rare Triumphs
of Love and Fortune* (Hazlitt's *Dodsley,*
vi. 150)—'What lives or draweth
breath, but I can pleasure or *despite?*'

35. *intend*] profess, pretend, as in *R3,*
iii. vii. 45—'*intend* some fear'.

39. *cozened*] cheated.

41. *instances*] proofs, as in *2H4,*
iii. i. 102-3—'I have receiv'd/A certain *instance* that Glendower is dead'.

hear Margaret term me Claudio; and bring them to
see this the very night before the intended wedding   45
—for in the meantime I will so fashion the matter
that Hero shall be absent—and there shall appear
such seeming truth of Hero's disloyalty that
jealousy shall be called assurance and all the preparation overthrown.   50

D. John. Grow this to what adverse issue it can, I will
put it in practice. Be cunning in the working this,
and thy fee is a thousand ducats.

Bora. Be you constant in the accusation, and my cunning shall not shame me.   55

D. John. I will presently go learn their day of marriage.

Exeunt.

[SCENE III]

Enter BENEDICK *alone.*

Bene. Boy!

[Enter Boy.]

Boy. Signior?

Bene. In my chamber-window lies a book; bring it
hither to me in the orchard.

Boy. I am here already, sir.   5

48. truth] *Q;* truths *F.*   54. you] *Q;* thou *F.*   56. S.D.] *QF (exit) subst.,*
Rowe.

Scene III

SCENE III] *Capell; not in QF;* ACT III *conj. Spedding.*   [*Location*] Leonato's
garden. *Pope;* Leonato's orchard. *Theobald; not in QF.*   1. S.D.] *Collier; not in*
QF.

44. *term me Claudio*] Theobald and
some others read 'Borachio' for
'Claudio', arguing that to hear
(supposed) Hero call a wooer 'Claudio' would suggest not that she was
false but that she was herself deluded
by an impersonator. But Borachio
means to persuade Margaret to disguise as her mistress, and to act with
him a love-scene in which the servants
masquerade as their 'betters'.

49. *jealousy*] suspicion, distrust.

52. *the working this*] For this form see
Abbott § 93.

53. *ducats*] silver or gold coins of
variable values, worth in former
times roughly from a sixth to a half of
a sovereign.

Scene III

Location] Leonato's garden or orchard.

Bene. I know that, but I would have thee hence and
here again. (*Exit Boy.*) I do much wonder that one
man, seeing how much another man is a fool when
he dedicates his behaviours to love, will, after he
hath laughed at such shallow follies in others, be-   10
come the argument of his own scorn by falling in
love: and such a man is Claudio. I have known
when there was no music with him but the drum
and the fife, and now had he rather hear the tabor
and the pipe. I have known when he would have   15
walked ten mile afoot to see a good armour, and
now will he lie ten nights awake carving the fashion
of a new doublet. He was wont to speak plain and to
the purpose, like an honest man and a soldier, and
now is he turned orthography—his words are a very   20
fantastical banquet, just so many strange dishes.
May I be so converted and see with these eyes? I
cannot tell; I think not. I will not be sworn but love

7. S.D.] *QF subst.* (*after l. 5*), *Johnson.*

11. *argument*] subject, theme. For a
different sense see III.i.96.

12–21. *I have known . . . dishes*] Lyly
offers amusing precedents for such
reversals when Alexander falls in love
with Campaspe—'Is the warlike
sou[n]d of drumme and trumpet
turned to the soft noyse of lire and
lute? the neighing of barbed steeds
. . . converted to dilicate tunes and
amorous glances?' etc., etc. When his
court turns from war to peace,
'youthes that were woont to carry
deuises of victory in their sheeldes,
engraue now posies of love in their
ringes: . . . instead of sword and target
to hazard their liues, vse pen and
paper to paint their loues', etc., etc.
(*Campaspe*, II.ii.35–9, IV.iii.13–18:
Works, ed. Bond, II.330, 347). Shakespeare had echoed this passage in the
opening soliloquy of *Richard III.*

13–15. *drum . . . pipe*] 'When I was a
boy, before the late civill warres, the
tabor and *pipe* were commonly used,

especially Sundays and Holy-dayes.
. . . Now it is almost all lost; the
drumme and trumpet have putte all
that peaceable music to silence' (John
Aubrey, *Lives*, ed. A. Clark, 1898,
II.319). *Tabor* = small drum for
festivities.

18. *doublet*] close-fitting body gar-
ment with attachable sleeves, the
upper part of a man's dress. 'So great
was the variety in shape, trimming,
and sleeve design that a young man
who wished to impress his lady might
well *need* to "lie ten nights awake
carving the fashion of a new doublet"'
(Linthicum).

20. *orthography*] i.e. the very spirit of
polished (even over-polished) style.
In *LLL*, v.i.20, Holofernes objects to
'rackers of orthography' who use newfangled terms.

22. *so converted*] Love's trans-
formations had already been satirized
in Speed's description of Valentine;
Gent., II.i.17–30.

Bene. [*Aside.*] Now, divine air! Now is his soul ravished!
Is it not strange that sheep's guts should hale souls
out of men's bodies? Well, a horn for my money,   60
when all's done.

The Song.

[*Balth.*]
 Sigh no more, ladies, sigh no more,
  Men were deceivers ever :
 One foot in sea, and one on shore,
  To one thing constant never.   65
 Then sigh not so, but let them go,
  And be you blithe and bonny,
 Converting all your sounds of woe
  Into Hey nonny, nonny.

 Sing no more ditties, sing no moe,   70
  Of dumps so dull and heavy :
 The fraud of men was ever so,
  Since summer first was leavy.
  Then sigh not so, etc.

D. Pedro. By my troth, a good song.   75
Balth. And an ill singer, my lord.

58. S.D.] *Capell subst.; not in QF.*   62. *Balth.*] *Capell subst.; not in QF.*   72.
was] *Q ; were / F.*

(C. J. Sisson, *New Readings*). The *o* in
nothing was long, and the *th* could be
sounded as *t* (as still in some regional
or plebeian speech). Cf. H. Kökeritz,
Shakespeare's Pronunciation (1953), p.
132; also as in *Wint.,* IV.iv.600—'No
hearing, no feeling, but my sir's song,
and admiring the *nothing* of it'—and
perhaps *Tp.,* III.ii.140—'I shall have
my music for *nothing.*'

60. *horn*] 'A hunting horn—something more masculine than these
stringed instruments' (Kittredge).

62–74.] See Appendix VI. The song
suggests more to the audience than to
the characters present, none of whom
knows of 'the fraud of man' against
Hero which is soon to give cause for

sighing, as that against Beatrice and
Benedick is to be 'blithe and bonny'.
It exemplifies Shakespeare's skill in
adapting his lyrics to the theme and
atmosphere of their contexts. Here
deception is a leading theme, whether
light-hearted and well-meant, or
sinister and malevolent. Balthasar
does not sound too solemn a note;
sighs of woe will turn to merriment.

70. *moe*] 'more in number (as distinguished from more, greater in
amount)' (*OED*, Mo, C. *adj.* 2).

71. *dumps*] A more dignified word
then than now, for either a sad mood
or the air of a song (often, but not
always, melancholy).

D. Pedro. Ha, no, no, faith; thou sing'st well enough for
    a shift.

Bene. [*Aside.*] And he had been a dog that should have
    howled thus, they would have hanged him, and I   80
    pray God his bad voice bode no mischief. I had as
    lief have heard the night-raven, come what plague
    could have come after it.

D. Pedro. Yea, marry, dost thou hear, Balthasar? I pray
    thee get us some excellent music; for tomorrow   85
    night we would have it at the Lady Hero's cham-
    ber-window.

Balth. The best I can, my lord.

D. Pedro. Do so: farewell. (*Exit Balthasar.*) Come
    hither, Leonato. What was it you told me of today,   90
    that your niece Beatrice was in love with Signior
    Benedick?

Claud. O, ay! [*Aside to Don Pedro.*] Stalk on, stalk on, the
    fowl sits.—I did never think that lady would have
    loved any man.   95

Leon. No, nor I neither, but most wonderful that she
    should so dote on Signior Benedick, whom she hath
    in all outward behaviours seemed ever to abhor.

Bene. [*Aside.*] Is't possible? Sits the wind in that corner?

Leon. By my troth my lord, I cannot tell what to think   100

---

79. S.D.] *Johnson; not in QF.*   89. S.D.] *QF (after l. 88), Steevens '93 subst.*
93. S.D.] *Johnson (after* sits.*); not in QF.*   99. S.D.] *Theobald (after* corner?*);
not in QF.*

82. *night-raven*] Tilley R33 gives as
proverbial 'The croaking raven bodes
disaster'; cf. *Faerie Queene*, II.xii.36, l. 5
—'The hoars *night-raven*, trump of
dolefull drere'—and Lyly, *Sapho and
Phao*, III.iii.59–60 (*Works*, ed. Bond,
II.397)—'the owle hath not shrikte at
the window, or the *night Rauen* croked,
both being fatall.'

85. *music . . . tomorrow*] One of the
play's loose ends—nothing further is
heard of this.

89–90. *Come hither, Leonato*] Leonato
bears a spirited part in the fun; he
would be too tragic a figure in the

church scene were he not here seen
with the decorum and weight of age
forgotten.

93–4. *Stalk on . . . sits*] As at l. 109,
and at Beatrice's gulling (III.i.24–36),
images of wild, elusive creatures to be
hunted are vivid and stimulating.

99. *Sits . . . corner*] Tilley W419
gives as proverbial 'Is the wind in that
door (quarter)?'

100–2.] An example of the flexible
syntax resulting from Q's light
punctuation, which allows the sentence
to mean both (i) 'I cannot avoid
thinking she loves him distractedly'

of it, but that she loves him with an enraged affection, it is past the infinite of thought.

D. Pedro. Maybe she doth but counterfeit.

Claud. Faith, like enough.

Leon. O God! Counterfeit? There was never counter-   105
feit of passion came so near the life of passion as she
discovers it.

D. Pedro. Why, what effects of passion shows she?

Claud. [*Aside.*] Bait the hook well, this fish will bite.

Leon. What effects, my lord? She will sit you—you   110
heard my daughter tell you how.

Claud. She did indeed.

D. Pedro. How, how, I pray you? You amaze me, I
would have thought her spirit had been invincible
against all assaults of affection.   115

Leon. I would have sworn it had, my lord, especially
against Benedick.

Bene. [*Aside.*] I should think this a gull, but that the
white-bearded fellow speaks it. Knavery cannot
sure hide himself in such reverence.   120

Claud. [*Aside.*] He hath ta'en th'infection; hold it up.

D. Pedro. Hath she made her affection known to
Benedick?

Leon. No, and swears she never will: that's her torment.

Claud. 'Tis true indeed, so your daughter says: 'Shall   125
I,' says she, 'that have so oft encountered him with
scorn, write to him that I love him?'

Leon. This says she now when she is beginning to write
to him, for she'll be up twenty times a night, and
there will she sit in her smock till she have writ a   130
sheet of paper: my daughter tells us all.

Claud. Now you talk of a sheet of paper, I remember a

101–2. it, ...affection,] *QF;* it; . . . affection, *Pope;* it, . . . affection; *Var. '78.*
109. S.D.] *Theobald (after* bite.) *; not in QF.*   118. S.D.] *Theobald (after l. 120);*
not in QF.   121. S.D.] *Theobald (after* up.) *; not in QF.*

and (ii) 'The degree to which she
loves him distractedly passes the utmost reach of thought'.
    101. *enraged*] frenzied (used of

various emotions, not only anger).
    107. *discovers*] reveals, discloses.
    118. *gull*] hoax.
    121. *hold it up*] keep the jest going.

pretty jest your daughter told us of.

Leon. O, when she had writ it, and was reading it over,
she found 'Benedick' and 'Beatrice' between the   135
sheet?

Claud. That.

Leon. O, she tore the letter into a thousand halfpence;
railed at herself, that she should be so immodest to
write to one that she knew would flout her. 'I   140
measure him', says she, 'by my own spirit, for I
should flout him, if he writ to me, yea, though
I love him, I should.'

Claud. Then down upon her knees she falls, weeps, sobs,
beats her heart, tears her hair, prays, curses: 'O   145
sweet Benedick! God give me patience!'

Leon. She doth indeed, my daughter says so, and the
ecstasy hath so much overborne her that my
daughter is sometime afeard she will do a desperate
outrage to herself: it is very true.   150

D. Pedro. It were good that Benedick knew of it by some
other, if she will not discover it.

Claud. To what end? He would make but a sport of it
and torment the poor lady worse.

D. Pedro. And he should, it were an alms to hang him.   155
She's an excellent sweet lady, and, out of all suspicion, she is virtuous.

Claud. And she is exceeding wise.

D. Pedro. In everything but in loving Benedick.

Leon. O my lord, wisdom and blood combating in so   160
tender a body, we have ten proofs to one that blood
hath the victory. I am sorry for her, as I have just
cause, being her uncle and her guardian.

D. Pedro. I would she had bestowed this dotage on me,
I would have daffed all other respects and made her   165
half myself. I pray you tell Benedick of it and hear
what a will say.

---

133. us of] *F*; of vs *Q*.   153. make but] *Q*; but make *F*.   167. a] *Q*; he *F*.

137. *That*] Yes, that's it.   160. *blood*] passion.
138. *halfpence*] = tiny pieces.   165. *daffed*] put to one side; variant
155. *alms*] good deed.   of 'doffed'.

Leon. Were it good, think you?

Claud. Hero thinks surely she will die; for she says she
    will die if he love her not, and she will die ere she   170
    make her love known, and she will die if he woo her,
    rather than she will bate one breath of her accus-
    tomed crossness.

D. Pedro. She doth well: if she should make tender of
    her love, 'tis very possible he'll scorn it, for the man,   175
    as you know all, hath a contemptible spirit.

Claud. He is a very proper man.

D. Pedro. He hath indeed a good outward happiness.

Claud. Before God, and, in my mind, very wise.

D. Pedro. He doth indeed show some sparks that are like   180
    wit.

Claud. And I take him to be valiant.

D. Pedro. As Hector, I assure you: and in the managing
    of quarrels you may say he is wise; for either he
    avoids them with great discretion, or undertakes   185
    them with a most Christian-like fear.

Leon. If he do fear God, a must necessarily keep peace:
    if he break the peace, he ought to enter into a
    quarrel with fear and trembling.

D. Pedro. And so will he do, for the man doth fear God,   190
    howsoever it seems not in him by some large jests he
    will make. Well, I am sorry for your niece. Shall we
    go seek Benedick, and tell him of her love?

Claud. Never tell him, my lord, let her wear it out with
    good counsel.   195

Leon. Nay, that's impossible, she may wear her heart out
    first.

D. Pedro. Well, we will hear further of it by your
    daughter; let it cool the while. I love Benedick well,

---

179. Before] *Q;* 'Fore *F.*   182. *Claud.*] *Q (Claudio); Leon. F.*   184. say] *Q;*
see *F.*   186. most] *Q; not in F.*   193. seek] *Q;* see *F.*

176. *contemptible*] contemptuous,
'inclined to scorn' (Johnson).

177. *proper*] fine, handsome.

178. *hath . . . happiness*] at least looks
handsome enough.

183–6.] A witty slander, much in

Beatrice's vein (cf. I.i. 35–41) and, by
its improbability, involving some risk
of alerting Benedick to the game going
on.

191. *large*] broad.

195. *counsel*] reflection.

and I could wish he would modestly examine him-   200
self, to see how much he is unworthy so good a lady.
Leon. My lord, will you walk? Dinner is ready.
Claud. [*Aside.*] If he do not dote on her upon this, I will
never trust my expectation.
D. Pedro. [*Aside.*] Let there be the same net spread for   205
her, and that must your daughter and her gentle-
women carry. The sport will be when they hold one
an opinion of another's dotage, and no such matter:
that's the scene that I would see, which will be
merely a dumb-show. Let us send her to call him in   210
to dinner.   *Exeunt* [*Don Pedro, Claudio, and Leonato*].
Bene. [*Coming forward.*] This can be no trick: the conference was sadly borne; they have the truth of this
from Hero. They seem to pity the lady: it seems
her affections have their full bent. Love me? Why,   215
it must be requited. I hear how I am censured: they
say I will bear myself proudly, if I perceive the love
come from her; they say too that she will rather die
than give any sign of affection. I did never think to
marry: I must not seem proud: happy are they that   220
hear their detractions and can put them to mend-
ing. They say the lady is fair—'tis a truth, I can
bear them witness; and virtuous—'tis so, I cannot
reprove it; and wise, but for loving me—by my
troth, it is no addition to her wit, nor no great argu-   225

201. unworthy] *Q; vnworthy to haue F.*   203. S.D.] *Theobald (after l. 204);*
not in QF.   205. S.D.] *Theobald (after l. 211); not in QF.*   206-7. gentle-
women] *Q; gentlewoman F.*   211. S.D.] *F (Exeunt.), Capell; not in Q.*
212. S.D.] *Theobald (advances from the Arbour), Globe; not in QF.*   215. their]
Q; the F.

213. *sadly*] seriously.
215-16. *Love me? . . . requited*]
'There is not a touch of vanity in the
amazement. The thing that dominates
his consciousness is not primarily that
Beatrice loves him, but that she is
suffering for his sake and he must love
her. . . . Neither [Benedick nor
Beatrice] stops to consider if they love.
What they do consider is how to
shield the other one from pain'

(Mackenzie, p. 135).
216. *censured*] judged. *Censure* did not
imply adverse criticism; cf. Greene's
Philomela (*Works*, ed. Grosart, xi. 127)
—'tell me her name, that I may
censure of her qualities'.
224. *reprove*] deny, disprove, as in
2H6, III.i.40—'*Reprove* my allegation
if you can'.
225-6. *argument*] evidence, proof.

ment of her folly, for I will be horribly in love with
her. I may chance have some odd quirks and rem-
nants of wit broken on me because I have railed so
long against marriage: but doth not the appetite
alter? A man loves the meat in his youth that he   230
cannot endure in his age. Shall quips and sentences
and these paper bullets of the brain awe a man from
the career of his humour? No, the world must be
peopled. When I said I would die a bachelor, I did
not think I should live till I were married. Here   235
comes Beatrice. By this day, she's a fair lady! I do
spy some marks of love in her.

Enter BEATRICE.

Beat. Against my will I am sent to bid you come in to
    dinner.
Bene. Fair Beatrice, I thank you for your pains.   240
Beat. I took no more pains for those thanks than you
    take pains to thank me; if it had been painful, I
    would not have come.
Bene. You take pleasure then in the message?
Beat. Yea, just so much as you may take upon a knife's   245
    point and choke a daw withal. You have no
    stomach, signior, fare you well.   *Exit.*
Bene. Ha! 'Against my will I am sent to bid you come in
    to dinner'—there's a double meaning in that. 'I
    took no more pains for those thanks than you took   250

227. *quirks*] quibbles, quips, twists.

231. *sentences*] saws, maxims.

233. *career of his humour*] course of his inclination.

233-4. *the world must be peopled*] 'His [Charles Kemble's] utterance of his grand final reason for marriage . . . with his hands linked behind him, a general elevation of his aspect, and a sort of look at the whole universe before him, as if he saw all the future generations that might depend on his verdict, was a bit of the right masterly gusto—the true perception and relish of the thing' (Leigh Hunt, *Dramatic*

Essays, 1894, p. 206, quoted in A. C. Sprague, *Shakespeare and the Actors*, p. 13).

246. *withal*] Emphatic form of *with*, at the end of a clause; cf. *Mac.*, II.i.15—'This diamond he greets your wife *withal*'.

249. *there's . . . that*] This comes off very comically on the stage, because of the evident absence of double meaning. Benedick wrests what Beatrice says to mean something like 'I have to bid you in to dinner, but I should prefer to stay out here with you'.

pains to thank me'—that's as much as to say, 'Any
pains that I take for you is as easy as thanks'. If I do
not take pity of her, I am a villain; if I do not love
her, I am a Jew. I will go get her picture.   *Exit.*

254. *a Jew*] a faithless rascal; cf. *1H4*, II. iv. 172—'*I am a Jew* else, an Ebrew *Jew*'—and *Mer.V.*, II. ii. 102— '*I am a Jew*, if I serve the Jew any longer'.

ACT III

[SCENE I]

Enter HERO *and two gentlewomen,* MARGARET *and* URSULA.

Hero. Good Margaret, run thee to the parlour;
There shalt thou find my cousin Beatrice
Proposing with the Prince and Claudio.
Whisper her ear, and tell her I and Ursley
Walk in the orchard, and our whole discourse   5
Is all of her; say that thou overheard'st us,
And bid her steal into the pleached bower
Where honeysuckles, ripen'd by the sun,
Forbid the sun to enter, like favourites,

ACT III

Scene 1

ACT III] F (*Actus Tertius.*); *not in Q.*   SCENE 1] *Rowe; not in QF.*   [*Location*]
the Garden. Pope; the Orchard. Theobald; not in QF.   S.D. *gentlewomen*] Q *subst.;*
Gentlemen F.   *Ursula*] Q (*Vrsley*), F.   4. Ursley] Q; *Vrsula* F.   8. ripen'd]
QF (ripened), *Rowe.*

Location] Leonato's orchard.

1.] 'Scan *Margaret* as disyllable, *parlour* as trisyllable, . . . since a sonant liquid [like 'r' or 'l'] may form a new syllable' (Warwick)— as in *tickling* (III.i.80) and *assembly* (V.iv.34).

3. *Proposing*] talking. Outside this scene (cf. also l. 12) *propose* does not in Shakespeare mean 'converse'. The nearest approach is *Oth.*, I.i.25-6 ('the toged consuls can *propose*/As masterly as he') but there the sense is formal and dignified.

4. *Whisper her ear*] For omitted prepositions see l. 12, and Abbott § 200.

7. *pleached*] See I.ii.8, note.

8. *honeysuckles*] Generally identified with the woodbine (l. 30), though the Elizabethans apparently sometimes distinguished them; cf. *MND*, IV.i. 41-2 – 'So doth the *woodbine* the sweet *honeysuckle*/Gently entwine' (where *woodbine* = bindweed or convolvulus); see New Arden edition, note. Gerard's *Herball* (ed. 1633) treats them as interchangeable, observing that '*Woodbine* or *Honisuckle* climbeth up aloft' (p. 890), and illustrating both with the same woodcut (p. 891).

9–11. *like favourites . . . bred it*] These words have been held to allude

143

    Made proud by princes, that advance their pride   10
    Against that power that bred it. There will she hide her
    To listen our propose. This is thy office;
    Bear thee well in it, and leave us alone.
Marg. I'll make her come, I warrant you, presently.   [*Exit.*]
Hero. Now, Ursula, when Beatrice doth come,   15
    As we do trace this alley up and down,
    Our talk must only be of Benedick.
    When I do name him, let it be thy part
    To praise him more than ever man did merit:
    My talk to thee must be how Benedick   20
    Is sick in love with Beatrice. Of this matter
    Is little Cupid's crafty arrow made,
    That only wounds by hearsay.

        Enter BEATRICE [*into the arbour*].

                      Now begin;
    For look where Beatrice like a lapwing runs
    Close by the ground, to hear our conference.   25
Urs. The pleasant'st angling is to see the fish
    Cut with her golden oars the silver stream,
    And greedily devour the treacherous bait:
    So angle we for Beatrice, who even now
    Is couched in the woodbine coverture.   30
    Fear you not my part of the dialogue.
Hero. Then go we near her, that her ear lose nothing
    Of the false sweet bait that we lay for it.
    [*Approaching the arbour.*] No, truly, Ursula, she is too
        disdainful;

---

12. propose] *Q;* purpose *F.*   14. S.D.] *F2; not in QF1.*   23. S.D. *Enter Beatrice*] *Q (after l. 25), F (after* begin).   *into the arbour*] *Theobald subst.; not in QF.*   34. S.D.] *Var. '78 subst.; not in QF.*

to some specific disturbers of the Queen's peace. But political allusions were risky, and the last thing Shakespeare would do is deliberately to insert a reference to so touchy a subject. As a purely general allusion the image is acceptable.

  14. *presently*] at once.

  16.] A cue for stage-action.

  23. *only wounds*] = wounds only; cf. 'only be bold', III.ii.7.

  24. *like a lapwing*] The lapwing runs or couches coweringly to escape notice.

  24–36.] As with the gulling of Benedick (II.iii.93–4, note), images of wild, elusive creatures are apt, and 'delightfully picturesque' (Hazlitt).

  I know her spirits are as coy and wild
As haggards of the rock.   35
Urs.   But are you sure
That Benedick loves Beatrice so entirely?
Hero. So says the Prince and my new-trothed lord.
Urs. And did they bid you tell her of it, madam?
Hero. They did entreat me to acquaint her of it;
  But I persuaded them, if they lov'd Benedick, 40
  To wish him wrestle with affection,
  And never to let Beatrice know of it.
Urs. Why did you so? Doth not the gentleman
  Deserve as full as fortunate a bed
  As ever Beatrice shall couch upon?   45
Hero. O god of love! I know he doth deserve
  As much as may be yielded to a man:
  But Nature never fram'd a woman's heart
  Of prouder stuff than that of Beatrice.
  Disdain and scorn ride sparkling in her eyes, 50
  Misprising what they look on, and her wit
  Values itself so highly that to her
  All matter else seems weak. She cannot love,
  Nor take no shape nor project of affection, 55
  She is so self-endeared.
Urs.   Sure, I think so;
  And therefore certainly it were not good
  She knew his love, lest she'll make sport at it.
Hero. Why, you speak truth. I never yet saw man,

58. she'll] *Q;* she *F.*

35. *coy*] This could mean (i) shy; (ii) 'Of distant or disdainful behaviour' (*OED*, Coy. †3). Here it connects the ideas of *disdainful* and *wild*.

36. *haggards*] A haggard is a 'wild [female] hawk at liberty until she has . . . her adult plumage' (Madden, p. 148), and so fiercer-spirited than a hawk trained from its nestling stage for hunting; cf. *Spanish Tragedy,* II. i. 4 (Kyd, *Works,* ed. Boas, p. 21)— 'In time all *haggard* Hawkes will stoope to lure'. They occasioned ungallant comparisons: cf. *Shr.,* IV. ii. 39—'this proud disdainful *haggard*'; and Lyly *Euphues* (*Works,* ed. Bond, 1. 219)— 'if she should yeelde at the first assault he woulde thinke hir a light huswife, if she should reiect him scornfully a very *haggard*'.

42. *affection*] his feeling.

52. *Misprising*] undervaluing.

55. *project*] conception, idea (an unusual sense): *OED* cites Defoe, *Acc. Scot.* 152—'A great deal of *project* and fancy may be employed to find out the ancient shape of the Church'.

59–67.] Lyly offers precedents:

How wise, how noble, young, how rarely featur'd,   60
But she would spell him backward: if fair-fac'd,
She would swear the gentleman should be her sister;
If black, why, Nature, drawing of an antic,
Made a foul blot; if tall, a lance ill-headed;
If low, an agate very vilely cut;   65
If speaking, why, a vane blown with all winds;
If silent, why, a block moved with none.
So turns she every man the wrong side out,
And never gives to truth and virtue that

60. featur'd] *Q* (featured), *F*.   61. fac'd] *Q* (faced), *F*.

'Dost thou not knowe that woemen deeme none valyaunt, vnlesse he be too venturesome? That they accompte one a dastarde, if he be not desperate, a pinch penny and if he be not prodigall, if silent a sotte, if ful of wordes a foole?' and 'If he be cleanly, then terme they him proude, if meane in apparel, a sloven, if talle, a longis, if shorte, a dwarfe, if bolde, blunte, if shamefaste, a coward' (*Euphues to Philautus, Works*, ed. Bond, 1.249, ll. 9–12, and 1.254, ll. 1–3).

59–80.] 'When they are both on the scene together, Hero has but little to say for herself. . . . But when she has Beatrice at an advantage, she repays her with interest. . . . The portrait is a little overcharged, because administered as a corrective' (Anna Jameson, *Characteristics of Women*, 1833, 1.136).

61. *spell him backward*] i.e. conjure up an unfavourable image, as witches say prayers backwards to raise the devil. Defoe in his *System of Magic* records a conversation with a credulous countryman: '*C*. . . . but draw a circle and turn round five times in it, the Devil can't help appearing, no more than if we said the Lord's prayer backward./*A*. Why, will he come if we say our prayers backward?/*C*. Ay, certainly, master; . . . I have heard of an old woman at Daventry used to raise the Devil that way very often'

(*Novels and Miscellaneous Works*, 1840, XII.225).

61–7. *if fair-fac'd . . . block*] Lyly's *Euphues* has similar contrasting wayward exaggerations: see *Works*, ed. Bond, 1.195, ll. 21–7; 1.249, ll. 9–15; 1.254, ll. 1–3 and 17–21. Davenport's *A New Tricke to Cheat the Divell*, 1.ii (Bullen's *Old English Plays*, New Series, III.203), describes the opposite process, when Slightall tells how he deals with women's defects: 'To her whose skin was blacke as *Ebone* was,/I have said ere now, Oh, 'tis a nutbrowne lasse;/Or if she lookt a squint, As I am true/So *Venus* looked; if she be bleake of hew,/Pale for the World, like *Pallas*; be she growne,/By *Jove, Minerva* up and downe;/If she be tall, then for her height commend her;/If she be leane, like envy, terme her slender'.

63. *black*] dark in complexion.

63–4. *Nature . . . blot*] Trying her hand at a comic grotesque, nature made an ugly blotch of it: *antic* (variously spelt) = grotesque figure, strange appearance, buffoon. For the adverb, see v.i.96.

65. *agate*] metaphorically, a dwarf, from figures cut in agate for rings, seals, etc.: cf. *Rom.*, 1.iv.55–6—'In shape no bigger than an *agate* stone/ On the forefinger of an alderman'; and *2H4*, 1.ii.19— 'manned with an *agate*' (= served by a midget).

Which simpleness and merit purchaseth.　　70
Urs. Sure, sure, such carping is not commendable.
Hero. No, not to be so odd and from all fashions
　　As Beatrice is, cannot be commendable:
　　But who dare tell her so? If I should speak,
　　She would mock me into air; O, she would laugh me　75
　　Out of myself, press me to death with wit!
　　Therefore let Benedick, like cover'd fire,
　　Consume away in sighs, waste inwardly.
　　It were a better death than die with mocks,
　　Which is as bad as die with tickling.　　80
Urs. Yet tell her of it; hear what she will say.
Hero. No; rather I will go to Benedick
　　And counsel him to fight against his passion;
　　And truly I'll devise some honest slanders
　　To stain my cousin with: one doth not know　85
　　How much an ill word may empoison liking.
Urs. O, do not do your cousin such a wrong!
　　She cannot be so much without true judgement—
　　Having so swift and excellent a wit
　　As she is priz'd to have—as to refuse　90
　　So rare a gentleman as Signior Benedick.
Hero. He is the only man of Italy,
　　Always excepted my dear Claudio.

---

77. cover'd] *Q;* couered *F.*　　79. than] *Q* (then); to *F.*

70. *simpleness*] integrity, plain honesty (as usually in Shakespeare): so in *MND*, v. i. 82–3—'never anything can be amiss/When *simpleness* and duty tender it'.

purchaseth] For the singular verb after two subject nouns see Abbott § 336.

71. *commendable*] The accent falls on the first and third syllables; similarly in l. 73.

72. *from*] contrary to.

76. *press me to death*] An allusion to the *peine forte et dure,* the loading of heavy weights upon an accused person to induce him to answer a charge: so in *R2,* III. iv. 72—'O, I am *press'd to death* for want of speaking'.

77. *cover'd fire*] 'Fire that's closest kept burns most of all' was proverbial; Tilley F265.

80. *tickling*] Trisyllabic; the *l* is syllablized like *r* in *parlour* (III. i. 1) and *l* in *assembly* (v. iv. 34).

84. *honest*] i.e. honest because well-intentioned, and, probably, such as would not dishonour Beatrice.

85–6. *one . . . liking*] Hero's mock-serious observation is soon to be poignantly appropriate to her own love-affair.

87–91.] A shrewdly judged shaft, pinning Beatrice's own most esteemed qualities to the cause of loving Benedick.

90. *priz'd to have*] valued for having.

Urs. I pray you be not angry with me, madam,
   Speaking my fancy: Signior Benedick,   95
   For shape, for bearing, argument, and valour,
   Goes foremost in report through Italy.
Hero. Indeed he hath an excellent good name.
Urs. His excellence did earn it ere he had it.
   When are you married, madam?   100
Hero. Why, every day, tomorrow! Come, go in;
   I'll show thee some attires, and have thy counsel
   Which is the best to furnish me tomorrow.
Urs. [*Aside.*] She's lim'd, I warrant you! We have caught her,
   madam.
Hero. [*Aside.*] If it prove so, then loving goes by haps: 105
   Some Cupid kills with arrows, some with traps.
                              Exeunt [*Hero and Ursula*].
Beat. [*Coming forward.*] What fire is in mine ears? Can this be
   true?

---

96. bearing,] *F4;* bearing *QF1–3.*   104. S.D.] *Capell; not in QF.*   104.] *as*
Pope (one line); two lines ending you,/. . . madame. *QF subst.*   lim'd] *Q* (limed),
Theobald; tane *F.*   105. S.D.] *Capell; not in QF.*   106. S.D. Exeunt] *F (Exit),*
Rowe; not in Q.   *Hero and Ursula*] *Malone; not in QF.*   107. S.D.] *Theobald*
(advancing), Camb.; not in QF.

96. *argument*] keenness of reasoning or debating.

101. *every day, tomorrow*] every day, from tomorrow on.

104. *lim'd*] caught as with bird-lime (continuing the fowling and fishing metaphors of ll. 24–36). John Ray's *Epitome of the Art of Fowling* (in Francis Willughby's *Ornithology,* ed. 1678) gives instructions 'How to take Water-Fowl with limed strings' (p. 30; Bk 1, Sec. 1, chap. II, § i); 'How to take several sorts of small Birds . . . with Bird-Lime' (ibid., chap. III, § 1); and so on.

107–16.] For the first time Beatrice breaks into verse (in what remains of the play she has only nine or ten verse.lines more). Her capitulation is delightfully marked by her lapse into metre, rhyme, and romantic sentiment. In 'Shakespeare and Elizabethan English' (*Shakespeare Survey 7,* 1954, p. 17) Gladys Willcock notes how Shakespeare's lovers delight in verbal artifice, and comments, 'this artifice they pursue not because they do not have feelings but because they do'. Ellen Terry saw the artifices of expression as coexisting with deep feeling, and there is no reason to dismiss the lines as immature: 'Very difficult words for an actress; not very effective, but charged with the passion of a strong, deep heart! I have played Beatrice hundreds of times and never done this speech as I feel it should be done' (*Four Lectures on Shakespeare,* 1932, p. 88).

107. *What . . . ears*] Tilley E14 gives as proverbial 'When your ear tingles (burns) people are talking about you'. But Beatrice is not merely echoing the proverb: she intensifies the idea almost beyond recognition in the image of the fire of newly realized love burning within her.

Stand I condemn'd for pride and scorn so much?
Contempt, farewell, and maiden pride, adieu!
No glory lives behind the back of such.   110
And, Benedick, love on, I will requite thee,
Taming my wild heart to thy loving hand.
If thou dost love, my kindness shall incite thee
To bind our loves up in a holy band;
For others say thou dost deserve, and I   115
Believe it better than reportingly.   *Exit.*

[SCENE II]

Enter Prince [DON PEDRO], CLAUDIO, BENEDICK, *and*
LEONATO.

D. Pedro. I do but stay till your marriage be consummate, and then go I toward Aragon.

Claud. I'll bring you thither, my lord, if you'll vouchsafe
me.

D. Pedro. Nay, that would be as great a soil in the new   5
gloss of your marriage as to show a child his new
coat and forbid him to wear it. I will only be bold
with Benedick for his company, for from the crown
of his head to the sole of his foot he is all mirth. He
hath twice or thrice cut Cupid's bow-string, and the   10

111. on] *Q corr., F; one Q uncorr.*

Scene II

SCENE II] *Pope; not in QF.*   [*Location*] *Leonato's House. Theobald; not in QF.*
S.D. *Don Pedro*] *Rowe; not in QF.*   1. *D. Pedro*] *QF (Prince) (so subst. through-*
out scene, except l. 49), Rowe (Pedro), Capell (D. Pe.).

110.] = Such faults are forerunners
of no glory.
112.] Another bird-life image.
Hearing herself compared to a
haggard, Beatrice makes fine use of
the idea. Madden cites Edmund
Bert's *Treatise of Hawks and Hunting*
(1619)—'your haggard is very loving
and kinde to her keeper, after he hath
brought her by his sweet and kind
familiarity to understand him'.

Scene II

Location] Leonato's house.
1–2. *consummate*] See I.i.124, note.
3. *bring*] escort (a frequent sense).
7. *only be bold*] be bold only; see
II.i.128, note.
9–10. *He hath . . . bow-string*] One of
several references creating the illusion
of long familiarity with the main
characters. It gives a different version
of what Beatrice alluded to in I.i.35–8
but throws no more light.

little hangman dare not shoot at him. He hath a
heart as sound as a bell, and his tongue is the clapper; for what his heart thinks his tongue speaks.

Bene. Gallants, I am not as I have been.

Leon. So say I; methinks you are sadder.   15

Claud. I hope he be in love.

D. Pedro. Hang him, truant! There's no true drop of
blood in him to be truly touched with love. If he be
sad, he wants money.

Bene. I have the toothache.   20

D. Pedro. Draw it.

Bene. Hang it!

Claud. You must hang it first, and draw it afterwards.

D. Pedro. What? Sigh for the toothache?

Leon. Where is but a humour or a worm.   25

Bene. Well, every one can master a grief but he that has
it.

---

26. can] *Pope;* cannot *QF.*

11. *hangman*] rascal, rogue—a sense
softened by *little* so as to become a
playful endearment. *Hangman* could
mean any sort of executioner (e.g.
'the *hangman's* axe'; *Mer.V.*, IV.i.125)
but also, even more loosely, any sort
of rascal (e.g. 'stolen from me by the
hangman boys'; *Gent.*, IV.iv.52).

11–13. *He hath . . . speaks*] 'As sound
as a bell' is proverbial; Don Pedro
develops the metaphor with 'his
tongue is the clapper' and, perhaps
subconsciously, echoes another proverb on the same figure—'as the fool
thinks, the bell chinks' (Tilley F445).

14.] 'It is a notable point in Shakespeare's contrivance that he gives both
wits their off-day as soon as love has
disturbed their freedom' (Rossiter, p.
69). See III.iv.40.

20.] Love and toothache were
associated (perhaps both as causes of
anguish): so in Beaumont and
Fletcher, *The False One*, II.iii.109–10—
'You had best be troubled with the
Tooth-ach too,/For *Lovers* ever are';
and Massinger, *The Parliament of Love*
Ib. 32 (*Plays*, ed. Edwards and Gib-

son, II.113)—'I am troubled/With the
tooth ach, or with *loue*, I know not
whether:/There is a worme in both'.
The *worm* is both metaphorical and
(supposedly) literal—see l. 25, note.

23.] Punning on the hanging and
drawing (disembowelling) of crimi-
nals. Chapman's *Monsieur D'Olive*,
III.ii. 111–13, quibbles similarly—'*M.
D'Olive*: But how will I *hang* myself,
good wits? Not in person, but in picture; I will be *drawn*—/*Roderigue*:
What, *hanged* and *drawn* too?'

25.] Stephen Batman, *Vppon Bartholome*, Lib. Quintus, cap. 20, 'Of
the Teeth', affirms that 'The cause of
such aking is *humors* that come downe
from the heade, . . . Also sometime
teeth be pearced with holes & sometime by *worms* they be changed into
yellow colour, greene, or black'.

26–7.] Tilley cites proverbial parallels, A124 ('all commend patience
but none can endure to suffer') and
M182 ('The healthful man can give
counsel to the sick'). For a tragic
application see Leonato's outcry at
v.i.34–8.

Claud. Yet say I, he is in love.

D. Pedro. There is no appearance of fancy in him, unless
it be a fancy that he hath to strange disguises—as to   30
be a Dutchman today, a Frenchman tomorrow, or
in the shape of two countries at once, as a German
from the waist downward, all slops, and a Spaniard
from the hip upward, no doublet. Unless he have a
fancy to this foolery, as it appears he hath, he is no   35
fool for fancy, as you would have it appear he is.

Claud. If he be not in love with some woman, there is no
believing old signs; a brushes his hat o' mornings,
what should that bode?

D. Pedro. Hath any man seen him at the barber's?   40

Claud. No, but the barber's man hath been seen with
him, and the old ornament of his cheek hath already
stuffed tennis-balls.

31–4. or . . . doublet.] *Q; not in F.*   36. it] *Q;* it to *F.*   38. o'] *QF* (a),
Theobald.

29–30. *fancy . . . fancy*] This quibbles
on *fancy* as (i) love; (ii) affectation,
and is repeated at ll. 35–6.

30. *strange disguises*] The English
aping of foreign fashions was often
satirized. Portia surmises that her
English suitor 'bought his doublet in
Italy, his round hose in France, his
bonnet in Germany' (*Mer.V.*, I.ii.67–
68). Both this and the passage in the
text have close parallels in Joseph
Hall's *Virgidemiarum Sixe Bookes* (1597),
III.i.64–9—'But thou canst maske in
garish gauderie/To suit a fooles far-
fetched liuery./A *French* head ioynd to
necke *Italian*:/Thy thighs from *Ger-
manie*, and brest from *Spaine*:/An
Englishman in none, a foole in all,/
Many in one, and one in seuerall'.

31–4. *or . . . doublet*] This passage, in
Q, was omitted from F, perhaps to
avoid offending (i) some foreign
minister, e.g. the Spanish ambassador
or the German, this being among the
plays done at Court during the

wedding festivities of the Princess
Elizabeth and the Elector Palatine in
1613; or (ii) King James, touchy
about 'foreign' aspersions; in *Mer.V.*,
I.ii.69, Q's 'the Scottish lord' becomes 'the other lord' in F.

33. *slops*] large loose breeches. 'The
Switzer's and German's slops were
paned with grotesquely full lining in
contrasting colour, which hung
between panes in limp puffs. Hence
[this passage]' (Linthicum, p. 209).

34. *no doublet*] i.e. all cape—the
hip-length Spanish cloak.

42–3. *the old . . . tennis-balls*] Lodo-
wick Barry's *Ram Alley*, III.i. (Hazlitt's
Dodsley, x.315) indicates that this was
an actual practice —'Thy beard shall
serve to stuff those *balls*, by which / I
get me heat at *tennis*': also Dekker's
Shoemaker's Holiday, v.v.23–4 (*Works*,
ed. Bowers, I.84), where Eyre says of
his beard, 'yet Ile shaue it off, and
stuffe tennis balls with it to please my
bully king'.

Leon. Indeed he looks younger than he did, by the loss of
    a beard.   45

D. Pedro. Nay, a rubs himself with civet; can you smell
    him out by that?

Claud. That's as much as to say the sweet youth's in love.

D. Pedro. The greatest note of it is his melancholy.

Claud. And when was he wont to wash his face?   50

D. Pedro. Yea, or to paint himself? For the which I hear
    what they say of him.

Claud. Nay, but his jesting spirit, which is now crept into
    a lute-string, and now governed by stops.

D. Pedro. Indeed that tells a heavy tale for him: con-   55
    clude, conclude he is in love.

Claud. Nay, but I know who loves him.

D. Pedro. That would I know too: I warrant, one that
    knows him not.

Claud. Yes, and his ill conditions, and in despite of all,   60
    dies for him.

D. Pedro. She shall be buried with her face upwards.

Bene. Yet is this no charm for the toothache. Old signior,

---

49. *D. Pedro.*] *F (Prin.), Rowe subst.; Bene. Q.*   56. conclude he] *Q*; he *F*.

44–5. *loss of a beard*] 'As a soldier,
Benedick was heavily bearded when
he returned from the campaign'
(Kittredge). And he doubtless knew
Beatrice's preference—II. i. 26–7.

46. *civet*] a modish perfume; see
AYL, III.ii. 57—'The courtier's hands
are perfumed with *civet*'; and *The
Returne from Parnassus*, ll. 1363–5—
'he is one, that wil draw out his pocket
glasse thrise in a walke; one that
dreames in the night of nothing, but
muske and *ciuet*'.

50–1. *wash . . . himself*] = use
cosmetics. *A Quippe for an Vpstart
Courtier* (Greene, ed. Grosart, XI. 247)
describes shaving preparations, including 'being curiously *washt* with no
worse than a camphire bal'.

53–4.] 'His jocular wit is now employed in the inditing of love-songs,
which in Shakespeare's time were

usually accompanied on the lute'
(Knight). The *stops* are the frets, the
points at which the string is *governed*,
or stopped, by the finger on the finger-
board. Benedick's spirit does not now
run freely; it is repeatedly checked.

60. *ill conditions*] bad qualities.

62.] i.e. the only 'death' for her
is to be buried under Benedick's
body.

63–6.] For the first time Benedick is
defenceless against raillery; love has
transformed him to an oyster.

63. *charm for the toothache*] Brand's
Popular Superstitions (ed. W. C. Hazlitt,
III. 256) quotes from Joseph Hall's
Characters (1608), an account of a
superstitious man—'Old Wives and
Starres are his Counsellors: his Night-
spell is his Guard, and *Charms his
Physicians. He wears Paracelsian Charac-
ters for the Tooth Ache.*'

> walk aside with me; I have studied eight or nine
> wise words to speak to you, which these hobby-   65
> horses must not hear.   [*Exeunt Benedick and Leonato.*]

D. Pedro. For my life, to break with him about Beatrice.

Claud. 'Tis even so. Hero and Margaret have by this
> played their parts with Beatrice, and then the two
> bears will not bite one another when they meet.   70

Enter [DON] JOHN *the Bastard.*

D. John. My lord and brother, God save you!

D. Pedro. Good den, brother.

D. John. If your leisure served, I would speak with you.

D. Pedro. In private?

D. John. If it please you; yet Count Claudio may hear,   75
> for what I would speak of concerns him.

D. Pedro. What's the matter?

D. John. [*To Claudio.*] Means your lordship to be married
> tomorrow?

D. Pedro. You know he does.   80

D. John. I know not that, when he knows what I know.

Claud. If there be any impediment, I pray you discover
> it.

D. John. You may think I love you not: let that appear
> hereafter, and aim better at me by that I now will   85
> manifest. For my brother, I think he holds you well,

66. S.D.] *Theobald; not in QF.*   70. S.D. *Don*] *Rowe; not in QF.*   71. *D. John.*]
QF (*Bastard*) *subst.* (*so subst. throughout scene*), *Rowe* (*John*), *Capell* (*D. Jo.*).
78. S. D.] *Rowe* (*after l. 79*); *not in QF.*   86–7. brother, I . . . heart] *Rowe;*
brother, I . . . heart, *Q uncorr.;* brother (I . . . heart) *Q corr., F.*

64–5. *I . . . you*] Benedick in fact first
broaches the matter to Leonato at
v. iv. 21–2. An audience will not
notice the lack of follow-up here, and
Benedick's withdrawal with Leonato
enables Don John to confine his
plotting to Claudio and Don Pedro.

65–6. *hobby-horses*] Here = buffoons.
The *hobby-horse* was a main figure in
the Morris dance, 'represented by a
man equipped with as much paste-
board as was sufficient to form the
head and hinder parts of a horse, the
quadrupedal defects being concealed

by a long mantle or footcloth, like the
housing on a horse, that nearly
touched the ground. The performer
. . . exerted all his skill in burlesque
horsemanship' (Douce, *Illustrations,*
II. 467).

68. *Margaret*] A slip for Ursula:
Margaret had played her part, but
was absent from the gulling.

69–70. *the two . . . meet*] Tilley W606
gives as proverbial 'One wolf (bear)
will not . . . bite . . . another'.

72. *Good den*] God give you good
even.

and in dearness of heart hath holp to effect your
ensuing marriage—surely suit ill spent, and labour
ill bestowed.

D. Pedro. Why, what's the matter?   90

D. John. I came hither to tell you; and, circumstances
shortened—for she has been too long a-talking of—
the lady is disloyal.

Claud. Who, Hero?

D. John. Even she—Leonato's Hero, your Hero, every   95
man's Hero.

Claud. Disloyal?

D. John. The word is too good to paint out her wickedness. I could say she were worse; think you of a
worse title and I will fit her to it. Wonder not till   100
further warrant: go but with me tonight, you shall
see her chamber-window entered, even the night
before her wedding-day. If you love her then, tomorrow wed her; but it would better fit your
honour to change your mind.   105

Claud. May this be so?

D. Pedro. I will not think it.

D. John. If you dare not trust that you see, confess not
that you know. If you will follow me, I will show
you enough; and when you have seen more, and   110
heard more, proceed accordingly.

Claud. If I see anything tonight why I should not marry
her tomorrow, in the congregation, where I should
wed, there will I shame her.

87. holp] *Q corr.* (holpe), *F*; hope *Q uncorr.*   92. has] *Q*; hath *F*.   of] *Q
corr.*, *F*; *not in Q uncorr.*   103. her then,] *Hanmer*; her, then *QF*.   113. her
tomorrow, in] *Rowe*; her to morrow in *QF*; her; tomorrow, in *Capell*; her, tomorrow in *Alexander*.

93. *disloyal*] unfaithful.

95–6. *Leonato's . . . Hero*] Imitated in
Dryden's *All for Love*, iv. 298–9—'*Venti-
dius*: Your Cleopatra; Dolabella's
Cleopatra;/Every man's Cleopatra'.

98. *paint out*] depict in full.

108, 109. *that . . . that*] = what . . .
what.

112–23.] Claudio shows up lamen-
tably in expressing no anger with Don
John, only momentary doubt over
Hero, and an immediate desire for a
public and shameful revenge. 'The
antithetical way in which Claudio and
Don Pedro now speak . . . shows how
thoroughly Don John is making them
his victims. . . . The exit of Don John
with this string of sinister sibilants
[ll. 122–3] cannot be accidental'
(Craik, p. 304).

D. Pedro. And as I wooed for thee to obtain her, I will   115
  join with thee to disgrace her.

D. John. I will disparage her no farther till you are my
  witnesses. Bear it coldly but till midnight, and let
  the issue show itself.

D. Pedro. O day untowardly turned!   120

Claud. O mischief strangely thwarting!

D. John. O plague right well prevented! So will you say
  when you have seen the sequel.   *Exeunt.*

[SCENE III]

Enter DOGBERRY *and his compartner* [VERGES], *with the*
Watch.

Dog. Are you good men and true?

118. midnight] *Q;* night *F.*   123. S.D.] *F1 (Exit.), F2;* not in *Q.*

Scene III

SCENE III] *Capell;* not in *QF.*   [Location] *The Street. Pope;* not in *QF.*   S.D.
Verges] Rowe; not in *QF.*

118. *coldly*] coolly, collectedly.

Scene III

Location] A street.

S.D. *compartner*] The word occurs nowhere else in Shakespeare. It is still common in Cornwall for partner, companion. 'Dogberry is Head Constable, Verges is Headborough—a constable of somewhat lower rank' (Kittredge).

Shakespeare left the Watch's speeches sometimes to be distributed at the actors' discretion, and this edition does not attribute all of them definitively. It does however make certain rearrangements, changing Q's 'Watch 1' at ll. 159 and 163 to 'Sec. Watch', and Q's 'Watch 2' at ll. 160 and 166 to 'First Watch'. What in this latter part of the scene Q calls 'Watch 1' (i.e. the group's chief) must be what it calls 'Watch 2' at ll. 17 and 27, the George Seacoal appointed at l. 13

as constable or leader; he is 'Watch 2' at the earlier stage not as being inferior but as being the second watchman to speak. Having started as 'Watch 2' he should remain so throughout. As leader he is doubtless also Q's undifferentiated 'Watch' of ll. 86, 94, 104, and 122 (in this last instance being presumably the same authority on the mysterious 'Deformed' as speaks l. 163). Doubtless, too, in the exercise of his leadership he speaks ll. 169–70, which in Q merely continue Conrade's speech at l. 168. Q affords no clues for distributing ll. 37, 44, 48, 53, and 66, so other members of the Watch may be allowed their turn. At IV.ii.36 and 50 Q's 'Watch 1', who takes the initiative in charging Borachio and Conrade, is presumably also the same George Seacoal.

1.] Lyly's *Endimion* (IV.ii) has a group of befuddled watchmen given to ludicrous logic, of whom a charac-

Verg. Yea, or else it were pity but they should suffer
    salvation, body and soul.

Dog. Nay, that were a punishment too good for them, if
    they should have any allegiance in them, being   5
    chosen for the Prince's watch.

Verg. Well, give them their charge, neighbour Dog-
    berry.

Dog. First, who think you the most desartless man to be
    constable?   10

First Watch. Hugh Oatcake, sir, or George Seacoal, for
    they can write and read.

Dog. Come hither, neighbour Seacoal. God hath blest
    you with a good name: to be a well-favoured man is
    the gift of fortune, but to write and read comes by 15
    nature.

Sec. Watch. Both which, Master Constable—

Dog. You have: I knew it would be your answer. Well,
    for your favour, sir, why, give God thanks, and
    make no boast of it; and for your writing and read- 20
    ing, let that appear when there is no need of such
    vanity. You are thought here to be the most sense-

---

17. Constable—] *Q* (Constable.), *Rowe subst.;* Constable *F.*

ter remarks, 'A watch, quoth you? a
man may watch 7. yeres for a wise
word, & yet goe without it. Their
wits are all as rustic as their bils.' They
sing a song, starting 'Stand: who goes
there?/We charge you, appeare/Fore
our Constable here./(In the name of
the Man in the Moone)/To us Belmen
relate,/Why you stagger so late,/And
how come you drunke so soone'
(*Works*, ed. Bond, II. 58). There may
be echoes at ll. 25–6 and 42–3, below;
see also v. i. 203, note.

    4–6.] 'While apparently an *opposite*
to the wit-crackers, [Dogberry] is also
a parallel, in that pride of self-opinion
and a nice apprehension of one's own
wisdom and cleverness is as much
theirs as his' (Rossiter, p. 77).

    10. *constable*] Here = leader of the
watch. Dogberry himself is Master
Constable.

    11. *George*] Halliwell changed
George to *Francis*, thinking this to be
the same Seacoal as has 'pen and inkhorn' at III. v. 54. This is likely enough
but there is no telling; the uses of
literacy may have run in the Seacoal
family. 'Seacoal' may hint at the constable's superior quality, alluding to
'coal imported by sea from Newcastle
with its considerably higher . . . value
. . . than the charcoal offered by
colliers' (J. Schäfer, 'Orthography of
Proper Names in . . . Shakespeare',
Studies in Bibliography, XXIII, 1970, p. 9).

    15. *gift of fortune*] Lyly's *Euphues*
offers a parallel — 'to bee rich is the
gift of Fortune, to bee wise the grace of
God' (*Works*, ed. Bond, II. 15, ll. 27–8).

    19. *favour*] appearance.

    22–3. *senseless and fit man*] Tilley
C616 gives as proverbial 'You might
be a constable for your wit'.

　　　less and fit man for the constable of the watch;
　　　therefore bear you the lantern. This is your charge:
　　　you shall comprehend all vagrom men; you are to　　25
　　　bid any man stand, in the Prince's name.
Sec. Watch. How if a will not stand?
Dog. Why then, take no note of him, but let him go, and
　　　presently call the rest of the watch together, and
　　　thank God you are rid of a knave.　　30
Verg. If he will not stand when he is bidden, he is none
　　　of the Prince's subjects.
Dog. True, and they are to meddle with none but the
　　　Prince's subjects. You shall also make no noise in
　　　the streets: for, for the watch to babble and to talk　　35
　　　is most tolerable, and not to be endured.
Watch. We will rather sleep than talk; we know what
　　　belongs to a watch.
Dog. Why, you speak like an ancient and most quiet
　　　watchman, for I cannot see how sleeping should　　40
　　　offend: only have a care that your bills be not
　　　stolen. Well, you are to call at all the ale-houses,
　　　and bid those that are drunk get them to bed.
Watch. How if they will not?
Dog. Why then, let them alone till they are sober: if　　45
　　　they make you not then the better answer, you may
　　　say they are not the men you took them for.
Watch. Well, sir.
Dog. If you meet a thief, you may suspect him, by virtue
　　　of your office, to be no true man; and for such kind　　50
　　　of men, the less you meddle or make with them,
　　　why, the more is for your honesty.

---

35. and to] *Q*; and *F*.　　43. those] *Q*; them *F*.

25. *vagrom*] vagrant.

29. *presently*] immediately.

41. *bills*] halberds, pikes (with spiked axe-heads fixed to a long pole).

50. *true*] honest. Dogberry probably uses *true man* in its legal sense, in contradistinction to thief; cf. *1H4*'s antithesis—'*true man* . . . false thief'

(II.i.91–2). W. L. Rushton's *Shakespeare Illustrated by the Lex Scripta* cites passages from Coke's *Institutes* in the technical sense, e.g. 'if thieves rob a *true man* and find but little about him . . .', 'if . . . the *true man* deliver his purse . . .' (pp. 56–7).

51. *meddle or make*] A proverbial tag; Tilley M852.

Watch. If we know him to be a thief, shall we not lay
    hands on him?

Dog. Truly, by your office you may, but I think they   55
    that touch pitch will be defiled. The most peaceable
    way for you, if you do take a thief, is to let him
    show himself what he is, and steal out of your com-
    pany.

Verg. You have been always called a merciful man,   60
    partner.

Dog. Truly, I would not hang a dog by my will, much
    more a man who hath any honesty in him.

Verg. If you hear a child cry in the night, you must call
    to the nurse and bid her still it.   65

Watch. How if the nurse be asleep and will not hear us?

Dog. Why then, depart in peace, and let the child wake
    her with crying, for the ewe that will not hear her
    lamb when it baas will never answer a calf when
    he bleats.   70

Verg. 'Tis very true.

Dog. This is the end of the charge: you, constable, are
    to present the Prince's own person; if you meet the
    Prince in the night, you may stay him.

Verg. Nay, by'r lady, that I think a cannot.   75

Dog. Five shillings to one on't, with any man that knows
    the statutes, he may stay him: marry, not without

---

77. statutes] *Q;* Statues *F.*

55-6. *they . . . defiled*] Proverbial;
Tilley P358, from Ecclesiasticus
XIII. I—'He that *toucheth pitch shall be
defiled*'.

64-5.] Whether or not Steevens was
right in suggesting a parody on *The
Statutes of the Night* (1595), a clause or
two is worth quoting for its own sake;
e.g. '22. No man shall blow any horn
in the night, within this citie, or
whistle after the hour of nyne of the
clock in the night, under paine of
imprisonment. . . . 25. No hammer-
man, as a smith, a pewterer, a founder, and all artificers making great
sound shall worke after the houre of

nyne at night. . . . 30. No man shall,
after the houre of nyne at night, keepe
any rule, whereby any suche suddaine
outcry be made in the still of the
night, as making any affray, or
beating his wyfe or servaunt, or
singing, or revyling in his house, to the
disturbaunce of his neighbours.'

68-70. *the ewe . . . bleats*] This sounds
proverbial, though Tilley does not
include it.

73. *present*] represent. Not a blunder;
cf. *2H4*, v.ii.79—'The image of the
King whom I *presented*'.

77. *statutes*] Q reads *statutes*, F
Statues. If Shakespeare wrote *statutes*,

the Prince be willing, for indeed the watch ought
to offend no man, and it is an offence to stay a man
against his will.   80

Verg. By'r lady, I think it be so.

Dog. Ha, ah ha! Well, masters, good night: and there
be any matter of weight chances, call up me: keep
your fellows' counsels and your own, and good
night. Come, neighbour.   85

Sec. Watch. Well, masters, we hear our charge: let us go
sit here upon the church-bench till two, and then all
to bed.

Dog. One word more, honest neighbours. I pray you
watch about Signior Leonato's door, for the   90
wedding being there tomorrow, there is a great
coil tonight. Adieu! Be vigitant, I beseech you.

Exeunt [Dogberry and Verges].

Enter BORACHIO *and* CONRADE.

Bora. What, Conrade!

Sec. Watch. [*Aside.*] Peace! Stir not.

Bora. Conrade, I say!   95

Con. Here, man, I am at thy elbow.

Bora. Mass, and my elbow itched; I thought there

---

86. *Sec. Watch.*] *Rowe; Watch QF.*   92. S.D.] *Dogberry and Verges/Pope; not in*
QF.   94. *Sec. Watch.*] *This edn; Watch QF.*   S.D.] *Rowe (after* not); *not in*
QF.

F's reading would be either mere
error (though felicitous) or intentional amendment, authoritative only
if Shakespeare had approved the
change. If Shakespeare wrote *statues*,
Q's compositor might set *statutes* as the
expected word (as the compositors of
F2 did, despite the *statues* before their
eyes in F1). F's compositor generally
follows his Q copy faithfully in this
play; his change is unlikely to be
made on his own initiative. It must
arise from a happy fluke, or from
stage practice known to whoever
prepared Q's text for F. But tempting
as F's reading is, Q's is by no means
certainly wrong.

83–4. *keep . . . own*] This is part of

the oath of a grand-juryman—'The
King's counsel your fellows and your
own you shall observe and keep secret'.
There is also a proverbial parallel—
'The counsel thou wouldst have an-
other keep, first keep thyself' (Tilley
C682).

92. *coil*] hubbub.

97. *Mass*] by the Mass. Earle's
Microcosmographie describes 'A Blunt
Man' who 'sweares olde out of date
innocent othes, as by the *Masse*, by our
Ladie, and such like'.

my elbow itched] An omen of uncertain
significance,   generally   warning
against doubtful company. Tilley E98
gives as proverbial 'My elbow itched,
I must change my bedfellow'.

would a scab follow.

Con. I will owe thee an answer for that: and now forward with thy tale.   100

Bora. Stand thee close then under this penthouse, for it
drizzles rain, and I will, like a true drunkard, utter
all to thee.

Sec. Watch. [*Aside.*] Some treason, masters; yet stand
close.   105

Bora. Therefore know, I have earned of Don John a
thousand ducats.

Con. Is it possible that any villainy should be so dear?

Bora. Thou shouldst rather ask if it were possible any
villainy should be so rich; for when rich villains   110
have need of poor ones, poor ones may make what
price they will.

Con. I wonder at it.

Bora. That shows thou art unconfirmed. Thou knowest
that the fashion of a doublet, or a hat, or a cloak, is 115
nothing to a man.

Con. Yes, it is apparel.

Bora. I mean, the fashion.

Con. Yes, the fashion is the fashion.

Bora. Tush! I may as well say the fool's the fool. But 120
seest thou not what a deformed thief this fashion is?

Sec. Watch. [*Aside.*] I know that Deformed; a has been a

---

104. *Sec. Watch.*] *This edn; Watch QF.*   S.D.] *Johnson; not in QF.*   122. *Sec.*
Watch.] *This edn; Watch QF.*   S.D.] *Capell subst.; not in QF.*

98. *scab*] Punning on *scab* as rogue,
the same quibble as in *Cor.*, i.i. 162–4
—'What's the matter, you dissentious
rogues,/That, rubbing the poor *itch* of
your opinion,/Make yourselves *scabs*?'

101. *penthouse*] shed or sloping
porch.

102. *true drunkard*] Borachio alludes
both to his name (see *Dramatis Personæ*,
notes) and to the proverb *in vino veritas*,
wine brings out the truth.

114–38. *Thou knowest . . . the fashion*]
'Borachio's elaborate introduction to
his story . . . seems closely linked with
the theme of "errors"—in his case
always coupled with dissimulation

. . .: here he dwells on the difference
between the form of the outer clothing
. . . and that of its wearer, . . . and
recounts Don John's plot in which
deceit worked upon disguise to produce error' (Craik, p. 304). '"Fashions
are always changing—they have no
constancy. But men are even less
constant than the fashion." He is
leading up to his statement that
Claudio has been suddenly transformed from Hero's lover to her enemy'
(Kittredge).

114. *unconfirmed*] inexperienced.

116. *nothing to a man*] quite different
from the actual man himself.

vile thief this seven year; a goes up and down like a
gentleman: I remember his name.

Bora. Didst thou not hear somebody?   125

Con. No, 'twas the vane on the house.

Bora. Seest thou not, I say, what a deformed thief this
fashion is, how giddily a turns about all the hot
bloods between fourteen and five-and-thirty, sometimes fashioning them like Pharaoh's soldiers in the   130
reechy painting, sometime like god Bel's priests in
the old church-window, sometime like the shaven
Hercules in the smirched worm-eaten tapestry,
where his codpiece seems as massy as his club?

Con. All this I see, and I see that the fashion wears out   135
more apparel than the man. But art not thou thy-
self giddy with the fashion too, that thou hast shifted
out of thy tale into telling me of the fashion?

Bora. Not so, neither; but know that I have tonight
wooed Margaret, the Lady Hero's gentlewoman,   140

---

123. year] *Q;* yeares *F.*   124. I] *Q corr., F; not in Q uncorr.*   135. and I]
Q; and *F.*

129–34. *sometimes . . . club*] References to *the reechy painting* and *the old
church-window* sound familiar and
recognizable. They may derive from
images lodged in Shakespeare's mind
from representations he had seen.
Halliwell mentions an inventory of
hangings at Kenilworth Castle in
1588, including 'six peeces of the
historie of Hercules'. But nothing can
be proved, and the allusions may
simply be general ones.

130. *Pharaoh's soldiers*] Pharaoh,
King of Egypt, pursuing the escaping
Israelites, was drowned with his
soldiers in the Red Sea (Exodus XIV.
23–8).

131. *reechy*] smoke-grimed, dis-
coloured.

god Bel's priests] Probably an allusion
to the overthrow of the priests of Bel
by Daniel in the reign of King Cyrus
of Persia, told in the story 'Bel and the
Dragon', part of the apocryphal *Book
of Daniel* in the Bible. They were slain

by the King when Daniel revealed
that they were imposing a false god on
the people.

132–3. *shaven Hercules*] The allusion
has not been traced. It seems unlikely
to refer to Hercules in the house of
Omphale, dressed as a woman and set
to spin with her maids (see II.i.236–7,
note), for Borachio's Hercules is in
man's dress with a club. Warburton
suggested that the reference might
really be to Samson, his locks shorn by
Delilah, since some Christian writers
identified the two heroes. But as the
Hercules–Omphale story seems ex-
cluded by the male garments, the
Samson one seems equally so by the
difference of names and the fact that
Samson's weapon was the jawbone of
an ass.

134. *codpiece*] projecting forepiece of
men's breeches.

137–8. *shifted out*] Pun on changing
out of one's *shift*, shirt.

by the name of Hero; she leans me out at her mistress' chamber-window, bids me a thousand times
good night—I tell this tale vilely—I should first
tell thee how the Prince, Claudio, and my master,
planted and placed and possessed by my master   145
Don John, saw afar off in the orchard this amiable
encounter.

Con. And thought they Margaret was Hero?

Bora. Two of them did, the Prince and Claudio, but the
devil my master knew she was Margaret; and partly   150
by his oaths, which first possessed them, partly by
the dark night, which did deceive them, but chiefly
by my villainy, which did confirm any slander that
Don John had made, away went Claudio enraged;
swore he would meet her as he was appointed next   155
morning at the temple, and there, before the whole
congregation, shame her with what he saw o'er-
night, and send her home again without a husband.

Sec. Watch. We charge you in the Prince's name, stand!

First Watch. Call up the right Master Constable; we   160
have here recovered the most dangerous piece of
lechery that ever was known in the commonwealth.

Sec. Watch. And one Deformed is one of them; I know
him, a wears a lock.

Con. Masters, masters—   165

148. they] *Q;* thy *F.*   159. *Sec. Watch.*] *This edn; Watch* 1 *QF.*   160. *First
Watch.*] *This edn; Watch* 2 *QF.*   163. *Sec. Watch.*] *This edn; Watch* 1 *QF.*
165. masters—] *QF* (masters.), *Theobald.*

145. *possessed*] informed, instructed;
with, possibly, 'the sense of demoniac
possession, inasmuch as Borachio
refers in his next sentence to "the
devil, my master"' (Furness). In l.
151 the same implications are present.

160. *right*] An honorific intensive, as
in 'right honourable', 'right worship-
ful'.

164. *lock*] a lock of hair, sometimes
adorned with favours, and called a
love-lock. The custom supposedly came
from France; see *A Quippe for an
Vpstart Courtier* (Greene, *Works*, ed.
Grosart, xi.247)—'Will you be

Frenchefied with a *loue lock* downe to
your shoulders, wherein you may
weare your mistresse favour?' Writers
derided and denounced it: William
Prynne wrote a tract against *The
Unlovelyness of Love-locks*. Cf. Lyly,
Midas, III.ii.37–44 (*Works*, ed. Bond,
III.133)—'I instructed thee in the
phrases of our elegant occupation, as
"how sir will you be trimmed? wil you
haue . . . a lowe curle on your head
like a Bull, or dangling *lock*, like a
spaniel? . . . your *loue-locks* wreathed
with a silken twist, or shaggie to fal on
your shoulders?"'

First Watch. You'll be made bring Deformed forth, I
    warrant you.
Con. Masters—
[*Sec. Watch.*] Never speak, we charge you, let us obey you
    to go with us.   170
Bora. We are like to prove a goodly commodity, being
    taken up of these men's bills.
Con. A commodity in question, I warrant you. Come,
    we'll obey you.   *Exeunt.*

[SCENE IV]

Enter HERO *and* MARGARET *and* URSULA.

Hero. Good Ursula, wake my cousin Beatrice, and desire
    her to rise.
Urs. I will, lady.
Hero. And bid her come hither.
Urs. Well.   [*Exit.*]   5
Marg. Troth, I think your other rebato were better.
Hero. No, pray thee good Meg, I'll wear this.
Marg. By my troth 's not so good, and I warrant your
    cousin will say so.

166. *First Watch.*] *This edn; Watch 2 QF.*   168–9. Masters—/*Sec. Watch·*
Never] *This edn; Masters,—/First Watch.* Never *Theobald; Masters, neuer QF*
subst.

Scene IV

SCENE IV] *Capell; not in QF;* ACT IV *conj. Spedding.*   [*Location*] Leonato's
House. Pope; Hero's Apartment in Leonato's House. Theobald; not in QF.
1. Good] *Q corr., F;* God *Q uncorr.*   5. S.D.] *Hanmer; not in QF.*   7, 10,
16. Hero] *Q;* Bero *F.*

171–2. *commodity . . . bills*] A sequence
of quibbles. *Commodity* = (i) article;
(ii) parcel of goods obtained on credit
(or *taken up*) from a usurer, usually at
exorbitant interest. *Taken up* = (i)
apprehended; (ii) received on credit.
Bills = (i) weapons; (ii) bonds given
as security for goods.
    173. *in question*] A further quibble:
= (i) sought after; (ii) 'subject to
legal trial or examination' (Steevens).

Scene IV

Location] Hero's apartment in Leonato's house.
    6. *rebato*] kind of stiff collar or ruff.
The word seems to cover both the
ruff itself and its support, 'a linen-
covered, wire frame . . . pinned . . . to
the neck of the kirtle, and then bent
back to make the most becoming
frame to the face' (Linthicum, pp.
167–8).

Hero. My cousin's a fool, and thou art another; I'll wear   10
    none but this.

Marg. I like the new tire within excellently, if the hair
    were a thought browner; and your gown's a most
    rare fashion, i' faith. I saw the Duchess of Milan's
    gown that they praise so.   15

Hero. O, that exceeds, they say.

Marg. By my troth 's but a night-gown in respect of
    yours—cloth o' gold, and cuts, and laced with
    silver, set with pearls, down sleeves, side sleeves,
    and skirts, round underborne with a bluish tinsel: 20
    but for a fine, quaint, graceful, and excellent
    fashion, yours is worth ten on't.

Hero. God give me joy to wear it, for my heart is ex-
    ceeding heavy.

Marg. 'Twill be heavier soon by the weight of a man.   25

Hero. Fie upon thee, art not ashamed?

---

17. in] *F; it Q.*   18. o'] *QF* (a), *Capell.*

12. *tire*] the complete head-dress, including the false hair and ornaments attached. Satirists were scornful: a 'Ballet' by one William Bagnall (*Satirical Songs and Poems on Costume*, ed. F. W. Fairholt, Percy Society, 1849, p. 146) has, 'And at the devill's shopps you buy/A dress of powdered hayre,/On which your feathers flaunt and fly,/But I'de wish you have a care/Lest Lucifer's selfe, who is not prouder,/Do one day dresse up your haire with powder'.

14–15. *the Duchess . . . gown*] 'Queen Elizabeth possessed many garments of tinsel [silk interwoven with gold or silver thread] in silver and colour, and . . . Shakespeare probably found at Court his inspiration for the Duchess of Milan's gown' (Linthicum, p. 117).

16. *exceeds*] excels.

17. *night-gown*] 'Dressing-gown' is a modern equivalent, here and in *Mac.*, II.ii. 70–1—'Get on your *night-gown*, lest occasion call us/And show us to be watchers'.

18. *cloth o' gold*] 'In the drama cloth of gold and silver symbolize[s] wealth or extravagance in dress' (Linthicum, p. 114).

cuts] Edward Hall describes Henry VIII and his gentlemen in gala attire as 'apparayled all in one sewte of shorte garmentes, . . . with long sleves, all *cut* and lyned with clothe of gold' (Joseph Strutt, *Complete View of the Dress and Habits*, etc., ed. Planché, 1847, I. 195).

19. *down sleeves, side sleeves*] 'The down sleeves were long sleeves to the wrist; the side sleeves [were] the hanging . . . sleeves, open from the shoulder' (Linthicum, p. 173), and generally arranged to fall away from the shoulders down the back.

20. *round underborne*] Either, as Capell (*Notes*) suggests, the pearls 'had under them strips of "a bluish tinsel"', or the skirts were edged with tinsel to hold them away from the feet, as was fashionable.

23–4.] A presentiment of disaster.

Marg. Of what, lady? Of speaking honourably? Is not
marriage honourable in a beggar? Is not your lord
honourable without marriage? I think you would
have me say, saving your reverence, 'a husband'.   30
And bad thinking do not wrest true speaking, I'll
offend nobody. Is there any harm in 'the heavier
for a husband'? None, I think, and it be the right
husband, and the right wife; otherwise 'tis light,
and not heavy. Ask my Lady Beatrice else; here she   35
comes.

Enter BEATRICE.

Hero. Good morrow, coz.
Beat. Good morrow, sweet Hero.
Hero. Why, how now? Do you speak in the sick tune?
Beat. I am out of all other tune, methinks.   40
Marg. Clap's into 'Light o' Love'; that goes without a
burden. Do you sing it, and I'll dance it.
Beat. Ye light o' love with your heels! Then, if your

30. saving . . . 'a husband'] *Pope subst.; 'saving . . . a husband' Camb.;* sauing . . .
a husband *QF.*   32–3. 'the . . . husband'] *Capell;* the . . . husband *QF.*
41, 43. o'] *QF* (a), *Rowe 3.*

27–8. *Is . . . beggar*] '*Marriage is
honourable*' was proverbial (Tilley
M683), deriving from Hebrews XIII. 4
– 'Marriage is honourable in all' – and
the Book of Common Prayer—'holy
Matrimony . . . is an *honourable* estate'.

30. *saving your reverence*] A version of
salva reverentia—'respect for you being
preserved' (Kittredge). Margaret implies that Hero is so bashful that even
the mention of a husband needs an
apology.

31–2. *And . . . speaking*] Tilley L65
gives as proverbial 'There were no ill
language if it were not ill taken'.

40.] See III. ii. 14, note.

41. *Clap's . . . Love*] 'Change your
tune immediately into the joy of
loving' (Kittredge). This popular
dance and song tune is referred to in
Gent., I. ii. 83, with similar quibbling—
'*Julia*: Best sing it to the tune of
"*Light o' Love*".*/Lucetta*: It is too

heavy for so light a tune./*Julia*: Heavy!
belike it hath some burden, then';
also in *The Two Noble Kinsmen*, v. ii. 54
—'[He] gallops to the tune of "*Light
o' Love*"'. See Appendix VI.

41–2. *without a burden*] i.e. (*i*) lightly
(as the title suggests); (*ii*) without an
undersong (the bass part, for the
man's voice), since no men are present.
'The tune "Light o' Love" . . . used to
go *without a burden* and was considered
a "light" tune on that account' (E. W.
Naylor, *Shakespeare and Music*, 1931, p.
24); cf. the quotations in l. 41, note.

43. *Ye . . . heels*] Beatrice retorts with
a double-edged pun: *light o' love* here
= 'be *light*', play the wanton; and
with your heels implies 'light-heeled' or
'short-heeled', slang for unchaste; cf.
Henry Porter's *Two Angry Women of
Abington* (Malone Society, l. 740)—
'*Light aloue*, shorte *heeles*, mistress
Goursey'.

husband have stables enough, you'll see he shall
lack no barns.   45

Marg. O illegitimate construction! I scorn that with my
heels.

Beat. 'Tis almost five o'clock, cousin, 'tis time you were
ready. By my troth, I am exceeding ill—heigh-ho!

Marg. For a hawk, a horse, or a husband?   50

Beat. For the letter that begins them all, H.

Marg. Well, and you be not turned Turk, there's no
more sailing by the star.

Beat. What means the fool, trow?

Marg. Nothing I, but God send everyone their heart's   55
desire!

Hero. These gloves the Count sent me, they are an
excellent perfume.

Beat. I am stuffed, cousin, I cannot smell.

Marg. A maid, and stuffed! There's goodly catching of   60
cold.

44. see] *Q;* looke *F.*

45. *barns*] 'A quibble between *barns*,
repositories of corn, and *bairns*, the old
[and still northern] word for children'
(Johnson). The form *barne* is found in
All's W., I. iii. 26 ('*barnes* are blessings')
and *Wint.*, III. iii. 70 ('a very pretty
barne'), both times from illiterate men.

46–7. *scorn . . . heels*] reject that with
scorn—a proverbial expression; cf.
Mer. V., II. ii. 9–10—'*scorn* running
with thy *heels*'.

48. *five o'clock*] W.S.'s *The Puritaine
Widdow*, v. i. 5–6, provides a parallel
for this early marriage hour—'hie
thee, tis past *fiue*, bid them open the
Church dore, my sister is almost ready'.

49. *heigh-ho*] This exclamation, and
the following question from Margaret,
recall Beatrice's light-hearted reference to the old tag at II. i. 301. She
sighs in earnest, yet invites 'a
quibble upon "*heigh*", a cry of
encouragement to a horse or hawk'
(*NCS*)—see l. 50.

51.] *Ache* used to be pronounced
'aitch', which led to quibbles on the

letter H. John Heywood's *Proverbs and
Epigrams* includes one 'Of the letter H'
(Spenser Society, 1869, p. 111)—'H,
is worst among letters in the crosse
row, / For if thou find him other in
thine elbow, / In thine arm, or leg, in
any degree, / In thy head, or teeth, in
thy toe or knee, / Into what place so
euer H, may pike him, / Where euer
thou finde ache, thou shalt not like
him'.

52. *turned Turk*] become a renegade
(by reneging on your scorn of love).
The phrase was proverbial; Tilley
T609.

53. *the star*] the Pole Star.

54. *trow*] I wonder.

57–8. *gloves . . . perfume*] Perfumed
gloves were highly favoured. Stubbes's
Anatomie of Abuses (ed. F. J. Furnivall,
1877–9, p. 79) mentions women's
'*sweet-washed gloves*, imbrodered with
golde, siluer, and what not'.

59. *am stuffed*] have a cold in the
head.

60. *stuffed*] A bawdy quibble.

Beat. O, God help me, God help me, how long have you
    professed apprehension?

Marg. Ever since you left it. Doth not my wit become
    me rarely?   65

Beat. It is not seen enough, you should wear it in your
    cap. By my troth, I am sick.

Marg. Get you some of this distilled *carduus benedictus*,
    and lay it to your heart; it is the only thing for a
    qualm.   70

Hero. There thou prick'st her with a thistle.

Beat. Benedictus! Why *benedictus*? You have some moral
    in this *benedictus*.

Marg. Moral? No, by my troth I have no moral mean-
    ing, I meant plain holy-thistle. You may think per-   75
    chance that I think you are in love, nay by'r lady
    I am not such a fool to think what I list, nor I list
    not to think what I can, nor indeed I cannot think,
    if I would think my heart out of thinking, that you
    are in love, or that you will be in love, or that you   80
    can be in love. Yet Benedick was such another and
    now is he become a man: he swore he would never
    marry, and yet now in despite of his heart he eats
    his meat without grudging: and how you may be
    converted I know not, but methinks you look with   85
    your eyes as other women do.

62–5.] See III.ii.14, note.

63. *apprehension*] quickness in the
uptake.

68. *carduus benedictus*] The 'blessed'
or 'holy thistle' was held to be a cure
for all afflictions: '*Carduus benedictus* or
blessed thistell, so worthily named for
the vertues that it hath, . . . may
worthily be called ⌐*Benedictus* or
Omnimorbia, that is, a salue for euery
sore' (Thomas Cogan, *Haven of Health*,
1574, quoted by Furness). W. L.
Rushton, *Shakespeare Illustrated by Old
Authors* (1887, p. 35) cites *The Garde-
ners Labyrinth* (1594) as crediting it
with curing 'perillous diseases of the
heart'. Gerard's *Herball* (ed. 1633,
pp. 1171–2) omits this significant

power but mentions many others,
against pestilence, fever, giddiness,
poisons, deafness, bitings of mad dogs,
etc., etc. 'The distilled water thereof
is of lesse vertue' but doubtless, as
Margaret says, 'the only thing for a
qualm'.

72. *moral*] hidden meaning.

75–81.] Q's light punctuation
(preserved here) allows this to be very
expressive of Margaret's 'pace' of
tongue (l. 87).

83–4. *in despite . . . grudging*] despite
his resolution to be heart-whole, he
has now become a normal man and
readily eats the diet (of food, and love)
before him.

Beat. What pace is this that thy tongue keeps?
Marg. Not a false gallop.

Enter URSULA.

Urs. Madam, withdraw! The Prince, the Count, Signior Benedick, Don John, and all the gallants of the   90
town are come to fetch you to church.
Hero. Help to dress me, good coz, good Meg, good
Ursula.   [*Exeunt.*]

[SCENE V]

Enter LEONATO, *and the Constable* [DOGBERRY] *and the Headborough* [VERGES].

Leon. What would you with me, honest neighbour?
Dog. Marry, sir, I would have some confidence with
you, that decerns you nearly.
Leon. Brief, I pray you, for you see it is a busy time with
me.   5

93. S.D.] *Rowe; not in QF.*

Scene v

SCENE v] *Capell; not in QF.*   [*Location*] *another Apartment in* Leonato's *House.*
Theobald; *not in QF.*   S.D. *Dogberry, Verges*] *Rowe; not in QF.*   2. Dog.] *QF*
(*Const. Dog.*), Rowe subst. (*so subst. to l. 43*).

88. *false gallop*] artificial canter,
forced burst of speed. Touchstone
calls his rhymes 'the very *false gallop* of
verses' (*AYL,* III.ii.103); see also
Nashe's *Terrors of the Night*
(McKerrow, I.368)—'I haue rid a
false gallop these three or foure pages;
now I care not if I breathe mee, and
walke soberly and demurely half a
dozen turnes, like a graue Citizen
going about to take the ayre'.

1. *honest neighbour*] 'Throughout ...,
the noblemen treat Dogberry as
humanely as Shakespeare does'
(Vickers, p. 196).

2. *confidence*] For similar misuse see
Rom., II.iv.144—'I desire some *con-*
fidence with you'; and *Wiv.,* I.iv.172—
'I will tell your worship more ... the
next time we have *confidence*'. *OED*
gives all three passages under '*Con-*
fidence: the confiding of private or
secret matters', but adds that in these
cases 'some take *confidence* as a
humorous blunder for *conference*'. They
are certainly meant so, but in all three
the idea is of confidential talk, so the
word is not entirely 'off the matter'.

Scene v

Location] Leonato's house.
S.D. *Headborough*] parish officer,
local constable.

Dog. Marry, this it is, sir.

Verg. Yes, in truth it is, sir.

Leon. What is it, my good friends?

Dog. Goodman Verges, sir, speaks a little off the
matter: an old man, sir, and his wits are not so   10
blunt as, God help, I would desire they were, but, in
faith, honest as the skin between his brows.

Verg. Yes, I thank God, I am as honest as any man
living, that is an old man, and no honester than I.

Dog. Comparisons are odorous: *palabras*, neighbour   15
Verges.

Leon. Neighbours, you are tedious.

Dog. It pleases your worship to say so, but we are the
poor Duke's officers; but truly, for mine own part, if
I were as tedious as a king, I could find in my heart   20
to bestow it all of your worship.

Leon. All thy tediousness on me, ah?

Dog. Yea, and 'twere a thousand pound more than 'tis,
for I hear as good exclamation on your worship as of

---

7. *Verg.*] *QF* (*Headb.*), *Rowe* (*so subst. to l. 29*).   9. off] *QF* (of), *Steevens '93*,
conj. Capell.   23. pound] *Q*; times *F*.

9. *Goodman Verges*] 'The fine comic
acting of little Keeley as Verges
"culminated", we are told, "when his
asinine chief patted him on the head,
and he at first bent under the honour,
and then became the taller for it,
gazing into his patron's face with an
expression of fatuous contentment
perfectly marvellous" (Walter Goodman, *The Keeleys on the Stage and at
Home*, 1895, p. 163, quoting from an
anonymous article attributed to
Dickens)' (A. C. Sprague, *Shakespeare
and the Actors*, 1944, p. 15).

12. *honest . . . brows*] A proverbial
phrase; Tilley S506. In the proverb
brows seems to mean *eyebrows*, the skin
between which (and not that of the
forehead) was taken to indicate
honesty. In V. S. Lean's collection of
Proverbs, II.126, occur the lines,
'Trust not the man whose eyebrows
meet,/For in his heart you'll find
deceit'.

15. *Comparisons are odorous*] Cf. *Sir
Gyles Goosecappe*, IV.ii.45 (Bullen's
Old English Plays, III.65)—'*Goosecappe*:
Be Caparisons odious, sir *Cut*; what,
like flowers?/*Rudsbie*: O asse they be
odorous'.

palabras] Variants of the Spanish
pocas palabras (= few words) were
popular tags; e.g. Kyd, *Spanish
Tragedy*, III.xiv.118 (*Works*, ed. Boas,
p. 78)—'*Pocas Palabras*, milde as the
lambe'; *Shr.*, Induction, i.5—'*paucas
pallabris*; let the world slide'; and
Middleton, *The Roaring Girl*, v.i.318
(*Works*, ed. Bullen, IV.135)—'disgrace
me not; *pacus palabros*, . . . farewell'.

18–19. *the poor Duke's*] A similar
transposition occurs in *Meas.*, II.i.46–
7—'I am *the poor Duke's* constable'.

21. *of*] See Abbott § 175 for *on* and
of interchanged.

24. *exclamation*] Dogberry probably
means 'acclamation'. What he says
gives just the wrong sense: *exclamation*

any man in the city, and though I be but a poor   25
man, I am glad to hear it.

Verg. And so am I.

Leon. I would fain know what you have to say.

Verg. Marry, sir, our watch tonight, excepting your
worship's presence, ha' ta'en a couple of as arrant   30
knaves as any in Messina.

Dog. A good old man, sir, he will be talking; as they
say, 'When the age is in, the wit is out', God help us,
it is a world to see! Well said, i' faith, neighbour
Verges; well, God's a good man, and two men ride   35
of a horse, one must ride behind. An honest soul,
i' faith, sir, by my troth he is, as ever broke bread;
but God is to be worshipped, all men are not alike,
alas, good neighbour!

Leon. Indeed, neighbour, he comes too short of you.   40

Dog. Gifts that God gives.

Leon. I must leave you.

Dog. One word, sir: our watch, sir, have indeed compre-
hended two aspicious persons, and we would have
them this morning examined before your worship.   45

Leon. Take their examination yourself, and bring it me;
I am now in great haste, as it may appear unto you.

Dog. It shall be suffigance.

---

30. ha'] *Q* (ha); haue *F*.   32. talking;] *Capell;* talking *QF*.   47. it] *Q;*
not in *F*.   48. *Dog.*] *Q (Constable),* F *(Const.),* Rowe.   suffigance.] *Rowe;*
suffigance. *(exit QF subst.*

= loud complaint; cf. *John,* ii. i. 558—
'we shall stop her *exclamation*'; and *R3,*
iv. iv. 153—'Thus will I drown your
exclamations'.

33. *When . . . out*] 'When ale is in,
wit is out' was proverbial; Tilley
W471.

34. *it is . . . see*] Proverbial; Tilley
W878.

35. *God's . . . man*] Proverbial;
Tilley G195. This odd expression
occurs, for instance, in *Lusty Juventus*
(Hazlitt's *Dodsley,* ii. 73)—'He will say
that *God is a good man,*/He can make
him no better, and say the best he
can'. W. C. Hazlitt in his *English*

Proverbs comments, 'In Germany they
have a similar saying—and it seems to
be used in this sense: God is a good
person, he lets things take their
course'. Burton's *Anatomy of Melancholy,* Pt iii, Sect. iv, Mem. i, Subs.
iii (Bohn edn, 1927, iii. 412),
describes certain devil-worshippers
who 'allege this reason in so doing:
God is a good man and will do no harm,
but the Devil is bad, and must be
pleased, lest he hurt them'.

35-6. *and . . . behind*] Proverbial;
Tilley T638. *And* = if.

36-7. *honest . . . bread*] Proverbial;
Tilley M68.

Leon. Drink some wine ere you go. Fare you well!

[*Enter a* Messenger.]

Mess. My lord, they stay for you to give your daughter   50
  to her husband.

Leon. I'll wait upon them; I am ready.   *Exit* [*with Messenger*].

Dog. Go, good partner, go, get you to Francis Seacoal,
  bid him bring his pen and inkhorn to the gaol: we
  are now to examination these men.   55

Verg. And we must do it wisely.

Dog. We will spare for no wit, I warrant you; here's that
  shall drive some of them to a non-come. Only get
  the learned writer to set down our excommunica-
  tion, and meet me at the gaol.   *Exeunt.*   60

---

49. S.D.] *Rowe; not in QF.*   52. S.D.] *Rowe (Ex. Leon.), Johnson subst.; exit
(after l. 48) QF subst.*   55. examination these] *Q; examine those F.*   60.
S.D.] *F; not in Q.*

53. *Francis*] See III. iii. 11, note.

56–7. *And . . . wit*] Tilley C582
gives as proverbial 'He that is wise in
his own conceit is a fool'.

58. *non-come*] *non plus*, bewilderment

(confused by Dogberry with *non compos*, of unsound mind), perhaps combined with the idea of not coming,
impasse.

ACT IV

[SCENE I]

Enter Prince [DON PEDRO], [DON JOHN *the*] *Bastard*, LEONATO,
FRIAR [FRANCIS], CLAUDIO, BENEDICK, HERO, *and*
BEATRICE [, *and* Attendants].

Leon. Come, Friar Francis, be brief: only to the plain
form of marriage, and you shall recount their particular duties afterwards.

Friar. You come hither, my lord, to marry this lady?

Claud. No.   5

Leon. To be married to her, friar: you come to marry
her.

Friar. Lady, you come hither to be married to this
Count?

Hero. I do.   10

Friar. If either of you know any inward impediment why
you should not be conjoined, I charge you on your
souls to utter it.

Claud. Know you any, Hero?

Hero. None, my lord.   15

Friar. Know you any, Count?

Leon. I dare make his answer, None.

Claud. O, what men dare do! What men may do! What

ACT IV

Scene 1

ACT IV] F (*Actus Quartus.*); *not in* Q.   SCENE I] Rowe; *not in* QF.   [*Location*]
A Church. *Pope; not in* QF.   S.D. *Don Pedro*] Rowe; *not in* QF.   *Don John*]
Rowe; *not in* QF.   *the Bastard*] QF *subst.* (*Bastard*), *Kittredge.*   *Francis*] *Dyce;*
not in QF.   *and Attendants*] *White; and others Dyce; not in* QF.   4. *Friar.*] QF
(*Fran.*), *Rowe.*   lady?] *Rowe 3; lady.* QF *subst.*   6. her, friar:] *Rowe 3;*
her; *Frier* QF.   9. Count?] *Rowe 3;* counte. QF *subst.*

Scene 1

Location] A church.   the English marriage service.
  11–13.] Close to, but not exactly,   18–19.] Unconsciously ironic.

172

men daily do, not knowing what they do!
Bene. How now? Interjections? Why then, some be of   20
    laughing, as ah, ha, he!
Claud. Stand thee by, friar. Father, by your leave:
    Will you with free and unconstrained soul
    Give me this maid, your daughter?
Leon. As freely, son, as God did give her me.   25
Claud. And what have I to give you back whose worth
    May counterpoise this rich and precious gift?
D. Pedro. Nothing, unless you render her again.
Claud. Sweet Prince, you learn me noble thankfulness.
    There, Leonato, take her back again.   30
    Give not this rotten orange to your friend;
    She's but the sign and semblance of her honour.
    Behold how like a maid she blushes here!
    O, what authority and show of truth
    Can cunning sin cover itself withal!   35
    Comes not that blood as modest evidence
    To witness simple virtue? Would you not swear,
    All you that see her, that she were a maid,
    By these exterior shows? But she is none:
    She knows the heat of a luxurious bed: 40
    Her blush is guiltiness, not modesty.
Leon. What do you mean, my lord?

19. not . . . do!] *Q; not in F.*   21. ah] *Q;* ha *F.*   28. *D. Pedro.*] *Q (Princn),*
F (Prin.), Rowe (Pedro), Capell (D. Pe.); so subst. throughout scene.

19. *not . . . do*] Omitted in F perhaps because the compositor overlooked the fourth phrase ending in 'do'.
    20–1. *Interjections . . . he*] An echo of William Lyly's *Short Introduction of Grammar* (1538), Sig. C. viiiᵛ—'An Interjection . . . betokenѕth a sudden passion of the minde. . . . Some are of . . . laughing: as Ha, ha, he'. Allusions are frequent; e.g. Lyly's *Endimion*, III. iii. 5 (*Works*, ed. Bond, III. 42)—'An interiection, whereof some are of mourning: as *eho, vah*'.
    29–30.] Claudio's switch from apparent graciousness to aggressive hostility is as histrionic as it is distasteful. 'Even at this crisis Claudio

takes his cue from the Prince. This preconcerted effect agrees well with the theatricality of Claudio's whole performance' (Warwick).
    29. *learn me*] *Learn* for 'teach', now a vulgarism, was then acceptable. Caliban uses both verbs in the same sense—'You *taught* me language and my profit on't/Is, I know how to curse. The red plague rid you/For *learning* me your language!' (*Tp.*, I. ii. 363–5).
    33.] Tilley B480 gives as proverbial 'Blushing is virtue's colour'.
    36. *modest evidence*] evidence of modesty.
    40. *luxurious*] lascivious.

Claud. Not to be married, not to knit my soul
    To an approved wanton.
Leon. Dear my lord, if you, in your own proof,   45
    Have vanquish'd the resistance of her youth,
    And made defeat of her virginity—
Claud. I know what you would say: if I have known her,
    You will say she did embrace me as a husband,
    And so extenuate the 'forehand sin.   50
    No, Leonato.
    I never tempted her with word too large,
    But, as a brother to his sister, show'd
    Bashful sincerity and comely love.
Hero. And seem'd I ever otherwise to you?   55
Claud. Out on thee, seeming! I will write against it.
    You seem to me as Dian in her orb,
    As chaste as is the bud ere it be blown;
    But you are more intemperate in your blood
    Than Venus, or those pamper'd animals   60
    That rage in savage sensuality.
Hero. Is my lord well that he doth speak so wide?
Leon. Sweet Prince, why speak not you?
D. Pedro.   What should I speak?
    I stand dishonour'd, that have gone about
    To link my dear friend to a common stale.   65

43-4. Not . . . wanton.] *as Dyce; lines ending . . .* married, . . . wanton. *QF.*
47. virginity—] *QF* (virginitie.), *Rowe.*   50-1.] *as Pope; one line, QF.*   53.
show'd] *QF* (shewed), *Rowe.*   56. thee,] *Collier;* thee *QF;* thy *Pope;* thee!
White, conj. Seymour; the *Knight.*

---

44. *approved*] proven, as in l. 300.
Usually the word means approved in
the modern sense, as at II.i.356.

45. *Dear*] A disyllable.

proof] test or trial (of Hero).

50. *extenuate . . . sin*] lessen or excuse
the sin of anticipating marriage.

52. *large*] broad, as in II.iii.191.

56.] The sense seems to be, 'Shame
on you, for thus pretending virtue! I
will denounce the pretence.'

57. *Dian in her orb*] Diana, the moon
(*orb*), goddess of chastity.

58. *chaste . . . bud*] This simile suggested itself after the mention of
Diana, whose buds (those of the
flower, Agnus Castus) were reputed
to preserve chastity. See *MND*,
IV.i.71-2 (and H. F. Brooks's note in
the New Arden edition)—'*Dian's bud*
o'er Cupid's flower / Hath such force
and blessed power'. Steevens quotes
Æmilius Macer's *Herball* (*c.* 1530), Sig.
Aiv–iir, about the *Agnus castus or
Chaste Tree*, to the effect that 'the
vertue of this herbe is, to kepe men
and women chaste . . . [for it]
destroyeth ye fowle lust of lechery'.

65. *stale*] wanton, as in II.ii.25.

Leon. Are these things spoken, or do I but dream?
D. John. Sir, they are spoken, and these things are true.
Bene. This looks not like a nuptial!
Hero.   'True'? O God!
Claud. Leonato, stand I here?
    Is this the Prince? Is this the Prince's brother?   70
    Is this face Hero's? Are our eyes our own?
Leon. All this is so, but what of this, my lord?
Claud. Let me but move one question to your daughter,
    And by that fatherly and kindly power
    That you have in her, bid her answer truly.   75
Leon. I charge thee do so, as thou art my child.
Hero. O God defend me, how am I beset!
    What kind of catechizing call you this?
Claud. To make you answer truly to your name.
Hero. Is it not Hero? Who can blot that name   80
    With any just reproach?
Claud.   Marry, that can Hero;
    Hero itself can blot out Hero's virtue.
    What man was he talk'd with you yesternight,
    Out at your window betwixt twelve and one?
    Now if you are a maid, answer to this.   85
Hero. I talk'd with no man at that hour, my lord.
D. Pedro. Why, then are you no maiden. Leonato,
    I am sorry you must hear: upon mine honour,
    Myself, my brother, and this grieved Count
    Did see her, hear her, at that hour last night,   90
    Talk with a ruffian at her chamber-window,

67. *D. John.*] *QF* (Bastard) *subst.*, Rowe (*John*), Capell (*D. Jo.*).   68. 'True'?]
F3 (True!), *Kittredge* ('True!'), *this edn;* True, *QF1–2.*   76. so] *Q; not in F.*
86. *Hero*] *Q corr., F; Bero Q uncorr.*   87. are you] *Q;* you are *F.*

69–71.] The rhetorical questions
suggest a Claudio over-conscious of
himself and his part.
    74. *kindly*] natural. See I.i.25, note.
    78–9.] 'What is your name?' is the
opening of the church catechism, the
questions and answers testing the
believer's faith. Hero's name stood for
loyal love, after the classical Hero's
love for Leander.

    82. *Hero itself*] the very name, Hero
    87. *Why, . . . maiden*] An inevitable
conclusion, since Claudio framed his
question so as to force Hero into what
must seem either a falsehood or a
confession of guilt.
    89. *this grieved Count*] However
regrettable his conduct, Claudio is at
least meant to show great distress; see
ll. 152–4.

Who hath indeed, most like a liberal villain,
Confess'd the vile encounters they have had
A thousand times in secret.
D. John. Fie, fie, they are not to be nam'd, my lord,   95
Not to be spoke of!
There is not chastity enough in language
Without offence to utter them. Thus, pretty lady,
I am sorry for thy much misgovernment.
Claud. O Hero! What a Hero hadst thou been,   100
If half thy outward graces had been plac'd
About thy thoughts and counsels of thy heart!
But fare thee well, most foul, most fair! Farewell,
Thou pure impiety and impious purity!
For thee I'll lock up all the gates of love,   105
And on my eyelids shall conjecture hang,
To turn all beauty into thoughts of harm,
And never shall it more be gracious.
Leon. Hath no man's dagger here a point for me?

                        [Hero swoons.]

Beat. Why, how now, cousin! Wherefore sink you down? 110
D. John. Come, let us go. These things, come thus to light,
Smother her spirits up.

             [Exeunt Don Pedro, Don John, and Claudio.]

Bene. How doth the lady?
Beat.   Dead, I think. Help, uncle!

95. *D. John.*] *QF* (*Iohn*), *Capell* (*D. Jo.*).   nam'd] *QF* (named), *Rowe*.
96. spoke] *Q;* spoken *F*.   101. plac'd] *QF* (placed), *Rowe*.   109. S.D.]
Hanmer; not in QF.   111. *D. John.*] *QF* (*Bastard*) *subst., Rowe* (*John*), *Capell*
(*D. Jo.*).   112. S.D.] *Rowe; not in QF*.

92. *liberal*] 'frank beyond honesty or
decency. Free of tongue' (Johnson).
93. *Confess'd*] The implausibility of
this confession is masked by the fact
that it takes place offstage.
99. *misgovernment*] misconduct.
100. *What a Hero*] Not 'What a hero'
but 'What an embodiment of loyal
love'.
103. *most foul, most fair*] Tilley F29
gives as proverbial 'Fair without but
foul within'.
106. *conjecture*] doubt, suspicion, as
in *Wint.*, II.i.176–8—'their famili-

arity,/Which was as gross as ever
touched *conjecture,*/That lack'd sight
only'.
113. *How . . . lady*] '[Benedick]
makes an important decision when he
does not leave the church with
Claudio, Don Pedro, and the Bastard,
as might be expected. He chooses, instead, to remain behind with Hero,
Leonato, the Friar, and Beatrice'
(Riverside, p. 329).
113–14.] For an odd bit of 19th-
century stage-business see Introduction, p. 36, n. 3.

Hero! Why, Hero! Uncle! Signior Benedick! Friar!

Leon. O Fate, take not away thy heavy hand!   115
Death is the fairest cover for her shame
That may be wish'd for.

Beat.   How now, cousin Hero?

Friar. Have comfort, lady.

Leon. Dost thou look up?

Friar.   Yea, wherefore should she not?

Leon. Wherefore? Why, doth not every earthly thing   120
Cry shame upon her? Could she here deny
The story that is printed in her blood?
Do not live, Hero, do not ope thine eyes;
For did I think thou wouldst not quickly die,
Thought I thy spirits were stronger than thy shames, 125
Myself would on the rearward of reproaches
Strike at thy life. Griev'd I, I had but one?
Chid I for that at frugal Nature's frame?
O, one too much by thee! Why had I one?
Why ever wast thou lovely in my eyes?   130
Why had I not with charitable hand
Took up a beggar's issue at my gates,
Who smirched thus, and mir'd with infamy,
I might have said, 'No part of it is mine;
This shame derives itself from unknown loins'?   135

---

120. Why, doth] *Theobald;* why doth *QF subst.*   126. rearward] *Q* (rereward) *;*
reward *F.*   127. Griev'd] *Q* (Grieued), *F.*   133. smirched] *Q; smeered F.*
mir'd] *Q* (mired), *F.*

119. *Yea, . . . not*] The Friar has had
no chance yet to assert the spiritual
authority he shows later, yet these
few words are significant of not only a
physical but also a religious looking
up. Leonato's 'every *earthly* thing' unconsciously confirms the different
values here implied.

120–43.] Leonato's outburst differs
totally from the unquestioning faith
in Fenicia's virtue which in Bandello
her family maintains. The whole
speech, like those Leonato voices in
v. i, has a vehemence and drive which
foretell the impassioned style of the
later tragedies, a marked advance on

Old Capulet's outbursts in *Romeo and
Juliet.*

122.] = 'The story which her
blushes discover to be true' (Johnson).
The Friar, with more discernment,
sees in these 'blushing apparitions' the
story of Hero's innocence.

126. *reproaches*] Does he mean his
own? Or the world's? Probably his
own; he is too engulfed in his personal
anguish to place others' reactions
before it.

128. *frugal Nature's frame*] 'Nature's
frugality in framing' (Capell, *Notes*);
frame as in l. 189—'Whose spirits toil
in *frame* of villainies'.

But mine, and mine I lov'd, and mine I prais'd,
And mine that I was proud on—mine so much
That I myself was to myself not mine,
Valuing of her—why, she, O, she is fall'n
Into a pit of ink, that the wide sea   140
Hath drops too few to wash her clean again,
And salt too little which may season give
To her foul-tainted flesh!

Bene.   Sir, sir, be patient.
For my part I am so attir'd in wonder,
I know not what to say.   145

Beat. O, on my soul my cousin is belied!

Bene. Lady, were you her bedfellow last night?

Beat. No, truly, not; although until last night,
I have this twelvemonth been her bedfellow.

Leon. Confirm'd, confirm'd! O, that is stronger made   ᶜ 150
Which was before barr'd up with ribs of iron.
Would the two princes lie, and Claudio lie,
Who lov'd her so, that, speaking of her foulness,
Wash'd it with tears? Hence from her, let her die!

136. lov'd] *Q* (loued), *F.*   138. mine,] *Rowe;* mine: *QF.*   143. foul-tainted]
QF (*foule tainted*), *Dyce, conj. W. S. Walker.*   143–5. Sir, . . . say.] *as verse, Pope;*
as prose, QF. ·   144. attir'd] *QF* (attired), *Pope.*   148. truly, not;] *Rowe;*
truly, not *Q;* truly: not *F.*   152. two] *Q; not in F.*   153. lov'd] *Q* (loued), *F.*

138–9. *I myself . . . her*] in my own
eyes I counted for nothing, in comparison with the value I set on her.

143. *foul-tainted*] QF's 'foule tainted'
has no hyphen, but presumably the
words are linked not as two adjectives
(virtually tautological) but by the
intensification which *foul* (adverbially)
affords to the relatively mild *tainted*.

143–5. *Sir, . . . say*] QF print this as
prose, as also ll. 155–8. Q's compositor
seems to have found himself with more
text than expected to fit on this page
(Sig. G1ʳ). He saved two lines by
prosifying the verse in both places
(getting seven lines of verse into five of
prose), extended his page by two
extra lines, and so managed. F's
compositor followed Q. See pp. 76–7.

144. *attir'd in wonder*] A somewhat
similar figure occurs in ll. 174–5.
Furness (p. 206) gives several examples of moods conceived as figurative
dressings of man's spirit: the most
remarkable is, 'Was the hope drunk/
Wherein you dress'd yourelf?' (*Mac.*,
I. vii. 35–6).

148–9.] Why Beatrice was absent,
and why neither she nor Hero was in
their usual room, are questions which
the headlong rush of the plot ignores.

154. *Wash'd . . . tears*] For the
omitted nominative see Abbott § 399.
How the actor combines Claudio's
vindictive rhetoric with heartfelt
tears is his problem, but clearly
Claudio should appear not only
vengeful but anguished.

Friar. Hear me a little;   155
       For I have only been silent so long,
       And given way unto this course of fortune,
       By noting of the lady. I have mark'd
       A thousand blushing apparitions
       To start into her face, a thousand innocent shames   160
       In angel whiteness beat away those blushes,
       And in her eye there hath appear'd a fire
       To burn the errors that these princes hold
       Against her maiden truth. Call me a fool;
       Trust not my reading nor my observations,   165
       Which with experimental seal doth warrant
       The tenor of my book; trust not my age,
       My reverence, calling, nor divinity,
       If this sweet lady lie not guiltless here
       Under some biting error.

Leon.   Friar, it cannot be.   170
       Thou seest that all the grace that she hath left
       Is that she will not add to her damnation
       A sin of perjury: she not denies it.
       Why seek'st thou then to cover with excuse
       That which appears in proper nakedness?   175

Friar. Lady, what man is he you are accus'd of?

Hero. They know that do accuse me; I know none.
       If I know more of any man alive
       Than that which maiden modesty doth warrant,
       Let all my sins lack mercy! O my father,   180
       Prove you that any man with me convers'd
       At hours unmeet, or that I yesternight

155–8.] *as verse, Rowe* 3 (*three lines, ending* . . . long/. . . Fortune,/. . . mark'd),
Pope; . . . been/. . . unto/. . . fortune—/. . . mark'd *Globe; as prose, QF.*
158. lady.] *Pope subst.;* lady, *QF subst.;* lady *Boas.*   mark'd] *F2 subst.;* markt,
Q; markt. *F1.*   161. beat] *Q* (beate)*;* beare *F.*

155–8.] See ll. 143–5, note.
162–3. *fire . . . errors*] Alluding to the
burning of heretics.
166–7. *Which . . . book*] i.e. which
guarantees as true, by the confirmation of experience, what my reading
tells me.
171–3. *grace . . . perjury*] As befits the

church setting there are recurrent
motifs of religious concepts (*grace . . .
damnation . . . perjury*) and fundamental
spiritual values. The situation is far
more than a mere social crisis: it involves spiritual good and evil; cf. ll.
178–80.

    Maintain'd the change of words with any creature,
    Refuse me, hate me, torture me to death!
Friar. There is some strange misprision in the princes.   185
Bene. Two of them have the very bent of honour;
    And if their wisdoms be misled in this,
    The practice of it lives in John the bastard,
    Whose spirits toil in frame of villainies.
Leon. I know not. If they speak but truth of her,   190
    These hands shall tear her: if they wrong her honour,
    The proudest of them shall well hear of it.
    Time hath not yet so dried this blood of mine,
    Nor age so eat up my invention,
    Nor fortune made such havoc of my means,   195
    Nor my bad life reft me so much of friends,
    But they shall find, awak'd in such a kind,
    Both strength of limb and policy of mind,
    Ability in means and choice of friends,
    To quit me of them throughly.
Friar.   Pause awhile,   200
    And let my counsel sway you in this case.
    Your daughter here the princes left for dead,
    Let her awhile be secretly kept in,
    And publish it that she is dead indeed;
    Maintain a mourning ostentation,   205

---

202. princes left for dead,] *Theobald subst., Evans;* princesse (left for dead,) *QF subst.*

186. *have the very bent of*] are wholly
constituted of, disposed to.

188. *practice*] deceitful contrivance
(the frequent bad sense); cf. *Oth.*,
v.ii.292—'Fall'n in the *practice* of a
damned slave'.

   lives] is active.

194. *invention*] Four syllables: =
power to plan.

197. *kind*] *Kind* may be wrong: it
makes less sense than, say, 'cause',
and it jingles with *find* and *mind*. If
kind is correct, *such a kind* = such a
manner (as will quit me of them
thoroughly).

200. *throughly*] thoroughly.

202.] QF's 'the princesse (left for
dead,)' makes fair sense, though one
wonders whether the Friar would call
Hero 'Princess'. Capell (*Notes*) points
out that Claudio is included in the
'princes' of l. 185 and of v.i.262 and
Hero might be thought his equivalent.
Yet Claudio as a count seems of higher
status than Leonato as a gentleman.
Theobald amended QF and is generally followed.

205. *ostentation*] formal show (not in
a bad sense), as in *Ham.*, IV.v.209–11
—'his obscure funeral—/ . . . /No
noble rite, nor formal *ostentation*'.

And on your family's old monument
Hang mournful epitaphs, and do all rites
That appertain unto a burial.
Leon. What shall become of this? What will this do?
Friar. Marry, this well carried shall on her behalf   210
　　Change slander to remorse; that is some good:
　　But not for that dream I on this strange course,
　　But on this travail look for greater birth.
　　She dying, as it must be so maintain'd,
　　Upon the instant that she was accus'd,   215
　　Shall be lamented, pitied, and excus'd
　　Of every hearer; for it so falls out
　　That what we have we prize not to the worth
　　Whiles we enjoy it, but being lack'd and lost,
　　Why then we rack the value, then we find   220
　　The virtue that possession would not show us
　　Whiles it was ours: so will it fare with Claudio.
　　When he shall hear she died upon his words,
　　Th'idea of her life shall sweetly creep
　　Into his study of imagination,   225
　　And every lovely organ of her life
　　Shall come apparell'd in more precious habit,
　　More moving-delicate and full of life,
　　Into the eye and prospect of his soul
　　Than when she liv'd indeed: then shall he mourn—   230
　　If ever love had interest in his liver—

---

206. family's] *QF* (families) *subst., Rowe.*

206-7.] At important funerals friends would affix short poems to the hearse. Jonson's *Epitaph on the Countess of Pembroke*, which begins, 'Underneath this sable hearse/Lies the subject of all verse', was evidently meant to be so affixed. Middleton's *A Chaste Maid in Cheapside* (*Works*, ed. Bullen, v. 109) begins with a stage-direction— 'enter . . . the coffin of Moll, adorned with a garland of flowers, and *epitaphs* pinned on it'.

218-22. *what . . . ours*] A proverbial idea; Tilley W924.

220. *rack*] stretch to the utmost.

225. *study of imagination*] imaginative reflection.

226.] An odd expression; presumably = 'and every aspect of her beauty'.

227. *in . . . habit*] i.e. more richly adorned.

228. *moving-delicate*] i.e. touchingly graceful.

229.] He will see her in all he surveys.

231. *love . . . liver*] The Elizabethans often locate the seat of love in the liver. So in *Tw. N.*, II. iv. 100-1— 'their *love* may be call'd appetite—/

And wish he had not so accused her:
No, though he thought his accusation true.
Let this be so, and doubt not but success
Will fashion the event in better shape   235
Than I can lay it down in likelihood.
But if all aim but this be levell'd false,
The supposition of the lady's death
Will quench the wonder of her infamy:
And if it sort not well, you may conceal her,   240
As best befits her wounded reputation.
In some reclusive and religious life,
Out of all eyes, tongues, minds, and injuries.

Bene. Signior Leonato, let the friar advise you;
And though you know my inwardness and love   245
Is very much unto the Prince and Claudio,
Yet, by mine honour, I will deal in this
As secretly and justly as your soul
Should with your body.

Leon.   Being that I flow in grief,
The smallest twine may lead me.   250

Friar. 'Tis well consented. Presently away;
For to strange sores strangely they strain the cure.
Come, lady, die to live; this wedding-day

No motion of the *liver,* but the palate';
Wiv., II.i.104—'*Ford: Love* my wife?
Pistol: With *liver* burning hot'; and
Lyly, *Endimion,* I.iii.7–9 (*Works,* ed.
Bond, III.26)—'I brooke not this idle
humor of *loue,* it tickleth not my
liuer'.

234–6.] Follow my advice and do
not doubt that the outcome will turn
out better than whatever likelihood I
can now foretell.

237–9.] But should all the rest of my
plan miscarry, in this particular it
must succeed: her supposed death will
silence those who would gossip about
her shame.

237. *levell'd*] aimed, directed.

240. *sort*] turn out, as at v.iv.7.

242. *reclusive*] secluded.

245. *inwardness*] intimacy; this usage
is not found elsewhere in Shakespeare.
OED cites Pepys's *Diary,* 23 August
1668—'The Duke of York . . . did,
with much *inwardness,* tell me what
was doing'.

246. *Is*] Abbott § 336 illustrates
singular verbs after two or more
singular nouns as subject.

251–4.] The quatrain, as it were a
ritual close, marks a turning-point.
Prose follows and the tragic tension is
relaxed.

251. *Presently*] At once.

252.] A proverbial idea: 'A
desperate disease must have a desperate remedy' (Tilley D357).

Perhaps is but prolong'd; have patience and endure.

Exeunt [all but Benedick and Beatrice].

Bene. Lady Beatrice, have you wept all this while?   255

Beat. Yea, and I will weep a while longer.

Bene. I will not desire that.

Beat. You have no reason, I do it freely.

Bene. Surely I do believe your fair cousin is wronged.

Beat. Ah, how much might the man deserve of me that   260
would right her!

Bene. Is there any way to show such friendship?

Beat. A very even way, but no such friend.

Bene. May a man do it?

Beat. It is a man's office, but not yours.   265

Bene. I do love nothing in the world so well as you—is
not that strange?

Beat. As strange as the thing I know not. It were as
possible for me to say I loved nothing so well as you,
but believe me not; and yet I lie not; I confess   270
nothing, nor I deny nothing. I am sorry for my
cousin.

Bene. By my sword, Beatrice, thou lovest me.

---

254. S.D. *Exeunt*] *QF* (*exit*) *subst., Rowe.   all . . . *Beatrice*] *Rowe* (*Manent Benedick and Beatrice.*); *not in QF.*

254. *prolong'd*] postponed, as in *R3*, III. iv. 46–7—'For I myself am not so well provided/As else I would be, were the day *prolong'd*'.

256–329.] Lecturing on the part of Beatrice, Ellen Terry delivered these exchanges with Benedick and noted in the margin, 'Not *emotion*. A *passion*.'

263. *even*] straightforward.

265. *but not yours*] Beatrice may mean, 'As a friend of Claudio and Don Pedro, you are not the man to right Hero', or, 'You have not deserved so well of me that I can ask this of you'.

266–9. *nothing . . . nothing*] 'They manage by a deft indirectness to put *nothing* into a syntax where the other person can choose either its negative or its positive meaning' (P. A. Jorgensen, *Redeeming Shakespeare's*

Words, 1962, p. 30); i.e. they are saying that they value each other at either (i) nothing, or (ii) more than anything.

268. *As . . . not*] Beatrice will not yet acknowledge that she *knows* what she admits is a strange fact.

273. *By my sword*] 'It seems to have been usual for men before the Christian era to swear by or upon their swords, but amongst Christians this custom may have originated in the form of the Cross the sword presents where the guard crosses the blade' (W. L. Rushton, *Shakespeare Illustrated by Old Authors*, p. 7). There is an apt significance when Hamlet swears his friends 'upon [his] *sword*' to secrecy about the ghost—Christian probity against infernal treachery (*Ham.*, I. v. 145–60).

Beat. Do not swear and eat it.

Bene. I will swear by it that you love me, and I will   275
make him eat it that says I love not you.

Beat. Will you not eat your word?

Bene. With no sauce that can be devised to it. I protest
I love thee.

Beat. Why then, God forgive me!   280

Bene. What offence, sweet Beatrice?

Beat. You have stayed me in a happy hour, I was about
to protest I loved you.

Bene. And do it with all thy heart.

Beat. I love you with so much of my heart that none is   285
left to protest.

Bene. Come, bid me do anything for thee.

Beat. Kill Claudio!

Bene. Ha, not for the wide world!

Beat. You kill me to deny it. Farewell.   290

Bene. Tarry, sweet Beatrice.

Beat. I am gone, though I am here; there is no love in
you; nay I pray you let me go.

Bene. Beatrice—

Beat. In faith, I will go.   295

Bene. We'll be friends first.

Beat. You dare easier be friends with me than fight with
mine enemy.

Bene. Is Claudio thine enemy?

Beat. Is a not approved in the height a villain, that hath   300
slandered, scorned, dishonoured my kinswoman?
O that I were a man! What, bear her in hand until

---

274. swear] *Q;* sweare by it *F.*   290. it] *Q; not in F.*   294. Beatrice—]*QF*
(Beatrice.), *Theobald subst.*

274. *eat it*] = have to eat the words
you swore on it. 'To eat one's words'
is, of course, a proverbial phrase;
Tilley W825.

280. *God forgive me*] Beatrice has
practically admitted she loves Benedick (ll. 268–71). She is on the brink
of infringing the convention that the
woman takes no initiative in love.

283. *protest*] solemnly affirm.

290. *to deny it*] i.e. by refusing it.

292–3.] The business—Benedick
detaining Beatrice—is clear, one of
the many indications of stage-activity.

300. *approved*] proven.

302. *bear . . . in hand*] lead on with
false hopes. Volpone explains the
process vividly—'still *bearing them in
hand,*/Letting the cherry knock against
their lips,/And draw it, by their
mouths, and back againe' (*Volpone,*
i.i.88–90: Jonson, H. & S., v.27).

they come to take hands, and then with public
accusation, uncovered slander, unmitigated rancour—O God that I were a man! I would eat his   305
heart in the market-place.

Bene. Hear me, Beatrice—

Beat. Talk with a man out at a window! A proper
saying!

Bene. Nay, but Beatrice—   310

Beat. Sweet Hero! She is wronged, she is slandered,
she is undone.

Bene. Beat—

Beat. Princes and counties! Surely a princely testimony,
a goodly count, Count Comfect, a sweet gallant   315
surely! O that I were a man for his sake, or that I
had any friend would be a man for my sake! But
manhood is melted into curtsies, valour into com-
pliment, and men are only turned into tongue, and
trim ones too: he is now as valiant as Hercules that   320

304-5. rancour—] *Rowe;* rancour? *QF.*   307, 310. Beatrice—] *QF subst.*
(Beatrice.), *Collier subst.*   313. Beat—] *Theobald;* Beat? *QF.*   315. count,
Count] *Q;* Count, *F.*   318. curtsies] *QF1* (cursies), *F2;* curtesies *F3;* court-
esies *Hanmer.*

304. *uncovered*] barefaced; also, perhaps, suddenly revealed.

305. *O . . . man*] 'Beatrice, the
woman who pretended, early in the
comedy, that she could not imagine
why anyone should think her life in-
complete without a man, . . . finds
herself in Act iv wishing no fewer than
three times "that I were a man". Her
appeal to Benedick, . . . and her
gratitude to him, represent, on her
part, as radical a transformation of
attitude as does his challenge to
Claudio' (Riverside, p. 330).

314. *counties*] See ii.i.176, note.

315. *goodly count*] 'A bitter pun: "A
handsome count and a fine story"'
(Kittredge). Meanings of *count* include
(*i*) the rank in question; (*ii*) accusation, item in an indictment—cf. *testimony* l. 314; (*iii*) tale, story—cf.
Stefano Guazzo's *Ciuile Conuersation*
(1586), fol. 6b—'*Comptes* and other

delightfull speach'.

Comfect] = Candy, Sugarplum ('a
sweet gallant'); with also the sense of
something speciously attractive and
made up.

318. *curtsies*] QF's 'cursies' can be
rendered 'curtsies' or 'courtesies', the
senses of 'formal obeisances' and
'courteous manners' intermingling.
Here, 'manhood is melted' suggests
that bold bearing has given place to
bowing and scraping. The *curtsy* was
not a feminine salutation only; *OED*
quotes—'1583 Hollybrand *Campo di
Fior* 57. Put of thy cappe boye. Make a
fine *curtesie,* Bowe thy right knee . . .
As it hath bene taught thee'. And in
Shr., iv.i.80, Petruchio's men are to
'*curtsy* with their left legs'.

320. *trim*] fine, nice (ironical, as
often); reflecting on (*i*) the finical
bearing of the men (cf. *LLL.,* v.ii.363
—'*Trim* gallants, full of courtship and

only tells a lie and swears it. I cannot be a man
with wishing, therefore I will die a woman with
grieving.

Bene. Tarry, good Beatrice. By this hand I love thee.

Beat. Use it for my love some other way than swearing   325
by it.

Bene. Think you in your soul the Count Claudio hath
wronged Hero?

Beat. Yea, as sure as I have a thought, or a soul.

Bene. Enough! I am engaged, I will challenge him. I   330
will kiss your hand, and so I leave you. By this hand,
Claudio shall render me a dear account. As you
hear of me, so think of me. Go comfort your cousin;
I must say she is dead: and so farewell.   [*Exeunt.*]

[SCENE II]

Enter the Constables [DOGBERRY *and* VERGES] *and
the* [Sexton *as*] *Town Clerk in gowns,*
BORACHIO [, CONRADE, *and the* Watch].

331. I] *Q; not in F.*   334. S.D.] *F2; not in QF1.*

Scene 11

SCENE 11] *Capell; not in QF.*   [*Location*] *A prison. Theobald; not in QF.*   S.D.]
*Bennett; Enter the Constables, Borachio, and the Towne clearke in gownes. QF subst.;
Enter Dogberry, Verges, Borachio, Conrade, the Town Clerk and Sexton in gowns. Rowe.*

of state'; (*ii*) the bland deceits of their
tongues.

331. *By this hand*] i.e. by Beatrice's
hand (which he is kissing); he has
already sworn by his own (l. 324):
another hint of stage-action.

Scene 11

Location] A prison.
S.D. *Dogberry . . . Verges*] Throughout this scene there is much variation
in QF's speech-prefixes. Dogberry's
lines are given to *Kemp* (variously
spelt, misspelt, or abbreviated), except for l. 4, where he is *Andrew*
(supposedly from Kemp's playing the

clown or Merry Andrew) and l. 64,
Constable. Verges is *Cowley* or *Couley*
(the actor, Richard Cowley), though
at l. 48 he is *Const*. Conrade's speech at
l. 66 is joined on to *Couley*'s of l. 65,
and that at l. 70 is likewise attributed
to *Couley*.

in gowns] Malone cited *The Black
Book* (1604) as evidence that black
gowns were Elizabethan constables'
official robes. The following passage
is relevant—'I [Lucifer, in disguise as a constable] leapt out of
master constable's night-gown into an
usurer's fusty furred jacket; whereat
the watchmen staggered and all their

Dog. Is our whole dissembly appeared?

Verg. O, a stool and a cushion for the sexton.

Sex. Which be the malefactors?

Dog. Marry, that am I and my partner.

Verg. Nay, that's certain, we have the exhibition to   5
examine.

Sex. But which are the offenders that are to be examined? Let them come before Master Constable.

Dog. Yea, marry, let them come before me. What is
your name, friend?   10

Bora. Borachio.

Dog. Pray write down 'Borachio'. Yours, sirrah?

Con. I am a gentleman, sir, and my name is Conrade.

Dog. Write down 'Master gentleman Conrade'. Masters, do you serve God?   15

Con., Bora. Yea, sir, we hope.

Dog. Write down that they hope they serve God: and
write 'God' first, for God defend but God should go
before such villains! Masters, it is proved already

---

1. *Dog.*] *QF* (*Keeper*), *Capell; To. Cl. Rowe.*   2. *Verg.*] *QF* (*Cowley*), *Capell;*
Dog. Rowe.   4. *Dog.*] *QF* (*Andrew*), *Capell; Verg. Rowe.*   5. *Verg.*] *QF*
(*Cowley*), *Capell; Dog. Rowe.*   9. *Dog.*] *QF* (*Kemp*), *Capell; To. Cl. Rowe.*
12. *Dog.*] *Q* (*Ke.*), *F* (*Kem.*), *Capell; To. Cl. Rowe.*   14. *Dog.*] *Q* (*Ke.*), *F*
(*Kee.*), *Capell; To. Cl. Rowe.*   16. *Con., Bora.*] *Q* (*Both*), *Evans; not in F.*
16–19. Yea, . . . villains!] *Q; not in F.*   17. *Dog.*] *Q* (*Kem.*), *Capell; To. Cl.*
Theobald; not in F.

---

bills fell down in a swoon; . . . when
they missed their constable and saw
the black gown of his office lie full in a
puddle' (Middleton, *Works*, ed.
Bullen, VIII. 28).

1. *dissembly*] A form not peculiar to
Dogberry: 'It occurs in 16th–17th
century as a perversion of assembly'
(*OED*, citing a passage where the
'perversion' is deliberate, from
Richard Baxter's *Twelve Arguments*,
1684, § 16. 27—'Their usual titles
were the Priestbyters, the Drivines,
the Sinners of Westminster, the
Dissembly men').

4. *Marry . . . partner*] 'When he is
really most absurd and ridiculous,
then it is precisely that he feels most
confident and grand' (Hudson, *Life*,

i. 323).

5–6. *exhibition to examine*] Verges is
partly recalling Leonato's 'Take their
examination yourself' (III. v. 46). Here
exhibition must be an attempt at
'commission', the proper legal term
for the delegated authority invested in
him by Leonato for examining the
accused.

12. *sirrah*] = fellow (contemptuous);
Conrade's reply is a reproof.

16–19. *Yea, sir . . . villains*] Omitted
in F, probably to avoid the penalties
of the 1606 statute against profanity or
to clear F's text from offensiveness;
literary bowdlerization was sometimes practised even before the 1606
Act.

18. *defend*] forbid; see II. i. 86, note.

that you are little better than false knaves, and it 20
will go near to be thought so shortly. How answer
you for yourselves?

Con. Marry, sir, we say we are none.

Dog. A marvellous witty fellow, I assure you, but I will
go about with him. Come you hither, sirrah, a word 25
in your ear, sir; I say to you, it is thought you are
false knaves.

Bora. Sir, I say to you we are none.

Dog. Well, stand aside. 'Fore God, they are both in a
tale. Have you writ down that they are none? 30

Sex. Master Constable, you go not the way to examine;
you must call forth the watch that are their accusers.

Dog. Yea, marry, that's the eftest way. Let the watch
come forth. Masters, I charge you in the Prince's
name, accuse these men. 35

First Watch. This man said, sir, that Don John the
Prince's brother was a villain.

Dog. Write down 'Prince John a villain'. Why, this is
flat perjury, to call a prince's brother villain.

Bora. Master Constable— 40

Dog. Pray thee, fellow, peace, I do not like thy look, I
promise thee.

Sex. What heard you him say else?

Sec. Watch. Marry, that he had received a thousand
ducats of Don John for accusing the Lady Hero 45
wrongfully.

Dog. Flat burglary as ever was committed.

---

24. *Dog.*] *QF* (*Kemp*), *Capell*; *To. Cl. Rowe.*   26. ear, sir;] *QF* (eare sir,), *Rowe;*
ear: sir, *Camb.*   29, 33, 38. *Dog.*] *QF* (*Kemp*), *Capell*; *To. Cl. Rowe.*   40.
Constable—] *QF* (Constable.), *Capell subst.*   41, 47. *Dog.*] *QF* (*Kemp*), *Capell;*
To. Cl. Rowe.

25. *go about with*] deal with (and outmanœuvre).

26. *in your ear*] Dogberry 'goes about' with Conrade, who has denied the charge, by stage-whispering it (in some productions by bellowing it) to Borachio, who has already heard it.

33. *eftest*] Dogberry's nonce-word is felicitous, and his meaning clear (= 'nearest, shortest, most convenient': Onions); 'aptest' affords the closest resemblance in form.

36, 44, 50.] On the allocation of the Watch's speeches see conclusion of headnote to III. iii.

Verg. Yea, by mass, that it is.

Sex. What else, fellow?

First Watch. And that Count Claudio did mean, upon   50
his words, to disgrace Hero before the whole
assembly, and not marry her.

Dog. O villain! Thou wilt be condemned into ever-
lasting redemption for this.

Sex. What else?   55

Watch. This is all.

Sex. And this is more, masters, than you can deny.
Prince John is this morning secretly stolen away:
Hero was in this manner accused, in this very
manner refused, and upon the grief of this suddenly   60
died. Master Constable, let these men be bound
and brought to Leonato's; I will go before and show
him their examination.   [*Exit.*]

Dog. Come, let them be opinioned.

Verg. Let them be in the hands—   65

[*Con.*] Off, coxcomb!

Dog. God's my life, where's the sexton? Let him write
down 'the Prince's officer coxcomb'. Come, bind
them. Thou naughty varlet!

48. Verg.] *Capell; Const. QF; Dog. Rowe.*   by] *Q;* by th' *F.*   53. *Dog.*] *QF*
(*Kemp*), *Capell; To. Cl. Rowe.*   62. Leonato's] *Q; Leonato F.*   63. S.D.]
Theobald; not in QF.   64. *Dog.*] *Rowe; Constable QF subst.*   65. *Verg.*] *Capell;
Couley Q; Sex. F; Conrade Theobald.*   65–6. be in the hands—/Con. Off, cox-
comb!] *Malone*; be in the hands of Coxcombe. *QF subst.;* be in hand. [*Exit.*]/
Conr. Off, coxcomb! *Warburton;* be in bands./Con. Off, coxcomb! *Capell;* be in
the—/Con. Hands off! coxcomb! *Lloyd, conj. Kinnear;* be in the hands of—/Con.
Coxcomb! *Staunton;* be—in the hands. [*he offers to bind Conrade*]/Conrade. Off,
coxcomb! *NCS, conj. Brae.*   67. *Dog.*] *Q (Kemp), F (Kem.), Rowe.*   69. them.
Thou] *F3 subst.;* them, thou *Q;* them thou *F1–2.*

60. *refused*] disowned, as at IV.i.184.

65–6.] Q gives these words, undivided, to *Couley* (Verges). Malone
settled the text as here. The compositor, NCS suggests, perhaps found
Cou. and *Con.* on successive lines and
took the speakers to be the same. F
gives the words, also undivided, to
Sex[ton], Theobald to *Conrade* (on the
grounds that neither Verges nor the
Sexton would refer to a watchman as

'coxcomb'). Warburton divided the
words as here, giving them to *Sexton*
and *Conrade*, though he read 'in hand'
for 'in the hands'. Capell retained
Warburton's division, giving the
speeches to *Verges* and *Conrade*, but
reading 'in bands'.

67. *God's my life*] God save my life.

69. *naughty*] worthless, wicked (as
often; cf. V.i.291); formerly stronger
in sense than now. Jeremiah XXIV.2

Con. Away! You are an ass, you are an ass.   70

Dog. Dost thou not suspect my place? Dost thou not
suspect my years? O that he were here to write me
down an ass! But masters, remember that I am an
ass: though it be not written down, yet forget not
that I am an ass. No, thou villain, thou art full of   75
piety, as shall be proved upon thee by good witness.
I am a wise fellow, and which is more, an officer,
and which is more, a householder, and which is
more, as pretty a piece of flesh as any is in Messina,
and one that knows the law, go to, and a rich   80
fellow enough, go to, and a fellow that hath had
losses, and one that hath two gowns, and everything
handsome about him. Bring him away! O that I
had been writ down an ass!   *Exeunt.*

70. Con.] *Rowe; Couley QF.*   71. Dog.] *QF (Kemp), Rowe.*   79. is] *Q; not in*
F.   84. S.D.] *QF (exit) subst., Pope.*

has, 'the other basket had very
naughty figs, which could not be eaten,
they were so bad'.

72–3. *years . . . ass*] Dogberry appears unwittingly to achieve a pun.
Years could be a variant of *ears*, as in
the phrase 'as long as donkeys' *years*'.
Craik (p. 309) cites the interlude
Misogonus, i. ii. 63–4 (*c.* 1570), where
the Fool says, 'Nothinge greues me
but my *yeares* be so longe/my master
will take me for balames asse'.

77–83.] The light punctuation
(Q's) admirably expresses his flurry of
indignation.

79. *as pretty . . . Messina*] Cf. *Tw.N.*,
i. v. 25–6—'thou wert *as witty a piece of*
Eve's *flesh as any* in Illyria'.

81–2. *hath had losses*]—and can still
boast of *two gowns, and everything handsome about him.* How can this expression
of wounded pride ever have been
thought incomprehensible, as Furness's long note on critics' bewilder-

ment indicates it was?

83–4. *O . . . ass*] 'Our pleasure is
not caused just by Dogberry and
Verges being funny but by their being
funny in a particular way. The encounters of Beatrice and Benedick are
brilliant, . . . but there is often a kind
of hardness about the brilliance. . . .
And then come in [Dogberry and
Verges] and furnish a not unwelcome
restorative to our self-conceit, since . . .
here are two of God's creatures who
have an alacrity of sinking to depths
that . . . we could never plumb—and
yet [it is to them and their fellows]
that the exposure of the plot is finally
due' (M. R. Ridley, *Shakespeare's
Plays: A Commentary*, 1937, pp. 106–7).
Actually, the credit for solving the
problem belongs to the sensible Sexton, as that for arresting the offenders
belongs to the Watch; left to Dogberry and Verges the whole matter
would remain inextricably confused.

ACT V

[SCENE I]

Enter LEONATO *and* [ANTONIO] *his brother.*

Ant. If you go on thus, you will kill yourself,
    And 'tis not wisdom thus to second grief
    Against yourself.
Leon.   I pray thee cease thy counsel,
    Which falls into mine ears as profitless
    As water in a sieve. Give not me counsel,   5
    Nor let no comforter delight mine ear
    But such a one whose wrongs do suit with mine.
    Bring me a father that so lov'd his child,
    Whose joy of her is overwhelm'd like mine,
    And bid him speak of patience;   10
    Measure his woe the length and breadth of mine,
    And let it answer every strain for strain,
    As thus for thus, and such a grief for such,

ACT V

Scene 1

ACT V] *F* (*Actus Quintus.*); *not in Q.*   SCENE 1] *Rowe; not in QF.*   [*Location*]
Before Leonato's *House. Pope; not in QF.*   S.D. *Antonio] Rowe; not in QF.*
1. *Ant.*] *QF* (*Brother*), *Rowe* (*so subst. throughout scene, except l. 100 where F reads Ant.*).
6. *comforter*] *Q; comfort F.*   7. *do*] *Q; doth F.*

Scene 1

Location] Before Leonato's house.

1–3. *If . . . yourself*] Tilley D126
gives as proverbial 'To lament the
dead avails not, and to the living it is
hurtful'.

2. *second*] reinforce.

10.] The line is short, but with
emphasis on *him* its brevity is expressive.

12. *strain*] (*i*) quality of emotion; cf.
Troil., II. ii. 153–5—'Can it be/That so
degenerate a *strain* as this/Should once
set footing in your generous bosoms?';
(*ii*) stretch, stress; (*iii*) perhaps with a
musical connotation, one phase or
phrase *answering* another.

In every lineament, branch, shape, and form.
If such a one will smile and stroke his beard,   15
Bid sorrow wag, cry 'Hem!' when he should groan,
Patch grief with proverbs, make misfortune drunk
With candle-wasters, bring him yet to me,
And I of him will gather patience.
But there is no such man: for, brother, men   20
Can counsel and speak comfort to that grief
Which they themselves not feel; but tasting it,

16. Bid sorrow wag, cry 'Hem!'] *Capell subst.; And sorrow, wagge, crie hem,
QF1–2;* And hallow, wag, cry hem, *F3, Rowe;* And hollow, wag, cry hem, *F4;*
And Sorrow wage; cry, hem! *Theobald;* And sorrow waive, cry hem, *Hanmer;*
And sorrowing, cry 'hem' *Halliwell, conj. Heath;* And, Sorrow wag! cry; hem,
Johnson; In sorrow wag; cry hem, *Malone;* Cry—sorrow, wag! and hem,
Steevens '93, conj. Johnson; And sorrow, wag! cry hem, *Collier.*

15–16. *stroke . . . 'Hem!'*] To stroke
the beard and cry 'Hem' were re-
garded as preliminaries to a dull
speech or senile platitudes, as in
Troil., I.iii.165–6—'Now play me
Nestor; *hem,* and *stroke thy beard/*As he
being drest to some oration'. *Cry
'Hem!'* = clear the throat.

16. *Bid sorrow wag, cry 'Hem!'*] drive
grief away by croaking out platitudes.
The only serious textual crux un-
fortunately occurs in one of the few
passionately expressive speeches. QF's
reading, 'And sorrow, wagge, crie
hem,' has been followed only by Johnson, whose interpretation is intolerably strained—'I point thus: "And,
Sorrow wag! cry; hem, when" etc.
That is, "If he will smile, and cry
Sorrow be gone, and hem instead of
groaning"'. Capell's reading (followed substantially here) has been
generally adopted.

17. *Patch . . . proverbs*] patch over
grief's wounds with moral tags.

17–18. *drunk . . . candle-wasters*]
Drunk suggests the drowning of grief
with strong drink. This would seem
the likeliest interpretation. Yet since
Leonato is scorning wise saws as
tokens of patience, drugging oneself on
philosophical precepts may be what
he means. For *candle-wasters* as ex-

pressing contempt for scholars see
Cynthia's Revels, III.ii.2–3 (Jonson,
H. & S., IV.84)—'a whore-sone booke-
worme, a *candle-waster*'; and for the
same idea, though the whole word
does not appear, *The Returne from
Parnassus,* ll. 1890–6, (ed. J. B.
Leishman, pp. 347–8)—'To thinke so
many actiue, able wits,/ . . . /Sitt now
immur'd within their priuate cells,/
Drinking a long, lank, watching
candles smoake,/ . . . /In fruitlesse
poring on some worme eaten leafe'.

18. *yet*] The word suggests some
emphasis, but what is not clear; probably, 'even now, when I am over-
whelmed' (Kittredge); or else, simply,
'then'.

20–31.] For proverbial parallels see
III.ii.26–7, note. *Gorboduc,* IV.ii.59–64,
is characteristic—'Many can yelde
right sage and graue aduise,/Of
patient sprite to others wrapped in
woe,/And can in speache both rule and
conquere kinde;/Who, if by proofe
they might feele nature's force,/Wold
shewe them selues men, as thei are in
dede,/Which now will nedes be gods'.
Shakespearean instances occur at *R2,*
I.iii.275–303; *Rom.,* III.iii.54–70; and
Oth., I.iii.199–219.

22. *not feel*] For the omission of *do*
before *not* see Abbott § 305 and *Tp.,*

Their counsel turns to passion, which before
Would give preceptial medicine to rage,
Fetter strong madness in a silken thread,   25
Charm ache with air, and agony with words.
No, no, 'tis all men's office to speak patience
To those that wring under the load of sorrow,
But no man's virtue nor sufficiency
To be so moral when he shall endure   30
The like himself. Therefore give me no counsel:
My griefs cry louder than advertisement.

Ant. Therein do men from children nothing differ.

Leon. I pray thee peace, I will be flesh and blood;
For there was never yet philosopher
That could endure the toothache patiently,   35
However they have writ the style of gods,
And made a push at chance and sufferance.

Ant. Yet bend not all the harm upon yourself;
Make those that do offend you suffer too.   40

Leon. There thou speak'st reason: nay, I will do so.
My soul doth tell me Hero is belied;
And that shall Claudio know, so shall the Prince,
And all of them that thus dishonour her.

Enter Prince [DON PEDRO] *and* CLAUDIO.

Ant. Here comes the Prince and Claudio hastily.   45

44. S.D. *Don Pedro*] *Rowe; not in QF.*

v. i. 38—'Whereof the ewe not bites'.

24. *preceptial medicine*] medicine consisting of precepts, the 'moral medicine' rejected by Don John (I. iii. 12). *OED* quotes this as the only pre-19th-century instance of *preceptial*.

27–31.] Tilley A124 gives as proverbial 'All commend patience, but none can endure to suffer.'

28. *wring*] writhe.

32. *advertisement*] good advice, admonitions.

35–6.] Similarly III. ii. 26–7.

38. *made a push*] Either (*i*) scorned (alternative form of *pish*) ; or (*ii*) defied, counterattacked — the philosopher professing to outface fortune.

sufferance] what one must endure, suffering, as in *Meas.*, II. iv. 166–7— 'thy unkindness shall his death draw out/To ling'ring *sufferance*'. The usual sense is patience, endurance, as at I. iii. 8–9.

45. *comes*] For singular verbs preceding plural subjects see Abbott § 335, and also v. iv. 52, 91.

D. Pedro. Good den, good den.
Claud.   Good day to both of you.
Leon. Hear you, my lords—
D. Pedro.   We have some haste, Leonato.
Leon. Some haste, my lord? Well, fare you well, my lord!
    Are you so hasty now? Well, all is one.
D. Pedro. Nay, do not quarrel with us, good old man.   50
Ant. If he could right himself with quarrelling,
    Some of us would lie low.
Claud.   Who wrongs him?
Leon. Marry, thou dost wrong me, thou dissembler, thou!
    Nay, never lay thy hand upon thy sword,
    I fear thee not.
Claud.   Marry, beshrew my hand   55
    If it should give your age such cause of fear.
    In faith, my hand meant nothing to my sword.
Leon. Tush, tush, man, never fleer and jest at me!
    I speak not like a dotard nor a fool,
    As under privilege of age to brag   60
    What I have done being young, or what would do
    Were I not old. Know, Claudio, to thy head,
    Thou hast so wrong'd mine innocent child and me,
    That I am forc'd to lay my reverence by,
    And with grey hairs and bruise of many days   65
    Do challenge thee to trial of a man.
    I say thou hast belied mine innocent child;
    Thy slander hath gone through and through her heart,
    And she lies buried with her ancestors—

46. *D. Pedro.*] *QF (Prince) subst. (so throughout scene)*, Rowe *(Pedro)*, Capell *(D. Pe.)*.
47. lords—] *Capell;* Lords? *QF.*   63. mine] *Q;* my *F.*

46. *Good den*] God give you good
even.

49. *all is one*] no matter.

53. *Marry, thou*] Slurred into two
syllables.

53–4. *thou dost . . . thy*] Leonato
respectfully addresses the Prince as
you. To Claudio he uses *thou, thee*, or
thy throughout this encounter.

58. *fleer*] sneer, gibe.

62. *to thy head*] Halliwell quotes
Robert Forby's *Vocabulary of East*

Anglia: 'We say, "I told him so *to his
head*, not to his face, which is the usual
phrase. Ours is as old as Shakespeare".' Cf. *MND*, I. i. 106—
'Demetrius, I'll avouch it *to his head*'.

69. *lies buried*] The time is a few
hours after the church scene: Dogberry and Verges have only just
finished the 'examination' Leonato
enjoined on them and have had no
chance to announce the result. Considered realistically (an inappropriate

    O, in a tomb where never scandal slept,   70
    Save this of hers, fram'd by thy villainy!
Claud. My villainy?
Leon.   Thine, Claudio; thine, I say.
D. Pedro. You say not right, old man.
Leon.   My lord, my lord,
    I'll prove it on his body if he dare,
    Despite his nice fence and his active practice,   75
    His May of youth and bloom of lustihood.
Claud. Away! I will not have to do with you.
Leon. Canst thou so daff me? Thou hast kill'd my child;
    If thou kill'st me, boy, thou shalt kill a man.
Ant. He shall kill two of us, and men indeed: 80
    But that's no matter, let him kill one first.
    Win me and wear me, let him answer me.
    Come follow me, boy, come, sir boy, come follow me,
    Sir boy, I'll whip you from your foining fence,
    Nay, as I am a gentleman, I will.   85
Leon. Brother—
Ant. Content yourself. God knows I lov'd my niece,
    And she is dead, slander'd to death by villains,
    That dare as well answer a man indeed
    As I dare take a serpent by the tongue.   90

---

86. Brother—] *QF* (Brother.), *Theobald.*   87. lov'd] *Q* (loued), *F.*

procedure) Hero's interment is extraordinarily prompt.

72. *My villainy?*] Claudio is indignant to be thought wrong. No word of
remorse or even grief passes his lips on
hearing of Hero's death.

75. *nice fence*] dexterous sword-play.

78. *daff me*] put me aside.

80–101.] Antonio's growing fury,
with Leonato's attempts to check it,
is both gripping and (since Dogberry's
discoveries are on the way) oddly
funny in its extravagance.

82. *Win . . . wear me*] Proverbial;
Tilley W408. Lyly's *Euphues* (*Works*,
ed. Bond, I.199, ll. 33–5) has 'Unto
hir had *Philautus* accesse, who *wanne*
hir by right of loue, and shoulde

haue *worne* hir by right of lawe'. The
sense is, 'Overcome me and I submit
to your purposes; you may have me
if you win me (in fight)'.

answer me] respond to *my* challenge.
Me is emphatic.

83. *sir boy*] In Lyly's *Sapho and Phao*,
v. ii. 48, 72, Venus twice angrily thus
addresses Cupid (*Works*, ed. Bond,
II. 413). 'Boy' is Aufidius' culminating
insult to Coriolanus: *Cor.*, v. vi. 101–
117.

84. *foining fence*] Foining is parrying
instead of striking. Antonio will force
Claudio to fight close, in earnest, and
will beat down his parryings.

90.] The hardihood of such an act
needs no argument; but a passage

Boys, apes, braggarts, Jacks, milksops!
Leon.   Brother Antony—
Ant. Hold you content. What, man! I know them, yea,
    And what they weigh, even to the utmost scruple,
    Scambling, outfacing, fashion-monging boys,
    That lie, and cog, and flout, deprave, and slander,   95
    Go anticly, and show outward hideousness,
    And speak off half a dozen dang'rous words,
    How they might hurt their enemies, if they durst,
    And this is all.
Leon. But brother Antony—
Ant.   Come, 'tis no matter;   100
    Do not you meddle, let me deal in this.
D. Pedro. Gentlemen both, we will not wake your patience.
    My heart is sorry for your daughter's death;
    But on my honour she was charg'd with nothing
    But what was true, and very full of proof.   105
Leon. My lord, my lord—

---

91. Antony—] *QF* (Anthony. *subst.*), *Theobald subst.*   96. anticly] *QF* (anti-
quely), *Rowe.*   97. off] *QF* (of), *Theobald.*   100. Antony—] *QF* (Anthonie.,
subst.), *Theobald subst.*   *Ant.*] *Q* (*Brother*), *F.*   106. lord—] *QF* (Lord.),
Pope subst.

---

from Stephen Batman, *Vppon Bartholome* (1582), Lib. xviii, chap. 9, p. 343,
is apt—'No beast moueth the tongue
so swiftly as the *serpent*, for it moueth
the tongue so swiftly, yᵗ it seemeth yᵗ
it hath three tongues, yet it hath but
one'.

91. *Jacks*] See I. i. 170, note.
94. *Scambling*] rough, contentious.
In *H5*, 1.i.4, the Archbishop refers to
the '*scambling* and unquiet time'.

fashion-monging] dandified, fashion-
dealing. *Monging* = trading, traffic-
king: *OED* quotes W. Baldwin,
Funeralles Edw. VI, Cij (Roxburgh
Club edition)—'Repent you, mer-
chantes, your straunge marchandises/
. . . Your *monging* of vitayles, corne,
butter, and cheeses'.

95. *cog*] cheat.
deprave] defame, vilify, as in
Paradise Lost, VI. 174–5—'Unjustly

thou *deprav'st* it with the name / Of
servitude'.

96. *anticly*] grotesquely, like a buffoon (as at III. i. 63).

97. *off*] QF read 'of', a normal
Shakespearean spelling; see III. v. 9.

102. *wake your patience*] Capell and
others think this ironical; not the
patience but the wrath of the two old
men has long since been waked. But
Don Pedro wishes to soothe their
tempers and avoid a quarrel. He seems
to mean, 'We shall not disturb your
patience any longer, but let it settle
into its quiet state'. The episode can be
effectively played (with a touch of
comedy appropriate to Antonio's
excitement) with Don Pedro and
Claudio in high embarrassment
walking rapidly up and down while
the old men pertinaciously fasten
upon them, not to be shaken off.

SC. I]   MUCH ADO ABOUT NOTHING   197

D. Pedro. I will not hear you.

Leon. No? Come, brother, away! I will be heard.

Ant. And shall, or some of us will smart for it.

Exeunt Leonato and Antonio.

Enter BENEDICK.

D. Pedro. See, see! Here comes the man we went to seek.   110

Claud. Now, signior, what news?

Bene. Good day, my lord.

D. Pedro. Welcome, signior; you are almost come to
part almost a fray.

Claud. We had like to have had our two noses snapped   115
off with two old men without teeth.

D. Pedro. Leonato and his brother. What think'st thou?
Had we fought, I doubt we should have been too
young for them.

Bene. In a false quarrel there is no true valour. I came to   120
seek you both.

Claud. We have been up and down to seek thee, for we
are high-proof melancholy, and would fain have it
beaten away. Wilt thou use thy wit?

Bene. It is in my scabbard; shall I draw it?   125

D. Pedro. Dost thou wear thy wit by thy side?

Claud. Never any did so, though very many have been
beside their wit. I will bid thee draw, as we do the
minstrels—draw to pleasure us.

D. Pedro. As I am an honest man, he looks pale. Art   130
thou sick, or angry?

Claud. What, courage, man! What though care killed a
cat, thou hast mettle enough in thee to kill care.

---

109. S.D. *Exeunt . . . Antonio.*] *QF* (*Exeunt amb.* [*after l. 108*]) *subst., Capell.
Enter Benedick*] *Q ; after l. 107, F.*   115. like] *F2 ;* likt *QF1.*

118. *I doubt*] I'm afraid.

123. *high-proof*] in the highest
degree. *Proof* in this sense means 'of
recognized strength or degree', and is
still so used of alcoholic strength.

128–9. *I . . . us*] Claudio sees no
serious meaning in Benedick's words.
Wishing to be cheered up, he says, in

effect, 'Draw out your wit to please
us, from where you are concealing it,
as musicians draw their instruments
from their cases (or their bows across
the strings)'.

132–3. *What . . . cat*] Proverbial;
Tilley C84.

Bene. Sir, I shall meet your wit in the career, and you
  charge it against me. I pray you choose another sub-   135
  ject.

Claud. Nay then, give him another staff; this last was
  broke cross.

D. Pedro. By this light, he changes more and more; I
  think he be angry indeed.   140

Claud. If he be, he knows how to turn his girdle.

Bene. Shall I speak a word in your ear?

Claud. God bless me from a challenge!

Bene. [*Aside to Claudio.*] You are a villain. I jest not; I will
  make it good how you dare, with what you dare,   145
  and when you dare. Do me right, or I will protest
  your cowardice. You have killed a sweet lady, and
  her death shall fall heavy on you. Let me hear from
  you.

Claud. Well, I will meet you, so I may have good cheer.   150

D. Pedro. What, a feast, a feast?

Claud. I' faith I thank him, he hath bid me to a calf's
  head and a capon, the which if I do not carve most

---

144. S.D.] *Camb.; not in QF.*

134. *career*] full charge, onset.

135. *charge it*] Both (*i*) level it; and
(*ii*) urge it on (like a charging horse).

137. *staff*] lance-shaft.

138. *broke cross*] Cf. *AYL*, III. iv. 36-9
—'He . . . swears brave oaths, and
breaks them bravely, quite *traverse*,
athwart the heart of his lover; as a
puny tilter, that spurs his horse but
on one side, *breaks his staff*'.

141.] A proverbial expression;
Tilley B698: of uncertain origin,
meaning (possibly) (*i*) a wrestler's
turning of his belt when accepting a
challenge, so that the buckle was behind him and did not affect his
opponent's hold—Richard Carew's
Survey of Cornwall (1713 edn, p. 16)
refers to wrestlers as 'wearing a girdle
to take hold by'; or (*ii*) 'the vulgarism,
"If he doesn't like it he can lump it"'
(Warwick, quoting Cromwell's words

of 17 September 1656—'If any man
be angry at it—I am plain and shall
use a homely expression: let him *turn*
the buckle of *his girdle* behind him! If
this were to be done again I would do
it'). Cf. Swift's *Polite Conversation*
(*Prose Works*, ed. T. Scott, 1907,
XI. 260-1)—'if miss will be angry for
nothing, . . . bid her *turn* the buckle of
her girdle behind her'. This second
sense may be what Claudio means,
but why it should mean this is uncertain.

144. S.D.] The original Cambridge
edition added the stage-direction
since it seems from Don Pedro's 'What,
a feast, a feast?' that he had overheard
no more than Claudio's reply about
'good cheer'.

146. *protest*] denounce.

152-5. *calf's head . . . woodcock*]
Calf's head = dolt; see John Davies,

curiously, say my knife's naught. Shall I not find a
woodcock too?   155
Bene. Sir, your wit ambles well; it goes easily.
D. Pedro. I'll tell thee how Beatrice praised thy wit the
other day. I said thou hadst a fine wit. 'True,' said
she, 'a fine little one.' 'No,' said I, 'a great wit.'
'Right,' says she, 'a great gross one.' 'Nay,' said I,   160
'a good wit.' 'Just,' said she, 'it hurts nobody.'
'Nay,' said I, 'the gentleman is wise.' 'Certain,'
said she, 'a wise gentleman.' 'Nay,' said I, 'he hath
the tongues.' 'That I believe,' said she, 'for he swore
a thing to me on Monday night, which he for-   165
swore on Tuesday morning; there's a double
tongue; there's two tongues.' Thus did she an hour
together transshape thy particular virtues: yet at
last she concluded with a sigh, thou wast the pro-
perest man in Italy.   170
Claud. For the which she wept heartily and said she
cared not.
D. Pedro. Yea, that she did; but yet for all that, and if
she did not hate him deadly, she would love him
dearly—the old man's daughter told us all.   175
Claud. All, all; and moreover, God saw him when he
was hid in the garden.

158–9. said she] *Q*; saies she *F*.

Scourge of Folly (*Works*, ed. Grosart,
II. 11)—'One call'd Calistus *calues
head*, in a fume'. There may have been
some further sense; W. C. Hazlitt's
English Proverbs, p. 5, gives, 'A *calf's
head* will feast a hunter and his
hounds', which is plainly ironical
though the bearing of it is lost. *Capon*,
as a term of abuse, betokened
stupidity, as in *Err.*, III.i.32—'Mome,
malt-horse, *capon*, coxcomb, idiot,
patch!' The *woodcock* was a byword
for foolishness, from the ease with
which it was caught; 'As wise as a
woodcock' was an ironic proverb
(Tilley W746).

161. *Just*] Just so (as at II.i.24).

163. *wise gentleman*] 'Perhaps "*wise
gentleman*" was in that age used
ironically, and always stood for *silly
fellow*' (Johnson).

163–4. *hath the tongues*] is a linguist.

168. *transshape*] transform (dis-
paragingly).

169–70. *properest*] finest. This praise
echoes III.i.95–7.

174–5. *hate . . . dearly*] The idea was
proverbial; cf. Tilley W651—'A
woman either loves or hates to ex-
tremes'. Lyly's *Euphues* may lie behind
this line (*Works*, ed. Bond, I.238)—'I
haue hearde that women eyther *loue
entirely* or *hate deadly*'.

176–7. *God . . . garden*] This openly

D. Pedro. But when shall we set the savage bull's horns
on the sensible Benedick's head?

Claud. Yea, and text underneath, 'Here dwells Bene-   180
dick, the married man'?

Bene. Fare you well, boy, you know my mind: I will
leave you now to your gossip-like humour. You
break jests as braggarts do their blades, which God
be thanked hurt not. My lord, for your many   185
courtesies I thank you: I must discontinue your
company. Your brother the bastard is fled from
Messina. You have among you killed a sweet and
innocent lady. For my Lord Lackbeard there, he
and I shall meet; and till then, peace be with him. [*Exit.*]

D. Pedro. He is in earnest.   191

Claud. In most profound earnest, and, I'll warrant you,
for the love of Beatrice.

D. Pedro. And hath challenged thee.

Claud. Most sincerely.   195

D. Pedro. What a pretty thing man is when he goes in
his doublet and hose and leaves off his wit!

Claud. He is then a giant to an ape; but then is an ape a
doctor to such a man.

D. Pedro. But, soft you, let me be: pluck up, my heart,   200
and be sad. Did he not say my brother was fled?

179. on] *Q* (one), *F.*   190. S.D.] *Rowe; not in QF.*   201. S.D.] *QF, after l.
197 (Enter Constables, [F, Constable,] Conrade, and Borachio), Hanmer subst.*

hints to Benedick that the conspirators knew of his presence when he
thought himself safely hidden, but it
is clear later (cf. v.iv.27) that he
received no inkling of the plot. The
allusion is to Genesis III.8, when Adam
and Eve 'heard the voice of the Lord
walking in the garden in the cool of
the day: and . . . hid themselves from
the presence of the Lord God amongst
the trees of the garden'.

178–81.] These jests take up
I.i.241–2 and 247–8.

182–90.] Benedick acts with dignity.
He ignores his friends' raillery about
Beatrice, and at last turns from them

with a stinging reproof to Claudio and
a cold farewell to Don Pedro.

184. *as braggarts . . . blades*] as
coward boasters break their swords
(pretending that this happened in
fight).

196–7. *goes . . . hose*] discards his
cloak (of intelligence) in readiness for
a fight.

198–9.] = He is a strutting ape
magnified, but the ape is a model of
intelligence compared with him.

200–1. *pluck . . . sad*] An odd expression: presumably, 'take hold of
yourself, my heart, and be serious'.
For *sad* see I.i.170.

Enter Constables [DOGBERRY, VERGES, *and the* Watch, *with*] CONRADE *and* BORACHIO.

Dog. Come you, sir, if justice cannot tame you she shall
ne'er weigh more reasons in her balance. Nay, and
you be a cursing hypocrite once, you must be looked
to.   205

D. Pedro. How now? Two of my brother's men bound?
Borachio one?

Claud. Hearken after their offence, my lord.

D. Pedro. Officers, what offence have these men done?

Dog. Marry, sir, they have committed false report, more-   210
over they have spoken untruths, secondarily they
are slanders, sixth and lastly they have belied a
lady, thirdly they have verified unjust things, and
to conclude, they are lying knaves.

D. Pedro. First I ask thee what they have done, thirdly   215
I ask thee what's their offence, sixth and lastly why
they are committed, and to conclude, what you lay
to their charge.

Claud. Rightly reasoned, and in his own division; and
by my troth there's one meaning well suited.   220

D. Pedro. Who have you offended, masters, that you are
thus bound to your answer? This learned constable

202, 210. Dog.] *QF* (*Const.*), *Rowe.*

203. *reasons*] Intentionally or not, Dogberry puns on 'raisins' (the two words being pronounced the same; see Kökeritz, *Shakespeare's Pronunciation*, p. 138), transforming the traditional picture of justice holding the scales which measure right and wrong into that of a shopkeeper weighing commodities. He seems to mean, 'If justice lets you escape, she must give up her claim to adjudicate causes.' In Lyly's *Endimion*, IV.ii.94-6 (*Works*, ed. Bond, III.57) the Second Watchman (though seemingly without punning) argues that rules applying to men apply also to boys—'If I saie to my wife, wife I will haue no Reysons in my pudding, she puts in Corance [currants], smal Reysons are Reysons, and boyes are men'. Shakespeare may half-consciously have recalled the comic-watch analogy in the earlier play; see note on III.iii.1. See also 1*H4*, II.iv.264 ('if reasons were as plentiful as blackberries . . . '), and *Troil.*, II.ii.33.

204. *a cursing hypocrite*] 'Dogberry seems to mean "a lying imposter"' (Kittredge).

once] = 'to sum you up in a word'.

210-18.] Another example of Q's light, expressive pointing.

220. *well suited*] thoroughly dressed.

222. *bound*] (*i*) coerced; (*ii*) tied up.

is too cunning to be understood. What's your
offence?

Bora. Sweet Prince, let me go no farther to mine answer.   225
Do you hear me, and let this Count kill me. I have
deceived even your very eyes: what your wisdoms
could not discover, these shallow fools have brought
to light, who in the night overheard me confessing
to this man, how Don John your brother incensed   230
me to slander the Lady Hero, how you were
brought into the orchard and saw me court Margaret in Hero's garments, how you disgraced her
when you should marry her. My villainy they have
upon record, which I had rather seal with my death   235
than repeat over to my shame. The lady is dead
upon mine and my master's false accusation; and
briefly, I desire nothing but the reward of a villain.

D. Pedro. Runs not this speech like iron through your blood?

Claud. I have drunk poison whiles he utter'd it.   240

D. Pedro. But did my brother set thee on to this?

Bora. Yea, and paid me richly for the practice of it.

D. Pedro. He is compos'd and fram'd of treachery,
And fled he is upon this villainy.

Claud. Sweet Hero! Now thy image doth appear   245
In the rare semblance that I lov'd it first.

Dog. Come, bring away the plaintiffs. By this time our
sexton hath reformed Signior Leonato of the
matter: and masters, do not forget to specify, when

274. *Dog.*] *QF* (*Const.*), *Rowe.*

223. *cunning*] ingenious.

225. *answer*] Both (*i*) reply to your
question; and (*ii*) punishment for my
wrong-doing.

230. *incensed*] instigated, as in *Wiv.*,
I. iii. 96—'I will *incense* Page to deal
with poison'; and *Lr*, II. iv. 305—
'what they may *incense* him to'.

233. *in Hero's garments*] 'This important touch is added for the first
time in this, the last account of the
midnight episode' (Warwick). It
would greatly increase the difficulty

of exonerating Margaret if one had
time to attend to it (as an audience
has not).

242. *practice of it*] deceitful effecting
of it; see IV. i. 188.

246. *that*] = in which; see Abbott
§ 394, and v. ii. 46—'let me go with
that I came' (= that for which I
came).

247–50.] Dogberry's speech (like
that at ll. 298–307) is superbly
designed to jolt the play back to
comedy.

time and place shall serve, that I am an ass.   250
Verg. Here, here comes Master Signior Leonato, and
the sexton too.

Enter LEONATO, [ANTONIO] *his brother, and the* Sexton.

Leon. Which is the villain? Let me see his eyes,
That when I note another man like him
I may avoid him. Which of these is he?   255
Bora. If you would know your wronger, look on me.
Leon. Art thou the slave that with thy breath hast kill'd
Mine innocent child?
Bora.   Yea, even I alone.
Leon. No, not so, villain, thou beliest thyself.
Here stand a pair of honourable men—   260
A third is fled—that had a hand in it.
I thank you, Princes, for my daughter's death;
Record it with your high and worthy deeds;
'Twas bravely done, if you bethink you of it.
Claud. I know not how to pray your patience,   265
Yet I must speak. Choose your revenge yourself,
Impose me to what penance your invention
Can lay upon my sin; yet sinn'd I not
But in mistaking.
D. Pedro.   By my soul, nor I:
And yet, to satisfy this good old man,   270
I would bend under any heavy weight
That he'll enjoin me to.
Leon. I cannot bid you bid my daughter live—
That were impossible—but I pray you both,
Possess the people in Messina here   275
How innocent she died; and if your love
Can labour aught in sad invention,
Hang her an epitaph upon her tomb,

251. *Verg.*] *QF (Con.* 2), *Rowe.*   252. S.D. *Antonio*] *Rowe; not in QF.*   his
brother, and the Sexton] *Q; not in F.*   257–8.] *as verse, Q; as prose, F.*   257.
thou] *Q;* thou thou *F.*

265. *patience*] A trisyllable.   Shakespeare as in modern usage.
267. *Impose me to*] Virtually combin-   275. *Possess*] inform.
ing 'impose on me' and 'subject me   277. *invention*] Four syllables.
to'. The verb is used elsewhere in

And sing it to her bones, sing it tonight.
Tomorrow morning come you to my house,   280
And since you could not be my son-in-law,
Be yet my nephew. My brother hath a daughter,
Almost the copy of my child that's dead,
And she alone is heir to both of us.
Give her the right you should have giv'n her cousin, 285
And so dies my revenge.
Claud.   O noble sir,
Your overkindness doth wring tears from me!
I do embrace your offer, and dispose
For henceforth of poor Claudio.
Leon. Tomorrow then I will expect your coming;   290
Tonight I take my leave. This naughty man
Shall face to face be brought to Margaret,
Who I believe was pack'd in all this wrong,
Hir'd to it by your brother.
Bora.   No, by my soul she was not,
Nor knew not what she did when she spoke to me, 295
But always hath been just and virtuous
In anything that I do know by her.
Dog. Moreover, sir, which indeed is not under white and
black, this plaintiff here, the offender, did call me
ass; I beseech you let it be remembered in his   300
punishment. And also the watch heard them talk
of one Deformed; they say he wears a key in his ear
and a lock hanging by it, and borrows money in

---

294. Hir'd] *Q* (Hyred), *F* (Hired), *Rowe*.   298, 309, 312, 315. *Dog.*] *QF*
(*Const.*), *Rowe*.

284.] What about Antonio's son, mentioned at I.ii.1–2? Doubtless one of the play's several small oversights.

293. *pack'd*] in league, an accomplice; cf. *Err.*, v.i.219–20—'That goldsmith there, were he not *pack'd* with her,/Could witness it'.

294–7.] 'Shakespeare's evident concern to distribute moral judgments clearly and justly appears from his care for the reputation of so minor a character as Margaret' (Craik, p. 34).

313). See also v.iv.4–6. 'As he turns to a happy close, Shakespeare contrives to give a redeeming touch to Borachio' (Warwick).

303–4. *in God's name*] The universal plea of beggars. *Tarlton's Jests* (Shakespeare Society edition, 1844) records encounters with two beggars, one of whom asked 'something of him *for God's cause*' (p. 16) and the other 'begged a peny *for the Lord's sake*' (p. 34).

God's name, the which he hath used so long, and
never paid, that now men grow hard-hearted and   305
will lend nothing for God's sake: pray you examine
him upon that point.

Leon. I thank thee for thy care and honest pains.

Dog. Your worship speaks like a most thankful and
reverent youth, and I praise God for you.   310

Leon. There's for thy pains.

Dog. God save the foundation!

Leon. Go, I discharge thee of thy prisoner, and I thank
thee.

Dog. I leave an arrant knave with your worship, which   315
I beseech your worship to correct yourself, for the
example of others. God keep your worship! I
wish your worship well. God restore you to health!
I humbly give you leave to depart, and if a merry
meeting may be wished, God prohibit it! Come,   320
neighbour.   *Exeunt [Dogberry and Verges].*

Leon. Until tomorrow morning, lords, farewell.

Ant. Farewell, my lords, we look for you tomorrow.

D. Pedro. We will not fail.

Claud.   Tonight I'll mourn with Hero.

Leon. [*To the Watch.*] Bring you these fellows on. We'll talk
with Margaret,   325
How her acquaintance grew with this lewd fellow. *Exeunt.*

321. S.D.] *F (Exeunt) (after l. 322), Camb.; not in Q.*   325. S.D.] *Camb.; not
in QF.*   325-6.] *as verse, Pope; as prose, QF.*

312.] The usual formula of those
who received alms, especially at
religious houses. In Marston's *Histrio-
Mastix*, II.i (*Plays*, ed. Wood, III.262)
the Morris dancers, hearing the hospitable order, 'Butler, make them

drinke their skinnes full', exclaim,
'*God blesse the founder!*'
326. *lewd*] worthless, rascally, as
often; e.g. Acts XVII.5—'the Jews . . .
took unto them certain *lewd* fellows of
the baser sort'.

[SCENE II]

Enter BENEDICK *and* MARGARET [*, meeting*].

Bene. Pray thee, sweet Mistress Margaret, deserve well
at my hands, by helping me to the speech of Beatrice.

Marg. Will you then write me a sonnet in praise of my
beauty?   5

Bene. In so high a style, Margaret, that no man living
shall come over it, for in most comely truth thou
deservest it.

Marg. To have no man come over me? Why, shall I
always keep below stairs?   10

Bene. Thy wit is as quick as the greyhound's mouth, it
catches.

Marg. And yours as blunt as the fencer's foils, which hit,
but hurt not.

Bene. A most manly wit, Margaret, it will not hurt a   15
woman. And so I pray thee call Beatrice; I give
thee the bucklers.

Marg. Give us the swords, we have bucklers of our own.

Bene. If you use them, Margaret, you must put in the
pikes with a vice, and they are dangerous weapons   20
for maids.

Scene 11

SCENE II] *Capell; not in QF.*   [*Location*] Leonato's House. Pope; Leonato's Gar-
den. Steevens '93; not in QF.   S.D. meeting] *Capell; not in QF.*

Scene 11

Location] The vicinity of Leonato's
house (cf. ll. 88–9—'yonder's old coil
at home')—probably his garden.

1. *sweet Mistress Margaret*] Whatever
Margaret's conduct has been, every
effort is made to re-establish her.

6–7. *style . . . over it*] Punning on
'stile', as in Chaucer, *Squire's Tale*, ll.
97–8—'Al be it that I can nat sowne
his *style,*/ Ne can nat clymen over so
high a *style.*'

7. *comely*] pleasing (referring to
truth, but implying some stage-action

complimenting Margaret's beauty).

10. *keep*] stay, dwell (still Cambridge
university usage).

below stairs] in the servants' quarters.

16–17. *give . . . bucklers*] throw down
my shield, acknowledge defeat.

18. *swords . . . bucklers*] Sexual
equivoques, perhaps prompted by *no
man come over me*, l. 9; cf. E. Partridge,
Shakespeare's Bawdy (1949), p. 199.

20. *pikes*] central spikes (in 16th
century round shields); with a bawdy
equivoque.

vice] A bawdy allusion to thighs

Marg. Well, I will call Beatrice to you, who I think
     hath legs.   *Exit.*
Bene. And therefore will come.

[*Sings.*]   *The god of love,*   25
                     That sits above,
                And knows me, and knows me,
                  How pitiful I deserve—

I mean in singing; but in loving, Leander the good
swimmer, Troilus the first employer of pandars, and   30
a whole bookful of these quondam carpet-mongers,
whose names yet run smoothly in the even road of a
blank verse, why, they were never so truly turned
over and over as my poor self in love. Marry, I
cannot show it in rhyme; I have tried. I can find   35
out no rhyme to 'lady' but 'baby'—an innocent
rhyme; for 'scorn', 'horn'—a hard rhyme; for
'school', 'fool'—a babbling rhyme; very ominous

---

23. S.D.] *QF* (*Exit Margarite*), *Rowe.*   25. S.D.] *Pope; not in QF.*   25–8.]
as verse, Capell; as prose, QF.   32. names] *Q; name F.*   35. in] *Q ; not in F.*
37. hard rhyme] *Q* (hard rime)*; hard time F.*   38. rhyme] *Q* (rime)*; time F.*

---

closed in intercourse.

25–8.] See Appendix VI.

29–30.] *Leander . . . Troilus*] *Much
Ado*'s probable date being late 1598,
the publication of Marlowe's *Hero and
Leander* in that year may have prompted the Leander allusion, though
clear echoes of the poem occur in
MND, proving that Shakespeare
knew it in MS.; see H. F. Brooks's
New Arden edition, lxiv with fn. 1.
Dekker and Chettle are known to have
worked on a *Troilus and Cressida* play
in 1599, and Shakespeare soon took
up the subject. Leander drowned in
the Hellespont, swimming to visit
Hero; Troilus gained access to
Cressida through her uncle Pandarus.

31. *quondam*] former.

carpet-mongers] Benedick has in mind
romantic lovers celebrated by poets,

and *carpet-mongers* seems to mean
those, like carpet-knights, distinguished for prowess not in war but 'on
carpet consideration' (*Tw.N.*, III.iv.
224) in the boudoir realms of courtship.

34. *over and over*] head over heels.

34–5. *I cannot . . . rhyme*] Yet he
manages 'a halting sonnet' (v.iv.87).
Love often reduces Shakespeare's
lovers to forebodings about versifying:
cf. Berowne (*LLL*, IV.iii.15–16)—'By
heaven, I do love: and it hath taught
me to *rhyme*, and to be mallicholy';
Henry V (*H5*, v.ii.132–3)—'Marry,
if you would put me to verses, or to
dance for your sake, Kate, why, you
undid me'; and Hamlet (*Ham.*,
II.ii.119–20)—'I am ill at these
numbers: I have not the art to reckon
my groans'.

endings! No, I was not born under a rhyming
planet, nor I cannot woo in festival terms.   40

Enter BEATRICE

Sweet Beatrice, wouldst thou come when I called
thee?

Beat. Yea, signior, and depart when you bid me.

Bene. O, stay but till then!

Beat. 'Then' is spoken; fare you well now. And yet ere I   45
go, let me go with that I came, which is, with knowing what hath passed between you and Claudio.

Bene. Only foul words—and thereupon I will kiss thee.

Beat. Foul words is but foul wind, and foul wind is but
foul breath, and foul breath is noisome; therefore I   50
will depart unkissed.

Bene. Thou hast frighted the word out of his right sense,
so forcible is thy wit. But I must tell thee plainly,
Claudio undergoes my challenge, and either I must
shortly hear from him, or I will subscribe him a   55
coward. And I pray thee now tell me, for which of
my bad parts didst thou first fall in love with me?

Beat. For them all together, which maintained so politic
a state of evil that they will not admit any good part
to intermingle with them. But for which of my good   60
parts did you first suffer love for me?

Bene. 'Suffer love'—a good epithet! I do suffer love
indeed, for I love thee against my will.

Beat. In spite of your heart, I think. Alas, poor heart!
If you spite it for my sake, I will spite it for yours,   65
for I will never love that which my friend hates.

Bene. Thou and I are too wise to woo peaceably.

Beat. It appears not in this confession; there's not one
wise man among twenty that will praise himself.

---

40. nor] *Q;* for *F.*   40. S.D.] *Q (after l. 42), F.*

40. *festival*] light-hearted, holiday-mood.

46. *with . . . came*] See v. i. 246, note.

55. *subscribe*] proclaim over my signature.

58. *politic*] canny, prudent.

69–71. *praise . . . neighbours*] Tilley N117 gives as proverbial 'He has ill neighbours that is fain to praise himself'.

Bene. An old, an old instance, Beatrice, that lived in the   70
time of good neighbours. If a man do not erect in
this age his own tomb ere he dies, he shall live no
longer in monument than the bell rings, and the
widow weeps.

Beat. And how long is that, think you?   75

Bene. Question: why, an hour in clamour and a quarter
in rheum. Therefore is it most expedient for the
wise, if Don Worm, his conscience, find no impediment to the contrary, to be the trumpet of his own
virtues, as I am to mys̓elf. So much for praising my-   80
self, who I myself will bear witness is praiseworthy.
And now tell me, how doth your cousin?

Beat. Very ill.

Bene. And how do you?

Beat. Very ill too.   85

Bene. Serve God, love me, and mend. There will I leave
you too, for here comes one in haste.

Enter URSULA.

Urs. Madam, you must come to your uncle—yonder's
old coil at home. It is proved my Lady Hero hath
been falsely accused, the Prince and Claudio   90
mightily abused, and Don John is the author of all,
who is fled and gone. Will you come presently?

Beat. Will you go hear this news, signior?

---

73. monument] *Q;* monuments *F.*   bell rings] *Q;* Bels ring *F.*   80. myself. So] *Rowe subst.;* my self so *QF subst.*   87. S.D.] *Q; after l. 85, F.*

70.] See Appendix V. iii.

73. *monument*] any memorial.

73–4. *the bell . . . weeps*] Two stories
in the *Hundred Merry Tales* (cf. ii.i. 120,
note) illustrate the situation. One
relates that a woman burying her
fourth husband lamented that at each
previous burial she had secured a
replacement before the corpse left the
house, but now 'I am sure of no other
husband'. For the second, see Appendix V. iii. In his *English Proverbs* W. C.
Hazlitt includes 'A good occasion for
courtship, when the widow returns

from the funeral'.

78. *Don . . . conscience*] A traditional
idea: 'the worm of conscience' occurs,
e.g. in Chaucer's *Physician's Tale*, l.
280, and *R3*, i. iii. 222. Halliwell cites
records of the Coventry mystery plays
for dresses for 'ij *wormes of conscience*,
xvj.d.'. The origin is doubtless Mark
ix. 46—'Their *worm* dieth not, and the
fire is not quenched.'

89. *old coil*] fine old rumpus.

91. *abused*] deceived, imposed upon.

92. *presently*] at once.

Bene. I will live in thy heart, die in thy lap, and be buried
   in thy eyes; and moreover, I will go with thee to thy   95
   uncle's.   *Exeunt.*

[SCENE III]

Enter CLAUDIO, *Prince* [DON PEDRO], *and three or four
with tapers* [, *followed by* BALTHASAR *and* Musicians].

Claud. Is this the monument of Leonato?
A Lord. It is, my lord.

Epitaph.

[*Claud.*] [*Reading from a scroll.*]
       'Done to death by slanderous tongues
           Was the Hero that here lies:
       Death, in guerdon of her wrongs,   5
           Gives her fame which never dies:
       So the life that died with shame
       Lives in death with glorious fame.'
                                        [*Hangs up the scroll.*]

   Hang thou there upon the tomb,

96. uncle's] *QF* (vncles) *subst., Malone.*   96. S.D.] *Q* (*exit.*), *F.*

Scene III

SCENE III] *Capell; not in QF.*   [*Location*] *A Church. Pope; A Church. A Stately
Monument in the Front. Capell; A Churchyard. Boas; not in QF.*   S.D. *Don Pedro*]
Rowe; not in QF.   followed by . . . Musicians] *Capell subst.; not in QF.*   2. *A*]
Camb.; not in QF.   3. Claud. . . . scroll] *Capell; not in QF.*   8. S.D.] *Capell
subst.; not in QF.*

Scene III

   Location] Conventionally, following
Pope, a church, though ll. 25–8
indicate a monument out of doors.
Wherever situated, an impressive
tomb (a stage-property, as in *Romeo
and Juliet*) is essential, to symbolize
the gravity of death and the purga-
torial nature of Claudio's reverence.
Short though the scene is, a conviction
of religious grief and awe is to be
evoked, creating depth and dignity of

emotion more by non-verbal than by
verbal means.
   3. *Claud.*] QF give no speech-
heading, as though the speaker continued to be the '*Lord*' of l. 2, Claudio
remaining silent until given l. 11 to
speak. It seems natural that Claudio
should himself deliver the epitaph,
and Capell's arrangement is therefore
adopted.
   5. *guerdon*] recompense, reward.
   9–10.] These lines are attached to
the epitaph in QF, though somewhat

Praising her when I am dumb.   10
Now, music, sound, and sing your solemn hymn.

Song.

[*Balth.*]   *Pardon, goddess of the night,*
              Those that slew thy virgin knight;
              For the which, with songs of woe,
              Round about her tomb they go.   15
                  Midnight, assist our moan,
                  Help us to sigh and groan,
                      Heavily, heavily:
              Graves, yawn and yield your dead,
              Till death be uttered,   20
                  Heavily, heavily.

Claud. Now unto thy bones good night!
          Yearly will I do this rite.

10. dumb] *F; dead Q*.   11. Now] *Capell; Claudio Now QF subst.*   12.
Balth.] NCS; not in QF.   16–17.] *as F3; one line, QF1–2*.   21. *Heavily,*
heavily] Q; Heauenly, heauenly F.   22. *Claud.] Rowe; Lo. QF*.   22–3.] *as*
Rowe 3; one line, QF.   23. rite] *QF (right), Pope*.

differentiated from it by indentation.
Since the couplet after the song is
marked to be spoken separately, it
seems right that this should be so too;
it is addressed to, not part of, the
epitaph, though the identical metre
maintains the ceremonial air.

12. *Balth.*] Having given Claudio
l. 11 to speak, QF name no singer and
leave it to be inferred that Claudio
was he. But in l. 11 Claudio has called
on some other performer and Balthasar is the obvious choice.

Pardon . . . night] See Appendix VI.
Since Hero is in fact not dead, a
Christian ceremony would be im-
proper and might have seemed
blasphemous to the play licenser.
Claudio's epitaph sounds a secular yet
solemn note, and the song is addressed
to Diana or Artemis, the moon,
protector of virgins, goddess of
chastity (as at IV.i.57). All the audience can perceive is 'a ritualistic
exorcism which drives away . . . the

somber shadow that temporarily
obscures the comic spirit' (J. H. Long,
Shakespeare's Use of Music, 1955, p.
134). Critics who detect 'extravagance
and insincerity', even 'something of
comedy', as signs of Claudio's deluded
sentimentality (P. J. Seng, *The Vocal*
Songs in the Plays of Shakespeare, 1967,
p. 69; R. Noble, *Shakespeare's Use of*
Song, p. 67), are postulating too
sophisticated a response.

13. *knight*] votary; follower; cf.
Two Noble Kinsmen, v.i.137—'O
sacred, shadowy, cold and constant
queene,/ . . . who to thy female *knights/*
Allow'st no more blood'.

15. *Round about her tomb*] The circ-
ling must be done clockwise, the
traditional way for averting evil, not
widdershins, which would have the
opposite effect.

19–20.] Various explanations have
been offered of these lines, none
entirely convincing. Midnight is to
assist their moan; graves are to yield

D. Pedro. Good morrow, masters; put your torches out.

      The wolves have prey'd, and look, the gentle day,   25

      Before the wheels of Phoebus, round about

      Dapples the drowsy east with spots of grey.

      Thanks to you all, and leave us. Fare you well.

Claud. Good morrow, masters—each his several way.

D. Pedro. Come let us hence, and put on other weeds,   30

      And then to Leonato's we will go.

Claud. And Hymen now with luckier issue speed's

      Than this for whom we render'd up this woe!   *Exeunt.*

[SCENE IV]

Enter LEONATO, BENEDICK, [BEATRICE,] MARGARET,
URSULA, *old man* [ANTONIO], FRIAR [FRANCIS], HERO.

Friar. Did I not tell you she was innocent?

Leon. So are the Prince and Claudio, who accus'd her

      Upon the error that you heard debated.

      But Margaret was in some fault for this,

---

24. *D. Pedro.*] *QF* (*Prince*) *subst., Rowe* (*Pedro*), *Capell* (*D. Pe.*).   24–7.] *as
Pope; ll.* 25, 27 *not indented, QF.*   25. prey'd] *QF1–3* (*preied*) *subst., F4.*   30.
D. Pedro.] *QF* (*Prince*) *subst., Rowe* (*Pedro*), *Capell* (*D. Pe.*).   32. speed's]
Theobald, conj. Thirlby; speeds *QF.*

Scene IV

SCENE IV] *Capell; not in QF.*   [*Location*] Leonato's House. *Pope; not in QF*
S.D. Beatrice] *Rowe; not in QF.*   Antonio] *Rowe; not in QF.*   Francis] *Rowe;
not in QF.*

up their dead; but how is death to be
uttered? That it is to be ousted or
expelled, as in Revelations xx. 14
('There shall be no more death'),
strains the sense intolerably. The
words are probably best taken as
parallel to *Help us to sigh and groan* and
as meaning 'Till we have fully voiced
our laments for her death', or 'Till all
that this death means has been fully
realized'.

24–7, 30–3.] The quatrains maintain a ritual air. Dawn's coming is
imaginatively appropriate to the
plot's emergence from the shadows of

evil and grief.

30. *other weeds*] different garments
(*weeds* now only in the expression
'widow's weeds'). Mourning black is
to change to wedding brightness as
the darkness of 'death' to the light of
revival.

32. *speed's*] = speed us.

Scene IV

Location] Leonato's house.

S.D. *Margaret*] Several editions
omit Margaret but QF include her,
reflecting the play's concern to gloss
over any apparent guilt.

Although against her will, as it appears   5
In the true course of all the question.
Ant. Well, I am glad that all things sort so well.
Bene. And so am I, being else by faith enforc'd
To call young Claudio to a reckoning for it.
Leon. Well, daughter, and you gentlewomen all,   10
Withdraw into a chamber by yourselves,
And when I send for you, come hither mask'd.

Exeunt Ladies.

The Prince and Claudio promis'd by this hour
To visit me. You know your office, brother:
You must be father to your brother's daughter,   15
And give her to young Claudio.
Ant. Which I will do with confirm'd countenance.
Bene. Friar, I must entreat your pains, I think.
Friar. To do what, signior?
Bene. To bind me, or undo me—one of them.   20
Signior Leonato, truth it is, good signior,
Your niece regards me with an eye of favour.
Leon. That eye my daughter lent her, 'tis most true.
Bene. And I do with an eye of love requite her.
Leon. The sight whereof I think you had from me,   25
From Claudio and the Prince. But what's your will?
Bene. Your answer, sir, is enigmatical:
But for my will, my will is, your good will
May stand with ours, this day to be conjoin'd
In the state of honourable marriage;   30
In which, good friar, I shall desire your help.
Leon. My heart is with your liking.
Friar.   And my help.
Here comes the Prince and Claudio.

7. *Ant.*] *QF (Old), Rowe.*   sort] *F;* sorts *Q.*   12. mask'd] *Q* (masked), *F.*
12. S.D.] *Camb.; after l. 16, QF.*   17. *Ant.*] *QF (Old), Rowe.*   33.] *Q; not in F.*

5. *against her will*] unintentionally. The sense cannot be that she was forced into wrong-doing.

6. *question*] investigation. The word is trisyllabic.

8. *faith*] my pledge to Beatrice.

17. *confirm'd countenance*] confident bearing, as in Valeria's account of Coriolanus' boy—'has such a *confirmed countenance*' (*Cor.*, I.iii.59); accented on *con-*.

21–2.] As noted at III.ii.64–5, Benedick's broaching of the subject then mooted has never occurred—an omission which allows it climactic force here.

Enter Prince [DON PEDRO] *and* CLAUDIO, *and two or three*
Others.

D. Pedro. Good morrow to this fair assembly.
Leon. Good morrow, Prince; good morrow, Claudio;   35
    We here attend you. Are you yet determin'd
    Today to marry with my brother's daughter?
Claud. I'll hold my mind were she an Ethiope.
Leon. Call her forth, brother; here's the friar ready.

                                        [*Exit Antonio.*]

D. Pedro. Good morrow, Benedick. Why, what's the matter,
    That you have such a February face,   41
    So full of frost, of storm, and cloudiness?
Claud. I think he thinks upon the savage bull.
    Tush, fear not, man, we'll tip thy horns with gold,
    And all Europa shall rejoice at thee,   45
    As once Europa did at lusty Jove,
    When he would play the noble beast in love.
Bene. Bull Jove, sir, had an amiable low,
    And some such strange bull leap'd your father's cow,
    And got a calf in that same noble feat   50
    Much like to you, for you have just his bleat.

Enter brother [ANTONIO], HERO, BEATRICE, MARGARET,
    URSULA [, *the ladies masked*].

Claud. For this I owe you: here comes other reck'nings.

33. S.D. *Don Pedro*] *Rowe; not in QF.*   *and . . . Others*] Q (*and two or three
other*); *with attendants* F.   34. *D. Pedro.*] QF (*Prince*) *subst., Rowe* (*Pedro*), *Capell*
(*D. Pe.*), *so subst. throughout scene.*   36. *determin'd*] Q (*determined*), F.
39. S.D.] *Theobald; not in QF.*   50. *And*] Q; A F.   51. S.D. *Antonio*]
Theobald; not in QF.   *the ladies masked*] *Theobald subst.; not in QF.*

34. *assembly*] Four syllables; cf. the
vocalic *l* in *tickling* (III.i.80) and the
rolled *r* in *parlour* (III.i.1).

38.] Claudio's response sounds
jaunty, but it is meant to express
entire submission and should be
spoken soberly, though cheerfully.

41–2. *February . . . cloudiness*] Only
for stage-effect would one expect
Benedick to look so formidable, but no
doubt he feels apprehensive over his

own emotions and Leonato's 'enigmatical' answers.

43. *savage bull*] The jest takes up
I.i.241–2 and v.i.178.

46. *Europa*] Europa's beauty fired
Jove to visit her in the form of a bull
and carry her on his back to Crete,
as Ovid relates in *Metamorphoses*,
Bk II.

52. *other reck'nings*] other matters to
be settled.

Which is the lady I must seize upon?

Ant. This same is she, and I do give you her.

Claud. Why then she's mine. Sweet, let me see your face. 55

Leon. No, that you shall not till you take her hand,
Before this friar, and swear to marry her.

Claud. Give me your hand before this holy friar.
I am your husband if you like of me.

Hero. [*Unmasking.*] And when I liv'd, I was your other wife;
And when you lov'd, you were my other husband. 61

Claud. Another Hero!

Hero.   Nothing certainer:
One Hero died defil'd, but I do live,
And surely as I live, I am a maid.

D. Pedro. The former Hero! Hero that is dead! 65

Leon. She died, my lord, but whiles her slander liv'd.

Friar. All this amazement can I qualify,
When after that the holy rites are ended
I'll tell you largely of fair Hero's death.
Meantime let wonder seem familiar, 70
And to the chapel let us presently.

Bene. Soft and fair, friar. Which is Beatrice?

Beat. [*Unmasking.*] I answer to that name. What is your will?

Bene. Do not you love me?

Beat.   Why, no, no more than reason.

Bene. Why then, your uncle, and the Prince, and Claudio 75
Have been deceiv'd—they swore you did.

---

54. *Ant.*] *Theobald; Leo. QF.*   60. S.D.] *Rowe (after* other wife.*); not in QF.*
61. lov'd] *Q* (loued), *F.*   63. defil'd] *Q; not in F.*   73. S.D.] *Capell (after*
name.*); not in QF.*   75–6.] *as verse, Q; as prose, F.*   76. deceiv'd] *QF* (de-
ceiued), *Rowe.*

---

54. *Ant.*] Since Antonio is the
bride's ostensible father, Theobald
transferred the attribution of this line
from QF's *Leo.* Some editors transfer
ll. 56–7 to Antonio also. But there it
is natural enough that Leonato should
break in to direct matters.

59. *like of*] 'Of after "to like" is
perhaps a result of the old impersonal
use of the verb, "me liketh", "him
liketh", which might seem to dis-

qualify the verb from taking a direct
object': Abbott § 177.

62. *certainer*] For similar compara-
tive inflections see Abbott § 7.

63. *defil'd*] slandered, under a
stain.

67. *qualify*] moderate, or appease.

69. *largely*] in full.

70. *let . . . familiar*] treat these
surprises as natural matters.

71. *presently*] forthwith.

Beat. Do not you love me?

Bene.   Troth, no, no more than reason.

Beat. Why then, my cousin, Margaret, and Ursula
     Are much deceiv'd, for they did swear you did.

Bene. They swore that you were almost sick for me.   80

Beat. They swore that you were well-nigh dead for me.

Bene. 'Tis no such matter. Then you do not love me?

Beat. No, truly, but in friendly recompense.

Leon. Come, cousin, I am sure you love the gentleman.

Claud. And I'll be sworn upon't that he loves her,   85
     For here's a paper written in his hand,
     A halting sonnet of his own pure brain,
     Fashion'd to Beatrice.

Hero.   And here's another,
     Writ in my cousin's hand, stol'n from her pocket,
     Containing her affection unto Benedick.   90

Bene. A miracle! Here's our own hands against our
     hearts. Come, I will have thee, but by this light I
     take thee for pity.

Beat. I would not deny you, but by this good day I
     yield upon great persuasion, and partly to save   95
     your life, for I was told you were in a consumption.

Bene. Peace! I will stop your mouth.   [*Kisses her.*]

D. Pedro. How dost thou, 'Benedick, the married man'?

Bene. I'll tell thee what, Prince; a college of wit-crackers
     cannot flout me out of my humour. Dost thou   100
     think I care for a satire or an epigram? No: if a
     man will be beaten with brains, a shall wear
     nothing handsome about him. In brief, since I do
     purpose to marry, I will think nothing to any pur-
     pose that the world can say against it; and therefore   105

80. that] *Q; not in F.*   81. that] *Q; not in F.*   82. such] *Q; not in F.*
me?] *F;* me. *Q.*   88. Fashion'd] *QF* (Fashioned), *Rowe.*   97. *Bene.] Theo-*
bald; Leon. QF.   97. S.D.] *Theobald subst.; not in QF.*

84. *cousin*] Used here of a niece, as
at I. ii. I of a nephew.

87–8. *sonnet . . . another*] In *LLL*,
IV. ii.–iii, the King of Navarre and his
companions likewise betray their true
feelings by composing secret poems.

96. *in a consumption*] 'wasting away
with lovesickness' (Kittredge).

101–3. *if a man . . . about him*] A
man whose wits can be mocked into
submission may as well give up all
personal display.

never flout at me for what I have said against it; for
man is a giddy thing, and this is my conclusion. For
thy part, Claudio, I did think to have beaten thee,
but in that thou art like to be my kinsman, live un-
bruised, and love my cousin.   110

Claud. I had well hoped thou wouldst have denied
Beatrice, that I might have cudgelled thee out of
thy single life, to make thee a double-dealer; which
out of question thou wilt be, if my cousin do not
look exceeding narrowly to thee.   115

Bene. Come, come, we are friends. Let's have a dance
ere we are married, that we may lighten our own
hearts and our wives' heels.

Leon. We'll have dancing afterward.

Bene. First, of my word! Therefore play, music. Prince,   120
thou art sad; get thee a wife, get thee a wife! There
is no staff more reverend than one tipped with horn.

106. what] *Q; not in F.*

107. *my conclusion*] 'My final anti-
cipation in reading the play is the
certainty that Beatrice will provoke
her Benedick to give her much and
just conjugal castigation' (Thomas
Campbell, *Dramatic Works of Shakespeare*, 1838, p. xlvi). 'I have no mis-
givings about the future happiness of
Benedick and Beatrice. . . . They will
always be finding out something new
and interesting in each other's
character. . . . She will prove the
fitness of her name as Beatrice (the
giver of happiness), and he will be
glad to confess himself blest indeed
(Benedictus) in having won her'
(Helen Faucit, Lady Martin, *On
Some of Shakespeare's Female Characters*,
1891, p. 325). Shakespeare winds
his play up with so complete a
restoration of harmony that foreseeing
a further instalment almost affronts
his artistic design—not, probably,
that he would at all object.

109. *kinsman*] Marrying Beatrice's
cousin, Claudio will become kin to
Beatrice's husband.

113. *make thee a double-dealer*] i.e.
I'd have beaten you out of single life
into (*i*) double (married) life, and
(*ii*) double-dealing (unfaithful) married life, at that.

121. *get thee a wife*] 'The complete-
ness of Benedick's recantation is
underlined by his wish to marry off
Don Pedro' (Craik, p. 314). Yet, as
with Antonio at the end of *The Merchant of Venice*, he who has done most
to further his younger friends' marriages (and in *Much Ado* has even
offered his hand to Beatrice) is left in
somewhat touching singleness. The
dramatic excellence of Benedick's
advice lies not only in the complete-
ness of his recantation but in the fact
that he recants without the slightest
loss of face and with a total refusal to
be disconcerted; moreover, he turns
the tables on the arch-plotter of the
jest against him: Don Pedro is now
the odd man out.

122. *staff . . . horn*] Probably an
allusion to the walking-sticks of
elderly folk, often horn-tipped; with,

Enter Messenger.

Mess. My lord, your brother John is ta'en in flight,
  And brought with armed men back to Messina.
Bene. Think not on him till tomorrow; I'll devise thee   125
  brave punishments for him. Strike up, pipers!

                                    Dance. [*Exeunt.*]
                      FINIS.

126. S.D. *Exeunt.*] *Rowe; not in QF.*

of course, an ironical fling at the dangers of cuckoldry. Benedick has the last word.

125–6.] 'Don John is a brief study in laconic villainy. But . . . the limits of his mischief are strictly defined. The "brave punishments" he has so richly deserved are left at the end to Benedick's invention, seemingly to add to the gaiety of the wedding festivities. The spirit of comedy prevails' (F. P. Wilson, *Shakespearian and Other Studies*, 1969, p. 87). Shakespeare is shrewd enough to leave out of his final reconciliations figures who, like Don John, would jar with the resolution into harmony—Jaques in *As You Like It*, Malvolio in *Twelfth Night*, and Antonio in *The Tempest*.

126. Dance] This is the only play of Shakespeare's that literally ends with a social dance, though *A Midsummer Night's Dream* finishes with the mechanicals' bergamask, Theseus' reference to 'nightly revels', and the fairies' song and dance before Puck's epilogue, and *As You Like It* has a dance followed only by Rosalind's epilogue. Any idea here of finishing in chapel (l. 71) is dismissed for the gayer symbol of happy marriage, the harmony of music and the measured figures of partnership in dance. 'Dancing is the most eloquent stage action which Shakespeare used to celebrate a call to order and decorum' (J. R. Brown, *Shakespeare and His Comedies*, 1957, p. 139).

APPENDIX I

SOURCE ANALOGUES

The following versions precede Shakespeare's treatment but seem not to have influenced it.

(i) *Peter Beverley: 'Ariodanto and Ieneura' (1565–6)*

Peter Beverley's verse narrative, one copy of which survives in the Huntington Library, California, is reprinted in C. T. Prouty's *The Sources of 'Much Ado About Nothing'* (1950). In worthy if pedestrian fourteener couplets it is the first version in English of any part of *Orlando Furioso*.

It adjusts Ariosto's story considerably, with a different intention in mind, this being to elaborate the romantic extremities of hazardous love. It virtually inverts the narrative sequence. In place of relating first Dalinda's rescue from assailants by Renaldo (here Raynaldo) and her disclosure of the villainies of Polynesso (Pollinesso), before treating Ariodanto's love and deception, it begins (and continues lengthily) with Jenevra's beauties and the adventurous travels of Ariodanto and his brother Lurcanio to the Scottish court, with their reception and prowess there (Lurcanio, a great hunter, saves the King from a lion; Ariodanto is idolized for courtly graces). Jenevra and Ariodanto, after hyperbolic ardours and despairs occupying hundreds of lines, realize their mutual love, and only then does the jealous Pollinesso enter the story, to tell Ariodanto, under feigned friendship, that he himself is the preferred lover. As evidence of Jenevra's unfaithfulness he shows a diamond ring Ariodanto had given her, which Dalinda had secretly secured. Though protractedly despairing, Ariodanto decides it is no proof, whereon Pollinesso proceeds to the bedroom trick, with Dalinda disguised as Jenevra. The story proceeds as in Ariosto, though Dalinda's rescue is held back to a late stage, just before the dénouement at court, with Lurcanio, Jenevra's accuser, prepared to fight to prove her guilt, against an unknown black-armoured champion (the returned Ariodanto). Pollinesso, himself now accused, denies the charge, but being overcome confesses, on which to universal rejoicing the lovers are reunited.

219

What Beverley is evidently interested in is not Ariosto's lively story of villainy confounded but the paroxysms of love endlessly elaborated in conventional emotional extravagances.

(ii) George Whetstone: 'The Rocke of Regard' (1576)

George Whetstone's story relates the love of Rinaldo and Giletta. Giletta is forced, for diplomatic reasons, to feign love for Rinaldo's rival Frizaldo. Frizaldo, to ruin her with Rinaldo, discovers through a disloyal maid, Rosina, that Giletta is sending Rinaldo a love-message hidden in an apple. He substitutes a contrary message, and Rinaldo, after rejoicing at the receipt of the apple, is horrified by reading what it contains, which gives him to understand that she is faithless. Like Ariodante in Ariosto he departs to drown himself, leaving with a peasant a scroll saying so. This is taken to the castle of Giletta's father, the Lord of Bologna, where Giletta is cast into despair at the news. Rinaldo, having leapt into the River Po, flounders out again and hides in a forest, hopelessly lamenting. Giletta overhears him from her window, discovers who he is, and is overjoyed.

She then, however, must suffer Frizaldo's suit, which is furthered by her father. Proclamation is made that unless Rinaldo (believed dead) claims Giletta's hand within a month she is to marry Frizaldo. Everyone rejoices whether in the know (like Rinaldo and Giletta) or not (like Frizaldo, the father, and friends), and Frizaldo makes great preparations.

But Rosina, the maid, has been promised marriage by Frizaldo and becomes jealous. Frizaldo protests that his courting Giletta is merely a blind, to punish her for her earlier refusals of him, and that on the eve of the wedding he will marry Rosina herself. In fact, he employs two accomplices to kill her in the forest where, as in Ariosto, Rinaldo rescues her. Rosina tells all this to Rinaldo and on the wedding morning, disguised in black armour, he accosts the wedding party and has Rosina relate her story. Frizaldo blusters a defence but Rinaldo challenges him and after a great fight kills him; upon which the marriage of Rinaldo and Giletta follows at once.

Shakespeare may have known Whetstone's story which, with picturesque variations, resembles Ariosto's, but there seem no actual debts, and the status of *The Rocke of Regard* is rather that of an analogue than of a source.

(iii) Edmund Spenser: 'The Faerie Queene' (1590)

The same is the case with Spenser's treatment in *The Faerie*

Queene, Book II, Canto IV. On the eve of a marriage promising every happiness Squire Phedon, in mutual love with Claribell, a lady of high degree, is deceived by his trusted friend Philemon, whose motives are either sheer envy (love-jealousy is never mentioned) or innate evil (II.iv.22). Philemon asserts that Claribell has 'distainde her honourable blood' and her vowed faith (II.iv. 22). Phedon falls wildly jealous. Philemon offers to prove Claribell faithless with a low-born groom and he flatters her maid, Pryene, that if she dresses in Claribell's finery she will outshine all beauties whatever. He arranges that Phedon 'in secret corner laid' (II.iv.27) shall that very night see the supposed Claribell (Pyrene disguised) receive the supposed groom (Philemon himself, also disguised). Phedon of course is deceived; he leaves in a fury and as soon as he meets Claribell he kills her. When he tells why, Pryene confesses her part and Philemon's guilt. Phedon poisons Philemon, and is pursuing Pryene until himself seized and overcome by Furor, from whom Sir Guyon rescues him.

The knightly-romance tone is like Ariosto, unlike Bandello, as indeed is the material on the whole. Spenser's treatment is far briefer and simpler than either of the others', and such features as the deluded Phedon's being sole witness of the supposed infidelity probably result from that fact rather than from any switch to Bandello. The hero's love for a high-born lady, the maid flattered by the wicked paramour into dressing as her mistress, and the villain killed in revenge by the hero—these elements are like Ariosto, not Bandello: only in the loosest of ways are they analogous to Shakespeare. The one thing that is nearer to Shakespeare than either of the others is the explanation of the villain's motive as pure envy or evil nature, but this similarity is probably pure coincidence.

APPENDIX II

THE EVOLUTION OF WIT STYLE

To trace the evolution of wit style for comedy would be too long a topic for the introduction, and would moreover tend to suggest that verbal figure-skating is the hallmark of *Much Ado*. This, largely true as it is of a writer like Oscar Wilde, is largely untrue of *Much Ado*, or rather is true only inasmuch as Shakespeare, from the tradition of precursors in sophisticated prose and from his own development in witty felicities, has by now at his fingertips a living style of pith and point.

Yet though artifice for the sake of artifice is at this stage evident only when affectation is to be mocked, the process by which dramatic prose evolved towards pith and point is worth tracing. And with this, Lyly's precursors and Lyly himself had much to do.

Euphuistic devices were not unprecedented before Lyly; they existed already in many quarters—alliterative patterns in Old and Middle English, balance and duplication of qualifiers in prose from Bede onwards, structural parallelism in the Bible.[1] Nearer to euphuism, however, are certain sixteenth-century prose forms —the patternings and alliterations of Berners's translations of Froissart (1523) and of Guevara's *Libro de Emperador Marco Aurelio* as *The Golden Boke of Marcus Aurelius* (1535), North's version of the same work in *The Diall of Princes* (1557), and George Pettie's *Petite Pallace of Pettie his Pleasure* (1576). Berners's preface to Froissart multiplies near-synonyms in formal and symmetrical flourishes:

> But onely hystorie, truely with wordes representyng the actes, gestes, and dedes done, complecteth all profyt; it moveth, stereth, and compelleth to honestie; detesteth, erketh, and abhorreth vices; it extolleth, enhaunceth, and lyfteth up such as ben noble and vertuous; depresseth, poystereth, and thrusteth downe such as ben wicked, yvell, and reprovable.[2]

From Guevara, 'one of the earliest European writers to realize

1. For further discussion see Thomas North, *The Diall of Princes*, ed. K. N. Colvile (1919), p. xxxv.
2. *The Cronycle of Syr John Froissart*, trans. Sir John Bourchier, Lord Berners, ed. W. P. Ker, Tudor Translations series (1901), I. 5.

that prose . . . has its pattern, intensifying the qualities of the abstract thought by the sound and the rhythm',[1] Berners transplanted into English many of the formulations on which euphuism was to thrive; for example,

> My herte being hole, thou hast deuyded, beinge in helth thou hast hurte, being aliue thou hast slayne. . . . Doest thou not thynke, that philosophers though they were neuer so sage, be not stryken with the cruelties of loue? and that vnder their cours clothes their fleshe is not smoth? Certaynely amo[n]ge the hard bones soft fleshe is bredde, vnder the sharpe huskes the chestnutte is nouryshed.[2]

The idea that prose should be—to adopt Sir Nathaniel's praise of Holofernes in *Love's Labour's Lost*—'sharp and sententious; pleasant without scurrility; audacious without impudency'—got off to a good start. North's later translation of Guevara made its contribution too, pointing its meaning by classical allusions, by simple natural similes, and by epigrammatic antitheses, paradoxes, and aphorisms. Of rivals courting a girl it declares,

> They both served her, they both followed her, they both loved her, and for her they both desired to die. For the dart of love is as a stroke with a clod of earth; the which being thrown amongst a company doth hurt the one, and blind the other;

and of claimants to knowledge,

> Amongst the sages he is most wise that presumeth to know least; and amongst the simple he is most ignorant that thinketh to know most. For if there be found one that knoweth much, yet always there is found another that knoweth more.[3]

North did not provide all that Lyly was to give but he notably developed the alert phrasing of choreographic patterns.

Pettie is closer to Lyly. In his *Petite Pallace*, alliterations, apostrophes, antitheses, analogies, rhymes, chimes, and patterns abound. In the story of *Sinorix and Canna* we learn that in happy marriage 'there is nothing fearful, nothing feigned; all things done faithfully, without doubting, truly, without flouting, willingly without constraint, joyfully without complaint';[4] in *Tereus and Progne* that plants feel 'neither the force of winter's blasts, nor the

1. North, op. cit., pp. xxxi–xxxii.
2. J. M. Galvez, *Guevara in England nebst Neudruck von Lord Berners' 'Golden Boke of Marcus Aurelius'* (*1535*), Palaestra, CIX (1916), p. 439.
3. North, op. cit., pp. 33, 54.
4. George Pettie, *Petite Pallace*, ed. I[srael] G[ollancz] (1908), I. 12: references in the following quotations are to this edition.

fire of summer's blaze', and that animals 'bear the brunt of their bodies only, and are not molested with the motions of the mind', whereas men suffer 'all storms of strife and pangs of pain', since they 'begin with cries and end with cares' (I. 50); in *Pygmalion and Luciano* that 'the flood of their felicity flowed from the fountain of most faithful friendship, the building of their biding together was raised on the rock of virtue' (II. 112–13). Procris cries in desire for Cephalus, 'Good God! what fiery flames do fry within me! what desire, what lust! what hope, what trust! what care, what despair! what fear, what fury!' (II. 52). And Pygmalion, afflicted by the veering of Panthea's love, expostulates thus (II. 114–15):

> O feigned fawning! O counterfeit courtesy! O deep dissembling! O honey mixed with gall! O heaven turned to hell! . . . And canst thou then prefer lewdness before learning, trifling before truth, clownishness before courtliness, vanity before virtue?

The attractions of prose art were not confined to elegant fictions or aphoristic moralizing; they offered themselves as a desirable social accomplishment. The early letters of Elizabeth show her fascination with witty point and excogitated effect, as in an undated letter to her brother Edward VI:

> Like as a shipman in stormy weather plucks down the sails tarrying for better wind, so did I, most noble King, in my unfortunate chance a' Thursday pluck down the high sails of my joy and comfort and do trust one day that as troublesome waves have repulsed me backward, so a gentle wind will bring me forward to my haven:

and again to Edward VI, from Hatfield, 15 May 1552:

> Like as the rich man that daily gathereth riches to riches, and to one bag of money layeth a great store till it come to infinite, so methinks your Majesty, not being sufficed with many benefits and gentleness showed to me afore this time, doth now increase them in asking and desiring where you may bid and command, requiring a thing not worthy the desiring for itself, but made worthy for your Highness' request. My picture, I mean, in which if the inward good mind toward your Grace might as well be declared as the outward face and countenance shall be seen, I would not have tarried the commandment but prevent[ed] it, nor have been the last to grant but the first to offer it. For the face, I grant, I might well blush to offer, but the mind I shall never be ashamed to present. . . . Of this although yet the proof could not be great, because the occasion hath been so small, notwithstanding as a dog hath a day, so may I

perchance have time to declare it in deeds where now I do write them in words.[1]

By Shakespeare's youth the current ran strongly toward a mannered vivacity of style. Lyly's climactic achievement may have owed something to Latin lectures given at Oxford by John Rainolds between 1572 and 1578.[2] These anticipate Lyly in syllabic echoing, alliteration, similes from real or fanciful natural history, and phrases patterned on similar length, syntax, or sound. They were popular while young men later prominent as euphuists were in residence; Rainolds noted that 'nostri adolescentuli' favoured him.[3] C. S. Lewis, however, observed that he sounds more pre-euphuistic in selected samples than in bulk, and concluded that Lyly himself was the true establisher of the style.[4]

Yet so many influences converged upon it that in effect 'Euphuism had attained full-blown existence before Lyly composed *Euphues*'.[5] Lyly himself said that he 'gleane[d] after an Others Cart',[6] and Gabriel Harvey observed that 'young Euphues . . . hatched the egges, that his elder freendes laid'.[7] Whatever their genesis, the full blossoming of these artifices, gathered in unmistakable totality in *Euphues, the Anatomy of Wit* (1578) and *Euphues and his England* (1579), intoxicated writers during the next two decades. Alliterations—simple, alternate, or patterned in other ways—syllabic echoes and assonances, puns and other semantic conjurings, fanciful variations on classical mythology and Plinyan natural-unnatural history, antithetical and paradoxical balances, incremental sequences and rhetorical apostrophes, became for a decade and more the hallmarks of the new sophistication. At first sight a mere flourish of ornamental mannerisms, euphuism showed the writer alertly calculating each verbal effect. Its general significance for drama is well expressed by Lyly's editor, R. W. Bond:

These [North, Pettie, and Lyly], and Lyly in particular,

---

1. G. B. Harrison (ed.), *The Letters of Queen Elizabeth* (1935, repr. 1968), pp. 15–16.

2. W. Ringler, 'The Immediate Source of Euphuism', *PMLA* (1938), vol. 53, pp. 678–86.

3. Ibid., p. 685, quoting Rainolds's *Orationes Duae* (1587). Lyly was at Oxford from 1569 to 1575, Lodge from 1573 to 1578, and Gosson from 1572 to 1576 (publishing his euphuistic *Ephemerides of Phialo*, dedicated to Sidney, in 1579, and saying it has 'some taste of the Vniversitie'). Pettie graduated in 1570 and apparently resided some time thereafter.

4. *English Literature in the Sixteenth Century* (1954), p. 313.

5. Lyly, *Works*, ed. R. W. Bond, I. 142.

6. Ibid., II. 5.

7. *Works*, ed. A. B. Grosart, II. 124.

recognised . . . the quality of mind in style, and treatment of the sentence not as a haphazard accumulation . . . but as a piece of literary architecture, whose end is foreseen in the beginning, and whose parts are calculated to minister to the total effect. Of this mental quality, this architectural spirit in style, Antithesis is the most powerful instrument.[1]

The prose of *Euphues* holds only limited dramatic promise. Sentences sprinkle themselves on the attention by pithy rhythm, spirited sound, and witty sense, but the array of artifice blunts their impact. The style of the comedies is much more dramatically effective; it is the language of light-footed onward-moving attention, enticing not only the ear but the mind by expectation of new stages of ingeniously provoked idea, and by stage-speech 'intensified, . . . infused with more point and emphasis, more wisdom and earnestness, . . . than common talk can ever be'.[2] It is, particularly, the language of tenderness, bravura self-analysis, and adroit repartee.[3] The effects were captivating, and were widely evident in Shakespeare's work of the 1590s, indeed up to Hamlet's exchanges with Rosencrantz and Guildenstern.

As important as any other virtue was its liveliness for vocal delivery—delivery not, indeed, of adult force, but of the light clarity of the boys' voices for which it was written. Phrasing like the following is equally apt for the mind which follows it, the memory which learns it, and the voice which speaks it:

Alexander as he tendereth virtue, so will he you; he drinketh not blood, but thirsteth after honour; he is greedy of victory, but never satisfied [i.e. satiated] with mercy. In fight terrible, as becometh a captain; in conquest mild, as beseemeth a king; in all things, than which nothing can be greater, he is Alexander.[4]

A brief anthology of Lylyan traits which Shakespeare (and others) must have found congenial and which led towards the sensitive refinements of good romance comedy follows.

1. Lyly, *Works*, ed. R. W. Bond, I. 145.
2. Ibid., II. 287.
3. 'The mood of *Euphues* and of the plays lies between sentimentality and acerbity, sentiment being sharpened by wit, and wit being humanized by sentiment. The ideal of life presented is one which will perfectly balance these two sides of human nature and social intercourse' (G. K. Hunter, *John Lyly*, p. 298).
4. *Campaspe*, I. i. 48 (*Works*, ed. R. W. Bond, II. 318).

(*i*) *Epigrammatic trimness*

Silvestris: The whole heauen hath but one Sunne.
Niobe: But starres infinite.
Silvestris: A woman hath but one heart.
Niobe: But a thousand thoughts.
Silvestris: My Lute, though it haue many strings, maketh a sweete consent; and a Ladies heart, though it harbour many fancies, should embrace but one.
Niobe: The strings of my heart are tuned in a contrarie keye to your Lute, and make as sweete harmonie in discord, as yours in concord.
Silvestris: Why, what strings are in Ladies hearts? Not the base.
Niobe: There is no base string in a womans heart.
Silvestris: The meane?
Niobe: There was neuer meane in a womans heart.
(*Loues Metamorphosis*, III.i. 109–24: *Works*, ed. Bond, III.313)

(*ii*) *Aphorisms*

Sybilla: Bee not coy when you are courted. Fortunes wings are made of times feathers, which stay not whilest one may measure them. Be affable and courteous in youth, that you may be honoured in age. Roses that lose their colours, keepe their sauours, and pluckt from the stalke, are put to the still.
(*Sapho and Phao*, II.i. 106–10: *Works*, ed. Bond, II.383)

(*iii*) *Gnomic dialogue*

Tellus: Why, she [Cynthia] is but a woman.
Endimion: No more was Venus.
Tellus: Shee is but a virgin.
Endimion: No more was Vesta.
Tellus: Shee shall haue an ende.
Endimion: So shall the world.
(*Endimion*, II.i. 79–84: *Works*, ed. Bond, III.33)

(*iv*) *Self-quizzing*

Mydas: Is *Mydas* that sought to bee Monarch of the world, become the mock of the world? are his golde[n] mynes turnd into water, as free for euery one that will fetch, as for himself that possessed the[m] by wish? Ah, poore *Mydas*! are his conceiptes become blockish, his counsells vnfortunate, his iudgements vnskilfulle? Ah, foolish *Mydas*.
(*Midas*, IV.i. 176–81: *Works*, ed. Bond, III.144)

(*v*) *Witty fantasy*

Sybilla: Litle things catch light mindes, and fancy is a worme, that feedeth first upon fenell. . . . Be prodigall in praises and

promises, bewtie must haue a trumpet, & pride a gifte. Pea-
cocks neuer spread their feathers, but when they are flattered,
and Gods are seldome pleased, if they be not bribed.

    (*Sapho and Phao*, II.iv.60–1, 66–9: *Works*, ed. Bond, II.390)

(*vi*) *Lucid delicacy*

Endimion: You know (fayre *Tellus*) that the sweet remembrance
of your loue, is the only companion of my life, and thy
presence, my paradise; so that I am not alone when no bodie
is with mee, and in heauen it selfe, when thou art with me.

    (*Endimion*, II.i.53–6: *Works*, ed. Bond, III.32)

Eumenides: It is *Semele*, *Cynthia*: the possessing of whose loue,
must onelie prolong my life.

Cynthia: Nay sith *Endimion* is restored, wee will haue all parties
pleased. *Semele*, are you content after so long triall of his faith,
such rare secresie, such vnspotted loue, to take *Eumenides*?
Why speake you not? Not a word?

Endimion: Silence, Madame, consents: that is most true.

Cynthia: It is true *Endimion*. *Eumenides*, take *Semele*. Take her I
say.

Eumenides: Humble thanks, Madame: now onely doe I begin to
liue.

    (*Endimion*, v.iii.205–14: *Works*, ed. Bond, III.77)

(*vii*) *Witty banter and mockery*

Mileta on men

    (*Sapho and Phao*, I.iv.15–40: *Works*, ed. Bond, II.379)

The mocking circle of women

    (*Midas*, III.iii: *Works*, ed. Bond, III.136ff.)

APPENDIX III

'THE LAW AGAINST LOVERS'

Pepys saw *The Law Against Lovers* at Lincoln's Inn Fields theatre on 18 February 1662 and thought it 'a good play and well performed, especially the Little Girle's (who I never saw act before) dancing and singing'. Such a feature being hardly expected by devotees of either *Much Ado* or *Measure for Measure*, it may be explained that Beatrice was furnished with a young sister Viola, who sang a song written by Benedick, 'Wake all the dead! What hoa! What hoa!', joined with Benedick, Beatrice, and Lucio in a chorus, 'Our Ruler has got the vertigo of State', and danced a saraband with 'castianetos'. Benedick (so called in the text, though Benedict in the *Dramatis Personae*) is Angelo's brother, Beatrice is Angelo's ward and a great heiress, Claudio is the Claudio not of *Much Ado* but of *Measure for Measure* and in love with Beatrice's cousin Julietta, and Lucio and Balthazar are friends of Angelo and Benedick. Hero and Don John do not appear at all. Benedick's lines are largely nondescript new composition save when he spars with Beatrice; Beatrice applies to the frosty Angelo some of *Much Ado*'s comments on Don John, and she is trapped into love when Lucio and Balthazar maintain that Benedick loves her. The early scenes retain something of Shakespeare's text for her and Benedick, but the rest largely abandons Shakespeare and sets the two conspiring to free Claudio and Julietta from gaol.

Of this unlikely work David Erskine Baker's *Companion to the Playhouse* (1764) reported that it 'met with great success' and that its substance was 'borrowed from that divine author, all that Sir William [Davenant] has done being to blend the circumstances of both plays together, so as to form some connexion between the plots' (a good idea, one would agree) 'and to soften and modernize those passages of the language which appeared rough or obsolete. The Scene, Turin' (edited by Stephen Jones as *Biographia Dramatica; or, a Companion to the Theatre*, 1812, II. 364).

APPENDIX IV

THE PROXY WOOING

Claudio's talk with Don Pedro (*i*) would presumably take place before Leonato's house (I.i.270ff.); (*ii*) Antonio's reference (I.ii.9) to a discussion in *mine orchard* would seem to point to another occasion; to which (*iii*) Borachio's report of an indoor meeting (I.iii.54–60) adds a third. In real life three discussions might be needed, but within the play surely not. The likeliest explanation is that Shakespeare scattered these references without troubling over consistency; an audience will hardly notice, and, if it should, the variations enhance that prevalence of hearsay and guesswork in which the play abounds. Critics, however, have sought to elucidate the matter. Borachio's report, originating in *a musty room*, clearly differs from the others, and suggests that Claudio and Don Pedro have had a resumption of their discussion. Some critics have thought occasions (*i*) and (*ii*) above also to be different. But as the New Cambridge edition observes, what Antonio learns is certainly (though distortedly) what Don Pedro had said. Both men refer to festivities 'tonight'/'this night', and to the 'break' (the subject-broaching) Don Pedro will undertake with Leonato. Kittredge sought to identify the two occasions by suggesting that Leonato and Antonio share an extensive house and grounds (orchard meaning 'garden', not the modern fruit-plantation), so that Leonato's courtyard and Antonio's orchard could be contiguous and accommodate both the initial talk and the report of it: Boas, to avoid a switch from Leonato's to Antonio's territory, read *the* (for *mine*) *orchard*. Such are the strategies of too literal criticism. The question is best left as part of that hinted offstage context which adds much to the play's perspectives even if, as with Beatrice and Benedick's former relationship, one is left guessing. The Warwick editor comments shrewdly: '[Antonio's] report is incorrect: so, though less seriously, is Borachio's version. Nothing comes of this mistake, except that it shows how the prince's plan might be misconceived, and so prepares us for Don John's machinations in Act II. But the discrepancy is none the less intentional. Shakespeare had noted that no two reports of an occurrence are, as a rule, precisely the same, except by collusion. Cf. *Oth.*, I.iii.5—"But though they jump not on a just account,/—As in these cases, where the aim reports,/'Tis oft with difference". These little discrepancies, like the two views in a stereoscope, help to create that sense of solidity of which Shakespeare is the greatest master.'

APPENDIX V

OLD TALES

(i) I. i. 200: 'Like the old tale, my lord'

A Mr Blakeway contributed to the Boswell–Malone Variorum edition in 1821, VII. 164–5, the tale given below, told him by a great-aunt born in 1715 who, he surmised, had heard it from a narrator born under Charles II. It has many analogues in European folklore on the general lines of the 'Robber-Bridegroom' type of story, the essentials of which are as given in *The Handbook of Folk-lore* (ed. C. S. Burne, 1914, Appendix c, p. 352): '1. A girl is engaged to a disguised robber. 2. She visits his castle and discovers his occupation. 3. She convicts him before her relatives by some token, and he is killed.' For a German version see 'The Robber Bridegroom' in Grimm's *Household Tales*, trans. M. Hunt (1884), 1. 40: the Nurse's story of Captain Murderer in Dickens's *The Uncommercial Traveller*, ch. xv, is an English variant. The *Journal of the Gypsy Lore Society*, New Series, II. 372–6, and Third Series, 1. 97–109, contains gypsy versions. Mr Blakeway's tale is as follows:

Once upon a time, there was a young lady (called Lady Mary in the story) who had two brothers. One summer they all three went to a country seat of theirs, which they had not before visited. Among the other gentry in the neighbourhood who came to see them, was a Mr. Fox, a batchelor, with whom they, particularly the young lady, were much pleased. He used often to dine with them, and frequently invited Lady Mary to come and see his house. One day that her brothers were absent elsewhere, and she had nothing better to do, she determined to go thither; and accordingly set out unattended. When she arrived at the house, and knocked at the door, no one answered. At length she opened it, and went in; over the portal of the hall was written *'Be bold, be bold, but not too bold'*: she advanced: over the staircase, the same inscription: she went up: over the entrance of a gallery, the same: she proceeded: over the door of a chamber,—'*Be bold, be bold, but not too bold, lest that your heart's blood should run cold.*' She opened it; it was full of skeletons, tubs full of blood, etc. She retreated in haste; coming down stairs, she saw out of a window Mr. Fox advancing towards the house, with a drawn sword in one hand, while with the other he dragged along a young lady by her hair. Lady Mary had just time to slip down, and hide herself under the stairs, before Mr. Fox and his victim arrived at the foot of them. As he pulled the young lady up stairs, she caught hold of one of the bannisters with her hand, on which was a rich bracelet. Mr. Fox cut it off with his sword: the hand and bracelet fell into Lady Mary's lap, who then contrived to escape unobserved, and got home safe to her brother's house.

After a few days, Mr. Fox came to dine with them as usual (whether by invitation, or of his own accord, this deponent saith not). After dinner, when the guests began to amuse each other with extraordinary anecdotes, Lady Mary at length said, she would relate to them a remarkable dream she had lately had. I dreamt, said she, that as you, Mr. Fox, had often invited me to your house, I would go there one morning. When I came to the house, I knocked, etc., but no one answered. When I opened the door, over the hall was written, '*Be bold, be bold, but not too bold.*' But, said she, turning to Mr. Fox, and smiling, *It is not so, nor it was not so;* then she pursues the rest of the story, concluding at every turn with *It is not so, nor it was not so,* till she comes to the room full of dead bodies, when Mr. Fox took up the burden of the tale, and said, *It is not so, nor it was not so, and God forbid it should be so*: which he continues to repeat at every subsequent turn of the dreadful story, till she came to the circumstance of his cutting off the young lady's hand, when, upon his saying as usual, *It is not so, nor it was not so, and God forbid it should be so,* Lady Mary retorts, *But it is so, and it was so, and here the hand I have to show,* at the same time producing the hand and bracelet from her lap: whereupon the guests drew their swords, and instantly cut Mr. Fox into a thousand pieces.

(*ii*) *II. i. 185: 'You strike like the blind man'*
This suggests a familiar tale, but the nearest analogy so far suggested is Diego Hurtado de Mendoza's *Lazarillo de Tormes*, in which the narrator steals a sausage from his master, a blind beggar, and is so harshly punished that in revenge he causes him to jump against a stone pillar. The story, translated by David Rowlands and published in London in 1586, was 'exceedingly popular with the Elizabethan reading public' (Sir Clement Markham's translation, Introduction, p. xxix). This differs in material respects, and Benedick's version may be only a loose reference or may refer to some other story. The

conclusion of this incident, told in Lazarillo's own words, is as follows (ed. cit., pp. 27–9):

Seeing all this, and how the blind man made me a laughing-stock, I determined that at all hazards I would leave him. This resolution was always in my mind, and the last game he played confirmed it. On another day we left the town to seek alms. It had rained a great deal in the previous night. It continued to rain in the day-time, and we got under some arcades in that town, so as to keep out of the wet. Night was coming on and the rain did not cease. The blind man said to me, 'Lazaro! this rain is very persistent, and as the night closes in it will not cease, so we will make for the inn in good time. To go there we have to cross a stream which will have become swollen by the heavy rain.' I replied, 'Uncle! the stream is now very broad, but if you like I can take you to a place where we can get across without being wet for it becomes much narrower, and by jumping we can clear it.' This seemed good advice, so he said, 'You are discreet and you shall take me to that place where the stream becomes so narrow, for it is winter time, and a bad thing to get our feet wet.' Seeing that things were going as I wished, I took him out of the arcade, and placed him just in front of a stone pillar that stood in the square. Then I said to him, 'Uncle, this is the narrowest part of the stream.'

As the rain continued and he was getting wet, we were in a hurry to get shelter from the water that was falling upon us. The principal thing was (seeing that God blinded my understanding in that hour) to be avenged. The old man believed in me and said 'Put me in the right place while you jump over the stream.' So I put him just in front of the pillar, and placed myself behind it. I then said, 'Jump with all your might so as to clear the stream.' I had hardly finished speaking, when the poor old man, balancing himself like a goat, gave one step backwards, and then sprung with all his force. His head came with such a noise against the pillar that it sounded like a great calabash. He fell down half dead. 'How was it you could smell the sausage and not the post? Oh! Oh!' I shouted. I left him among several people who ran to help him, while I made for the gate of the town at a sharp trot, so that before nightfall I might be in Torrijos, not knowing nor caring what afterwards happened to my blind man.

(*iii*) *V. ii. 70: 'An old, an old instance, Beatrice'*
The following story from *A Hundred Merry Tales*, mentioned by W. A. Wright, may or may not have prompted Benedick's remarks concerning the short-lived memory of widows. It is a

fair specimen of the collection and at least serves to show why Beatrice should resent the charge of having borrowed her wit from these tales (II.i.120):

XI. *Of the woman that sayd her wooer came to late.* Another woman there was that knelyd at yᵉ mas of requiē whyle the corse of her husbande lay on the bere in the chyrch. To whom a yonge man came to speake wyth her in her ere as thoughe hyt had bene for som matre concernynge the funerallys/howe be yt he spake of no such matter but only wowyd her that he myghte be her husbande/ to whome she answeryde & sayde thus/Syr by my trouthe I am sory that ye come so late/for I am sped all redy/For I was made sure yester day to a nother man.

By thys tale ye may perceyue that women ofte tymes be wyse and lothe to lose any tyme.

APPENDIX VI

THE SONGS

It has proved impossible to include in this edition contemporary settings of the songs sung or mentioned; of one of the two texts Shakespeare gives in full ('Pardon, goddess of the night': v. iii. 12) no setting seems extant earlier than Thomas Arne's, for soprano solo, the eighteenth-century style of which, however agreeable, nowadays sounds inappropriate. It may be found, if needed, in John Caulfield's *Collection of the Vocal Music in Shakespeare's Plays*, 1864, II. 128. Furness's New Variorum edition prints (p. 181) a setting for 'Light o' Love' (III. iv. 41) from William Chappell's *Popular Music of the Olden Time* [1855], I. 221, attributed to an edition of 1570; the original words seem to be lost. Since the ditty is merely referred to, not sung, no musicological finesse is called for.

Of 'The God of Love' (v. ii. 25) Benedick sings only a snatch. His lines are the start of a song by the actor and balladist William Elderton, printed in 1562 and often quoted or imitated. It had hardly appeared when a printer named Griffith took out a licence for 'the answere to the iiijth ballett made to the godes of loue'; another printer produced 'The ioy of Virginitie, to the Godes of Loue' (that is, to the tune so named). The first lines of this run, 'I iudge and finde/how God doth minde,/to furnish, to furnish/his heauenly throne aboue'. Several lines have the repetitive form of Benedick's l. 27; e.g. 'without misse, without misse', 'and credite, and credite', 'with Iesu, with Iesu'. Alexander Lacy procured a licence in 1567–8 to reprint 'The Gods of Love' (Hyder E. Rollins, 'William Elderton', in *Studies in Philology*, 1920, XVII, 203 ff.). 'The ioy of Virginitie' mentioned above, a moralized imitation, appeared in Clement Robinson's *A Handefull of Plesant Delites* (1584) (ed. Hyder E. Rollins, 1924, p. 42). Elderton's text was known only in Benedick's fragment and in imitations until James M. Osborn in 1958 found a complete version and published it, modernized, in the London *Times*, 17 November 1958, p. 11. The first stanza, unmodernized, begins: 'The gods of loue yᵗ sytts aboue/& knowe me & knowe me/how sorrofull I do serue/Graunt my request yᵗ at the least/she showe me she showe me/some pitty

236

whan I deserue' (Peter J. Seng, *The Vocal Songs in the Plays of Shakespeare*, 1967, p. 63). The tune is preserved in the Francis Willughby Lute Book (fols. 88ᵛ–89) in the University of Nottingham library; a modernized transcription was published by John Ward in 'Music for *A Handefull of plesant delites*' (*Journal of the American Musicological Society*, 1957, pp. 164–5).

Thomas Ford's setting, 'Sigh no more' (II.iii. 62), published by Philip Heseltine (pseud. Peter Warlock) in *Four English Songs of the Early Seventeenth Century* (1925), hardly fits Shakespeare's version, requiring an extra line between Shakespeare's first and second lines and considerable repetition in the refrains. Ford was born about 1580, and might perhaps have been old enough to compose the original music for the song, but it is likelier that his setting is a revision of another composer's work, or a later composition (Peter J. Seng, op. cit., p. 60).

Successful
Business
Writing

in a week

Gordon R. Wainwright

Headway · Hodder & Stoughton

British Library Cataloguing in Publication Data

Wainwright, Gordon R.
 Successful Business Writing in a Week. –
 (Successful Business in a Week Series)
 I. Title   II. Series
 658.4

ISBN 0 340 59813 1

First published 1993
Impression number   10   9   8   7   6   5   4   3   2   1
Year   1998   1997   1996   1995   1994   1993

Typeset by Multiplex Techniques Ltd, St Mary Cray, Kent.
Printed in Great Britain for the educational publishing
division of Hodder & Stoughton Ltd, Mill Road,
Dunton Green, Sevenoaks, Kent TN13 2YA by Colorcraft, Hong
Kong.